NATO ASI Series

Advanced Science Institutes Series

A series presenting the results of activities sponsored by the NATO Science Committee, which aims at the dissemination of advanced scientific and technological knowledge, with a view to strengthening links between scientific communities.

The Series is published by an international board of publishers in conjunction with the NATO Scientific Affairs Division

A	Life Sciences	Plenum Publishing Corporation
B	Physics	London and New York
C	Mathematical and Physical Sciences	Kluwer Academic Publishers Dordrecht, Boston and London
D	Behavioural and Social Sciences	
E	Applied Sciences	
F	Computer and Systems Sciences	Springer-Verlag Berlin Heidelberg New York
G	Ecological Sciences	London Paris Tokyo Hong Kong
H	Cell Biology	Barcelona Budapest
I	Global Environmental Change	

NATO-PCO DATABASE

The electronic index to the NATO ASI Series provides full bibliographical references (with keywords and/or abstracts) to more than 30 000 contributions from international scientists published in all sections of the NATO ASI Series. Access to the NATO-PCO DATABASE compiled by the NATO Publication Coordination Office is possible in two ways:

- via online FILE 128 (NATO-PCO DATABASE) hosted by ESRIN, Via Galileo Galilei, I-00044 Frascati, Italy.

- via CD-ROM "NATO-PCO DATABASE" with user-friendly retrieval software in English, French and German (© WTV GmbH and DATAWARE Technologies Inc. 1989).

The CD-ROM can be ordered through any member of the Board of Publishers or through NATO-PCO, Overijse, Belgium.

The ASI Series Books Published as a Result of
Activities of the Special Programme on
ADVANCED EDUCATIONAL TECHNOLOGY

This book contains the proceedings of a NATO Advanced Research Workshop held within the activities of the NATO Special Programme on Advanced Educational Technology, running from 1988 to 1993 under the auspices of the NATO Science Committee.

The books published so far as a result of the activities of the Special Programme are:

Vol. F 67: Designing Hypermedia for Learning. Edited by D. H. Jonassen and H. Mandl. 1990.

Vol. F 76: Multimedia Interface Design in Education. Edited by A. D. N. Edwards and S. Holland. 1992.

Vol. F 78: Integrating Advanced Technology into Technology Education. Edited by M. Hacker, A. Gordon, and M. de Vries. 1991.

Vol. F 80: Intelligent Tutoring Systems for Foreign Language Learning. The Bridge to International Communication. Edited by M. L Swartz and M. Yazdani. 1992.

Vol. F 81: Cognitive Tools for Learning. Edited by P.A.M. Kommers, D.H. Jonassen, and J.T. Mayes. 1992.

Vol. F 84: Computer-Based Learning Environments and Problem Solving. Edited by E. De Corte, M. C. Linn, H. Mandl, and L. Verschaffel. 1992.

Vol. F 85: Adaptive Learning Environments. Foundations and Frontiers. Edited by M. Jones and P. H. Winne. 1992.

Vol. F 86: Intelligent Learning Environments and Knowledge Acquisition in Physics. Edited by A. Tiberghien and H. Mandl. 1992.

Vol. F 87: Cognitive Modelling and Interactive Environments in Language Learning. Edited by F. L. Engel, D. G. Bouwhuis, T. Bösser, and G. d'Ydewalle. 1992.

Vol. F 89: Mathematical Problem Solving and New Information Technologies. Edited by J. P. Ponte, J. F. Matos, J. M. Matos, and D. Fernandes. 1992.

Vol. F 90: Collaborative Learning Through Computer Conferencing. Edited by A. R. Kaye. 1992.

Vol. F 91: New Directions for Intelligent Tutoring Systems. Edited by E. Costa. 1992.

Vol. F 92: Hypermedia Courseware: Structures of Communication and Intelligent Help. Edited by A. Oliveira. 1992.

Vol. F 93: Interactive Multimedia Learning Environments. Human Factors and Technical Considerations on Design Issues. Edited by M. Giardina. 1992.

Interactive Multimedia Learning Environments

Human Factors and Technical Considerations on Design Issues

Edited by

Max Giardina

Université de Montréal
Faculté des Sciences de l'Education
Pavillon Marie-Victorin
90 Vincent d'Indy
Montréal H3C 3J7, Canada

Springer-Verlag
Berlin Heidelberg New York London Paris Tokyo
Hong Kong Barcelona Budapest
Published in cooperation with NATO Scientific Affairs Division

Proceedings of the NATO Advanced Research Workshop on Interactive Multimedia Learning Environments, held at Laval University, Quebec, June 17–20, 1991

CR Subject Classification (1991): D.2.6, H.1.2, H.4.2, K.3.2, I.2.5

ISBN 3-540-55811-X Springer-Verlag Berlin Heidelberg New York
ISBN 0-387-55811-X Springer-Verlag New York Berlin Heidelberg

© Springer-Verlag Berlin Heidelberg 1992
Printed in Germany

Typesetting: Camera ready by authors
45/3140 - 5 4 3 2 1 0 - Printed on acid-free paper

Preface

Multimedia environments suggest to us a new perception of the state of changes in and the integration of new technologies that can increase our ability to process information. Moreover, they are obliging us to change our idea of knowledge. These changes are reflected in the obvious synergetic convergence of different types of access, communication and information exchange. The multimedia learning environment should not represent a passive object that only contains or assembles information but should become, on one side, the communication medium of the pedagogical intentions of the professor/designer and, on the other side, the place where the learner reflects and where he or she can play with, test and access information and try to interpret it, manipulate it and build new knowledge.

The situation created by such a new learning environments that give new powers to individuals, particularly with regard to accessing and handling diversified dimensions of information, is becoming increasingly prevalent in the field of education. The old static equilibrium, in which fixed roles are played by the teacher (including the teaching environment) and the learner, is shifting to dynamic equilibrium where the nature of information and its processing change, depending on the situation, the learning context and the individual's needs.

Within this conceptual framework, we defined interactivity by the integration of its physical and cognitive dimension (Giardina, 1989; Giardina, 1991) as a consequence of the different possible contacts shared by the learner and the system to progress quickly through the network of available information. Also, more importantly, this definition of interactivity evinces the learner's cognitive choices as dependent on his or her manipulations of available information.

In this way, the concept of interactivity acquires a new dimension by focusing particularly on each individual's strategies during the learning process. This encourages the exchange of relevant information and knowledge between the IMLE (interactive multimedia learning environment) and the learner.

In this context, we emphasize the idea that the learner is a fundamental component of the interactivity concept, since he or she is the starting factor and the final receiver of a multimodal transaction defined as an exchange cycle of information that is more or less meaningful for generating significance or understanding of a phenomena or a particular state (Merrill, 1990; 1991). Accordingly, when conceiving pedagogical interactivity we should ensure that the learner feels satisfied at each stage of his or her development and experiences a genuine relationship based on congenial interaction with the mediatized environment.

More specifically, we focused our attention on several elements, among others, that we consider to be important issues in the design of truly personalized multimediated interactivity: student modelling strategies, multimodal knowledge representation, intelligent advisory strategies, and diagnostic learning strategies. Our main purpose was to elaborate diversified design strategies for processing information and to integrate them into a general design model applicable to the different levels of a multimedia learning system.

Acknowledgements

We would like to thank Philippe Marton, director of the G.R.A.I.M. research group (groupe de recherche sur l'apprentissage interactif multimédia), Université Laval, for his support and cooperation in making possible the workshop "Interactive Multimedia Learning Environments". We would also like to thank Philippe Duchastel of EDS, Troy, Michigan, for the insightful suggestions he had for improving and focusing our work. Special thanks are due to Hans Wössner at Springer-Verlag for making our publication process an enjoyable one. Finally, we owe a great deal of appreciation to Ileana de La Teja, who did a tremendous job managing the paper and electronic collection of the texts submitted by the authors.

April 1992   Max Giardina

Table of Contents

4. Multimedia Learning Projects: Applications

1. Multimedia Learning Environment: A New Paradigm?

Learning in the Twenty-First Century Interactive Multimedia Technology

Alfred Bork

Educational Technology Center, Information and Computer Science, University of California, Irvine, California 92717, USA. Tel. (714) 856 6945 (messages 856 7403)

Introduction

Most learning systems in the world today are remarkably similar. This similarity extends over a wide range of student ages, and extends geographically almost everywhere. Although we hear a great deal about cultural differences, and undoubtedly differences can be found, there is also a tremendous similarity in educational strategies. The lecture/textbook approach to learning, teacher directed classes, with a teacher in front of a group of students, is almost universal, whether one is talking about a class of ten year olds in Japan, or whether one is talking about a class of twenty-two year olds in the United States.

This strategy for learning that dominates today is old. It has changed little over a long time, in spite of the talk of new media and new approaches that permeates the literature. Even the presence of the computer, and its associated equipment, has to this point made little difference in educational systems. Classes using the computer today are fundamentally the same, on a statistical basis, as classes that do not use the computer, of as older classes before the computer was present at all.

Yet many believe that the computer, although poorly used in education to this point, has great potential for making massive improvements in learning for almost everybody in the world. This paper considers aspects of new educational systems using interactive information technologies extensively. These new educational systems can be vastly superior for most of our students to the systems they use today.

A first step in moving toward better educational systems is to consider desirable aspects that such a system should have. This paper might be described as a set of visions for future educational systems, goals that those systems could aim toward. Systems of the type that I will be describing with these goals, are achievable today, using interactive technologies, at costs no greater, and probably less than, those of current educational systems. But they represent radical changes in the current system, and so are not easy to implement. A conservative educational strategy, that has continued for long periods of time essentially unchanged, is not one that is easily moved to a new and higher plateau.

1. All Students Should Learn Everything

This issue is fundamental to the notion of democracy. While people may be born equal, they often are not offered equal educational opportunities. There is no reason that every student, regardless of age or subject area, should not be learning to that student's full capability.

I proclaim it a right for every individual to be immersed in the best possible learning environment. Furthermore this environment should be lifelong, starting at birth, and continuing until death.

In our current schools this does not happen. Even the system of giving grades, such as A, B, etc., shows that we do not expect all students to learn the material fully. In a system where all students are learning fully all grades would be A, so there would be no necessity for grading. The fact that this does not happen is a condemnation of our current mode of assisting learning.

In the present system when someone does not learn, that person is often blamed. Yet the mastery learning theorists, from Benjamin Bloom to more recent ones, have long argued that the evidence is that every student can learn in the right learning environment. So if a student does not learn we can say that the learning environment is not the best for that student. Learning environment is a very complex issue, which refers to a variety of factors.

Experimental studies show that almost everybody learns in a one-on-one environment. That is if a student has an individual tutor, or competent teacher working with that student, everything is possible. But the possibility of having everyone tutored by a skilled teacher is not realistic, because of lack of skilled teachers and the cost involved. Hence the problem is to find reasonable methods for mastery learning, methods which are practical in our society today. Benjamin Bloom has called that in a recent paper the "Two Sigma" problem, meaning that we want to make an improvement in the average learning of students by two Sigmas.

To assure mastery learning we must have more than one learning strategy. A strategy which may be very useful for a particular person to learn something, may not be useful for another person. We do not currently know enough to know which strategies will work best for which individual, but if we provide a variety of learning strategies we have a good chance of achieving learning with one or the other of these strategies. Strategies can vary enormously - they can use different media, they can use different pedagogical directions, and they can be tailored in different ways to individual difficulties.

Mastery implies that we must have some way of knowing when people have mastered things, or when further learning is necessary. Vast numbers of things need to be mastered. Our current exam systems are totally inadequate for this. We cannot be giving exams constantly. In systems of the future there should be NO distinction between learning and examination; these should be one continuous seamless process.

The notion of mastery is an equity issue, the assurance that in a democracy everyone can be educated. This is by no means happening today and indeed in countries such as the United States there is evidence that discrepancy in education has increased.

2. Learning Should be Interesting

A second important factor for twenty-first century learning is that it must be interesting to the student. The learning material must be motivating, encouraging the student to learn more. Thus we not only want all students to learn to the mastery level, we want all students to enjoy learning.

Enjoying learning is important for a variety of reasons. First we want students to learn during their entire life. That is we must get people to think of learning as a lifelong activity that they *want* to engage in.

If learning is a terrible task, students will keep at it only through the use of external threats. These threats are common in American education. At one time they were mostly physical threats, but now many of them are threats concerning grades and parental reaction to grades. This almost universally used tactic is I believe highly undesirable. Students will never be encouraged to continue in the learning practice throughout their entire life unless they find learning a pleasant and rewarding experience.

Enjoying learning also has another positive factor. Many studies for years have shown that the amount of quality time spent at a learning task is one of the most important factors in determining how much and how well students learn. People will spend more time learning if they like what they are doing.

Motivation is another issue, such as the best method of learning mentioned in the last section, about which we know little at present. But we can determine empirically which material is motivating and which is not motivating, by testing people in free environments, environments in which students are able to leave at any time, and with no threats. Places in the learning material where many people leave are weak motivationally.

I hasten to say that I do not equate motivation with entertainment. The notion which seems to be prevalent in some educational circles that we must make all learning a game-like activity is not reasonable.

3. Learning Should Be Active

I begin with two extremes in the learning process. In one the learner behaves in a passive fashion. He or she is a spectator in the learning process. A typical example might be a large lecture environment, in which no questions occur whatsoever, and where the instructor is not available outside the lectures. I have seen examples of this, although it is an extreme case. The image is of drilling a hole into the student's head and inserting a funnel, and pouring "knowledge" into this funnel. A few students can make such a process interactive, but no many.

The other extreme is one in which the student is constantly involved in the learning process, playing an active role every moment. A typical example might be with a friend showing someone how to cook a Chinese dinner. I assume the friend is already knowledgeable, and the friend is working alongside of the person. But the person is in a learning situation so he or she does much of the activity. Any wrong step is immediately pointed out to the person. If some things are a matter of choice those too are indicated directly. This apprentice environment, working with a skilled teacher in the area, is typical of many highly active learning situations. Here the learner is no longer a spectator, but is participating fully in all aspects of the process. This represents fully interactive learning.

To say that I am illustrating two extremes emphasizes that there are intermediate positions. This is often overlooked in the current literature about technology in education. There is a great deal of talk of interaction - interactive computer material, interactive video, interactive multimedia - but little discussion of how interaction is to be measured, and little discussion of the several spectra involved. It is not simply a case of whether the material is interactive, or not interactive, but of HOW interactive.

Degree and quality of interaction are aspects of interaction that should be considered. Each of these might eventually be represented numerically. That is we might say that something is 6.7 in degree of interaction, and 4.3 in quality of interaction. I do not claim to be able to do this at present, but it does not seem to be inconceivable in the future that we will be able to judge material in such a way. Alternatively we could also speak of a slight degree of interaction, or a poor quality of interaction, indicating with these verbalisms that interaction is not spectacular on either scale.

3.1   Degree of Interaction

With regard to the degree of interaction the issue is how frequently is meaningful interaction occurring? A situation where one must listen to an hour of lecture, and then have a chance of asking one question, has a low degree of interaction. Or a situation where one goes to a class for a time, and then takes a test which shows what the student did and did not understood, is also typically of low degree of interaction because of the long amount of "instructional" time that passes before the student is tested. For an active learner there should be frequent interaction.

How can one begin to establish measurement of frequency of interaction? We ask how frequently the interaction occurs, as compared to the total learning process. Thus if in a lecture each student in the class were able to ask a question once every minute of lecture time, that would be a reasonably high degree of interaction. This is impossible in a lecture with large numbers of students, indicating that one can not achieve anything except a very small degree of interaction in an environment of this kind. This is not to say that a few students may not ask questions frequently, often students who do not need the information, but are just trying to bring themselves to the attention of the instructor!

There is a reciprocal relationship, but probably not linear. As the time between interactions becomes longer, the degree of interaction becomes less. But there are some limits. Some thinking time is needed with many types of interaction. So a student who replies immediately to a question from an instructor, without thinking about the answer, is perhaps proceeding too quickly. Some time is needed in a thoughtful learning process for reflection, so if the time between interactions becomes too small the student is neglecting one of the important aspects of learning, their own consideration about what is happening.

How can one decide on the optimal time? The experimental work in this area is limited, but our work at Irvine may shed light on this. When we test material in public libraries, we find that if the time between the interaction is greater than fifteen or twenty seconds, we start to lose students. In this environment a student is free to leave at any time.

So, if a student leaves, the material is not holding the interest of the student. Viewed in terms of the discussion of this section, if the degree of interaction gets too small, the material loses motivational capability. Or putting it another way a student actively involved in learning is more likely to stay at difficult tasks than a student who is only involved passively.

3.2 Quality of Interaction

The issue of the quality of interaction is more complicated. Intuitively(?), we know that some interactions are of relatively poor quality. But much of what we know in this area seems to be based only on the intuition of skilled teachers, rather than any careful experimental studies. Furthermore since there are many interactions in a sizable learning sequence; if degree of interaction is high, we must integrate over these different interactions for a total measure of quality of interaction for a given set of material.

It may help us to gain insight if we look at several examples of pre-technology highly interactive learning situations. They give us clues as how we can proceed in a technology-based educational system for the future.

3.3 Examples of Highly Interactive Learning in the Past

Surprisingly little literature exists on this topic, and as far as I know very little research exists on it. But widely quoted examples are thought of as showing high interaction. Some examples are old, some of them are more modern extensions of an older example.

3.3.1 The Socratic Dialog

One of the most famous examples of highly interactive learning is twenty five hundred years ago, the method that Socrates used in working with students, at least as reported by Plato in the Dialogs.

These literary works are different than an actual learning situation, and it is not clear to what extent Socrates taught in the way Plato shows. Furthermore a variety of different techniques are shown by Plato. I do not wish to defend everything "Socratic" in this discussion, but only to point out interactive features.

The essence of interaction in the Socratic dialog is that Socrates proceeded almost entirely by asking questions. There was very little in the way of lecturing going on. Rather Socrates asked questions, and the students are expected, in answering these questions, to "discover" the ideas involved. The purpose of the questions is presumably to stimulate active thinking on the part of the students. It is also interesting to note that Socrates tackles very difficult issues in this way, not simply rote learning. We see few examples of rote learning in Plato's Socratic dialogs.

In the Socratic procedure there are usually about two or three students involved, for one "teacher". That is it is a cooperative small group environment, but not just involving the students themselves. Socrates imposes structure on the group. This might come from other materials in the learning process too, a more modern variance of this tactic. In these small group environments every person is an active person. This might be simply a literary device introduced by Plato, but I choose to view it as more than that. If learning takes place in small group environments we do not want some people to survive only passively.

3.3.2 Tutors and Students

A modern variant of the Socratic approach, although with far less formality, and certainly much less study, happens when a teacher works with a single student, or with a small group of students. The typical situation is the teacher's office hours. The teacher announces that he or she will be in the office for a period of time, and students are free to come in during that time. How much time is actually used, and what happens during this time, is worth serious study.

Skilled teachers vary greatly as to what happens in these situations. Typically they will begin with the student asking a question, sometimes a question that the teacher does not want to answer in any direct fashion. For example in a science or mathematics course the question might be "how does one work problem 7.32?". A common way of responding to this, although I believe not by the best teachers, is for the teacher to simply work the problem. That is the easiest strategy to follow, because the teacher knows how to work the problem.

But often a more skilled teacher will move the situation into a Socratic one, answering the students' questions by other questions that the student must reply to. That is the student is led to solve the problem, in this example, by an active process, with the student coming up with most of the important steps along the way. Another frequent tactic for the instructor is to suggest additional reading on the part of the student. Perhaps textbooks cover the same material as that used in the class, but with different emphasis and pedagogical style.

This conversational interaction between a teacher and one to three students is a good model for thinking about interactivity in technology-based learning material. It is a model that we stress in our design groups in the Educational Technology Center at the University of California, Irvine. In these pedagogical design sessions some advice is needed for the designers. Most of the designers will have dealt with students primarily through lectures and textbooks, and we want to produce a much more interactive environment than that found in lectures and textbooks. So they need some guidance as to how they should work. Thinking about the situation as an interactive conversation in the office is one of the most valuable models we have been able to develop.

3.4 Examples of Low Quality of Interactivity

In contrast to the examples of a high degree of interactivity, particularly the conversational mode, one can see examples where interactivity, while existing, is of low quality.

Perhaps the most common example of poor quality of interaction is multiple choice. Multiple choice was never used in education until recently, and even now it tends to be primarily an American idiom. It came about at a time when we were dealing increasing numbers of students, and with increasing attention on national examinations. But it was a tactic of desperation, rather than a desirable educational tactic. It is not a tactic that is necessary in modern material, because modern computers can deal very well with free form English input, particularly in the situations where multiple choice is often used. It stimulates a type of guessing on the part of the students, and it leads to students studying tactics which could be described as "how do I do well on a multiple choice exam without my knowing anything about the subject matter." It also has a low student approval. Students refer to multiple choice as multiple guess frequently.

A second example of low quality in interaction is seen by the many hypertet and hypermedia materials that are available today. This is not inherent in the notion of hypertext and hypermedia, but it does represent what is usually done, simply because it is the most common tactic.

The usual hypertext of hypermedia material has active areas on the screen. Various things that the students can touch or point to lead to new things happening. Touch might refer to pointing by a mouse, to a touch screen, or to the use of the arrow keys. So the student can move off at a given point in any direction that he or she wants to, following down a very large number of different paths through the material.

What do students learn as compared to what have they been "exposed" to? Often particularly with other than the best students, paths through hypertext or hypermedia material appear to be almost random. A person at a given point has no reason for making one decision over another, and so pushes almost anything at that particular point. A few good students can explore a problem, and can work in a unaided discovery mode. But few of the students in our schools, and few teachers, can profit by such a strategy. So the typical student use of hypertext material is low quality interaction.

The problem is not with the concept of hypertext of hypermedia. This can still be a very useful technique. Most students need some kind of guidance, some kind of advice, some kind of help, to progress in an effective way with the learning process. The elements of discovery can still be preserved with help of this kind. Indeed everyone can make a discovery, but different discoveries may be made by different people, depending on their conceptual background. I know however of no examples of hypercourses that are highly interactive, in the sense of paying attention to the users problems. Most keep no information about the user problems, and let the user move through the material without any indication that learning took place.

3.5 Features of Highly Interactive Material

Looking at the examples we can see common features. First these interactions are conducted in the native languages of the teacher and students involved, and in the case of mathematics and science, with considerable supplementation with more technical language. A key to highly interactive learning, through all of human history, has been the very powerful tool of natural language, and the powerful tools of other symbolic systems that have been developed by humankind for thousands of years. This critical factor is often overlooked in developing technology-based learning material, unfortunately, and so we often see materials that are only very weakly interactive. Pointing environments with no other input permit only weak interactivity.

A second important point to notice in these examples is that small groups are involved. One of the major problems with education has been to try to provide interactive environments where we have increasing numbers of students to educate. What is often overlooked in attempts in this direction is the role of peer learning. In Socrates, as already mentioned, it is not just Socrates that plays a role, but the other students too. Likewise if several students are together in the instructor's office the skilled instructor will often be able to have an interplay between these students going on, so that peer learning between the students becomes an important part of the process. When groups become too large, this is no longer possible. Industry studies show that the best size for cooperative groups is about four; although few such studies have been made in education, I would feel that it is a similar issue there. There have been studies on cooperative groups.

A third important feature to note in this situation is the cumulative aspect of what is going on. Each question and each response in Socrates leads to a new kind of question. These new kinds of questions will in general be different for each of the learners involved. There is a clear recognition of a problem of individualization. The help that each student gets in a highly interactive learning environment is very much dependent on that student. It is interaction that makes individualization possible. A technology-based learning system which pays no attention to what the student already knows, and pays no attention to what is being learned, is not likely to be useful. There is an enormous difference between "exposing" students to learning material, and to learning itself.

4. Learning Materials Should Use Many Media

Recently we have gained the capability of allowing computers to control a great variety of different media. These media can include sound, still pictures (either those created by the computer, or those from external sources), and video sequences. Areas such as virtual reality also bring in touch as a possibility, although this is still impractical for typical use today.

In spite of the sizable amount of discussion in the literature of multimedia interactive material, relatively little of this material is available for use in schools and universities, and much of what is available is of relatively low quality in terms of interaction.

One area that has had perhaps more exploration than any other is in the teaching of languages. Here much of the video needed can be repurposed video, already existing, and the use of high quality spoken material is essential for language instruction.

An example of this is a project that we have been working on at Irvine, Understanding Spoken Japanese. The hardware so far includes the computer and the videodisc, and all the media mentioned above are used. This program is highly interactive, in the sense described earlier. It makes a serious attempt to find out what the students comprehend and do not comprehend about the language (Japanese in this case) and to provide help just where it is needed.

We believe that the potential in this area has scarcely been scratched however as vastly more material is needed to support the various languages that are taught. In the United States in particular we have a major problem with English as a Second Language. Over half the students, for example, in computer science at my university, the University of California, Irvine, do not have English as their first language! But I stress that very little quality material is available, and furthermore it is not easy to get funding in this area.

A quite different kind of interactive multimedia material is seen in some of the recent hypertext productions. Again there is little available, but there is soon to be a sizable set of material. IBM will announce in October two multimedia programs which probably can be considered in the humanities, although they span a good many different areas. These programs, ULYSSES and COLUMBUS, are to my mind the most elaborate attempts at hypermedia. They both have the advantage too that they are done by very competent development groups, at least as far as the visual material is concerned. They also have the advantage that they have had large amounts of money. Their problem will be to try to find out how teachers and students can make best use of them. Unlike the Japanese material mentioned above they do not try to find out what the students' needs are. Rather they provide a very rich exploration environment for the student to move around in.

The key to the future I would argue is in providing both of the two kinds of capabilities just noted for multimedia material. That is we can work in a hypertext environment, but we can also try to find frequently what the student is actually learning, and to govern further learning experiences on that basis. But I know of no example of such a product at the moment.

5. Learning Should Be Individually Paced

One aspect of individualization of learning needs particular attention. This aspect ties in closely with interactivity and motivation. We can no expect all students to learn all material in the same period of time. A well-prepared student, with some background already, may move through a given area very rapidly. With another student, with various weaknesses in background, it make take longer. Furthermore it may not be clear with a given student what is the best learning approach, and some time may be devoted to ineffective learning approaches. If we insist on the mastery criteria, that all students learn everything well, as described above, then we must insist on variable pacing.

This implies that in our twenty-first century educational systems the notion of "courses" will vanish. Learning will be a continuous seamless process, with many branches. We can still offer students vast amounts of choice, probably far more than with the current system. But as our theories of learning become better, perhaps over hundreds of years, and as we have more knowledge as to what material is appropriate for what students, the differences between different students in time required may decrease.

6. We Need New Educational Environments

We need to consider new organization patterns for the learning process. This would imply new course structures, new possibilities for schools, and new roles for teachers. These considerations apply to teachers at all levels, but there may be different possibilities at different levels.

6.1 Course Structures

Most of our courses now have approximately the same structure. There are lecture or textbook expositions for weeks on end, followed by an occasional quiz. These quizzes are given entirely for grading purposes, since feedback to the student is often not sufficient to allow the student to understand what learning problems occur. Furthermore the part of the course being tested has already passed so the teacher's strategies are usually not affected by the quiz either. Teachers usually interpret uniformly poor performance on the quiz as a problem of the students, not a problem of how they structure the learning experiences.

We can expect this to change with the new approaches made possible by interactive technology. The existence of new and powerful learning modes allows us to structure courses quite differently. I discuss this in more detail elsewhere. Although few full scale technology-based courses have yet to be developed, we can already begin to see some different patterns emerging. Two seem to have particular potential for using with the computer. Furthermore these two can be combined, using features of both into a single structure.

6.1.1 Quiz-based Mastery Learning Strategies

The idea is that the course will be organized around the tests, the quizzes, rather than around the lecture material. An example was the introductory level physics course developed by the Educational Technology Center at the University of California, Irvine. Students took a test in a given unit (there were fifteen tests in ten weeks) until they did essentially perfectly on that test, receiving a new test each time but one testing the same concepts. Tests were not used for "grading", but rather to determine whether the student needed more work in a given area. Thus mastery was required, as seen by this test.

The test also had built within it all the instructional material for the course. But this material was not presented until after the student had trouble with the particular material. Thus the student was never "taught" material that they knew already.

6.1.2   Hypercourses

Another strategy comes out of the hypertext environment, combining it with all the different media present in a full multimedia learning situation. Here a student has considerable control as to how to move through the material, and a rich variety of resources can be provided. Recent examples include the COLUMBUS and ULYSSES material from IBM.

6.1.3   Mastery-based Hypermedia Course

The two strategies just mentioned can be combined, providing a very rich environment, but also making certain that students are learning, and offering direct aid specific to the individual student's need.

6.2   School Structure and Location

Again there is a great similarity as to how many of the schools and universities are organized today. The lecture/text strategy of a given course is reflected in the fact that almost all of the rooms in schools and universities are constructed in a lecture type environment, with seats for the students, and with a podium, table, or some strategy to delineate the teacher at the front of the room. "discussion" strategies seldom have any rooms which are build explicitly for discussion purposes. I have had that trouble myself in several universities, since I am fond of running discussion-based classes.

Some experiments in elementary school, particularly the CHILD project in Florida, begin to show new possibilities for room organization. In this project there is no lecture strategy. Rather the room is organized as a series of tables, with only a few chairs at each table. Each table has in it a limited amount of learning material, used only by a group of about three students at any one time. Students move from one of these tables to another.

One can see at all levels of education new possibilities here. In many cases classrooms in the conventional sense will no longer be needed at all, and only a versatile multimedia resource center may be sufficient for the entire organizational structure.

We can also consider the possibility that learning takes place already in many different environments, and perhaps this situation may be extended in the future. There is no reason why sizable components of learning should not take place in the home, the public library, or other institutional or informal settings. It may well be that school as we know it today will gradually cease to exist.

6.3 Teacher Roles in Learning

Another new organizational structure to consider. As is already been indicated here several times, teachers today have a fixed lecture-based role in most of our present situations. They also serve unfortunately as authoritarian figures, even in science classes where no authority should be possible. This situation is worse at universities than at elementary schools. Nolan Estes has referred to the current situation as "the stage on the stage".

New courses will inevitably bring in new roles for the teacher. In the CHILD environment, already described, the teacher does not lecture, but rather moves from station to station, offering help to the students. This environment, in turn, is derived from the Writing to Read environment, which used a similar strategy for the teacher. A new technology-based course, when developed, should not only define the role of the teacher, but should provide, in technology-based learning form, all the material necessary for the teacher both to run the course, and to understand the particular role that he or she is assigned in that course.

7. We Need a New Curriculum With Extensive Use of Interactive Technology

This section is a culmination of everything that has come before. If we look at the key issues already raised, the notion that all students should learn everything to the mastery level, the notion that learning should be individualized, the notion that learning should be interactive, and the notion that learning should be interesting, it is clear that we do not achieve these in present courses. Present courses too never allow students to move at their own pace, except in very few exceptional situations. And we can not depend, for rebuilding the educational systems of the world, on these exceptional situations that involve a few very competent teachers, or that involve extensive resources not available in most schools.

It we were to make it a national law, in any country, that all schools and all teachers must satisfy the key points just raised, we would be in considerable trouble. One can not do this with the courses that we now have on hand, and with the technology on which those courses are based, the lecture/textbook technology. Only a very few exceptional teachers can take a class of thirty students (and thirty could vary considerably) and teach it in an interactive individualized mastery fashion, using our current dominant delivery systems. To my mind it is wishful thinking to believe otherwise, although as I keep stressing there will always be exceptional teachers who can do this.

But we are interested in education for *all* children and *all* adults, far more than can be reached by these exceptional teachers or special situations. At the same time we would like to consider policies that allow us to increase the number of exceptional teachers, to lure back into teaching just the brightest and most competent individuals that we do not often get at the present time. So our new strategies must be aimed at increasing the numbers of *excellent* teachers.

For most courses, and for most students, what happens is heavily dependent on existing curriculum material, and on the educational environment for which that curriculum material was prepared. Thus, although there are some exceptions, the vast majority of all courses are determined by available textbooks in those areas. This differs some from country to country, and from subject area to subject area, but statistically the textbook determines most of our courses. As long as the courses are fundamentally text based and lecture based courses they will not be different from today, no matter how much additional technology and media are introduced into the courses.

I am not concerned with small percentage changes, but the major changes implied by mastery, individualization, interaction an motivation. But all of these factors can be attained, I argue, in environments where a course is developed, from the beginning, around the interactive technologies. The word course is no longer appropriate because in a truly student-based environment, insisting on mastery, the entire notion of a course will vanish. Rather education will be a continuous process, without the artificial distinction of breaking it up into "courses". I will continue to use the word "course", but in a broader sense corresponding to any length segment of learning material.

The critical point is that we will not achieve the goals in education as suggested in this paper by halfway measures. Rather we need to reconstruct *all*, or almost all, of our current learning material. Thus we need to engage, in any one country and in all countries, in a sizable curriculum effort to provide the capabilities suggested. We are not doing that at the present time. Indeed many of the very large expenditures of money, such as the Model Schools Program, completely ignore the issues of how the new technology-based curriculum is to be attained. I contend that it is only through such a new curriculum that we will be able to achieve our goals.

We have had little experience with either developing or using full technology-based courses. One can count such courses in the United States on the fingers. Perhaps the first ones were the Logic and Set Theory courses developed by Patrick Suppes at Stanford University. We developed a full quarter of beginning physics at the University of California, Irvine. Suppes also developed a series of language courses. Perhaps the only recent example is the Writing to Read course, developed by John Henry Martin and marketed by IBM, intended for five and six years old. So our experience in this area is at present very limited.

This implies that additional experience, both in development and in use with students, is necessary before we can proceed to full scale development of a new curriculum. I have discussed elsewhere strategies for conducting such an experiment which would bring us the necessary knowledge to proceed further.

It should be emphasized that these courses might be quite different in their total structure than existing courses. When the delivery system is changed, with the new possibilities presented by the new information technologies, then we can have very different strategies for organizing and conducting the course, not at all like the typical structure today. Thus we can have a much more intimate blend of testing and learning, in a way that these become almost indistinguishable. And we can use, within this blend, a hypermedia environment. Only further experimentation will show us which of these course structures are most viable for student use. This type of thing can not be predicted on a philosophical basis, but need empirical information.

8. How Do We Develop the New Curriculum Material?

I have discussed extensively in my papers strategies for production of high quality technology-based multimedia learning materials, particularly aiming toward future sizable development of such materials. So the present section only gives a bare outline of that extensive activity.

There are four critical features in the development of any type of curriculum material. In any sizable effort these features need to be considered as separate activities, since the best people for each are different.

First there is the issue of overall management. If a project is going to produce material at reasonable costs, and is actually going to produce material (it is surprising how many curriculum projects do not) then careful consideration needs to be given to management.

The second important feature, and perhaps the most important of all, is that of pedagogical design. This is the domain of very good teachers, experienced individuals who work daily with the types of students that are to be involved here. I do not believe that competent material that is highly sensitive to student problems can be written by traditional instructional design strategies. Nor do I believe that the various authoring languages now available are of much use here either. Rather these teachers should be allowed to work in a free environment, doing what they think is best, and without the bonds of either behavioral psychology or authoring languages.

The third stage is technical implementation. It is important to separate this from the second stage, since we do not want good teachers to be concerned at all with how the material is to be running on the computer. Here there is considerable promise in recent work we have done with the University of Geneva, for considerable improvement in the tactics here, through the use of automatic programming.

The final stage is evaluationand improvement. Here we are using evaluation in the sense of formative evaluation. The material must not only be tested internally for consistency, but must be used by typical students from the target group. Then based on the results the materials can be considerably improved.

9. Conclusion

We can have in the twenty-first century a much superior educational system, at all levels and in all countries, than we have at the present time. In this paper I have tried to outline some of the important features of such a system. These features are not attained today, and will not be attained by any of the strategies for improving education that are currently receiving large amounts of attention.

To my mind the issue is fundamentally a curriculum problem. Courses all over the world depend heavily on existing curriculum material, for most teachers and for most students. In only a few instances is the teacher, given all the large amount of work assigned to teachers in a position to develop extensive curriculum. Developing effective learning material is a difficult and time-consuming process. The development of the new courses must be undertaken on a national or international scale. Very little of this is happening at the present time.

Although I have not explored the issue in this paper there is considerable gain in considering these projects internationally. Thus development involving several countries working together would be much less expensive than the same development done independently in several countries. Furthermore I believe the courses themselves can be much richer courses, because they can draw on the differing educational strengths of the countries involved.

References

1. Bloom, B.: The 2 Sigma Problem: The Search for Methods of Group Instruction as Effective as 1-on-1 Tutoring. Educational Researcher, Vol. 13, pp. 4-16. June/July, 1984
2. Highly Interactive Software With Videodiscs of Learning to Comprehend Spoken Japanese. Proceedings of the Ninth Annual Conference on Interactive Instruction Delivery. Society for Applied Learning Technology. Orlando, Florida. February 20-22, 1988
3. Interaction: Lessons From Computer Based Learning. Interactive Media: Working Methods and Practical Applications. (Diana Laurillard, ed). Ellis Horwood Limited. Chicester, England. 1987
4. International Development of Technology-Based Learning Courses. Journal of Research on Computing in Education, Vol. 23, No. 2. Winter, 1990

5. Let's Test the Power of Interactive Technology. Educational Leadership, Vol. 43, No. 6. March 1986
6. New Structures for Technology-Based Courses. Education and Computing, Vol. 4, pp. 109-117, (1988)
7. Schools for Tomorrow (Draft available)
8. Pedagogical Development of Computer-Based Learning Material, *Designing Computer-Based Learning Materials,* NATO ASI Series, Series F: Computer and Systems Sciences, Vol. 23. Springer-Verlag, Berlin, Germany. 1989
9. Production of Technology-Based Learning Material Tools vs. Authoring Systems. Instruction Delivery Systems, Vol. 3, No. 2. March/April, 1989
10. Production Systems for Computer-Based Learning. Instructional Software: Principles and Perspectives for Design and Use. (Walker, D.F., and Hess, R.D, eds.). Wadsworth Publishing Company. Belmont, California. 1984

Research and Theory on Multi-Media Learning Effects

Richard E. Clark and Terrance G. Craig

University of Southern California, USA. Correspondence address in 1992: Richard E. Clark, 7 Asgard Building, Balscdden Road, Howth, County Dublin, Republic of Ireland (bitnet electronic mail: RCLARK@VAX1.TCD.IE)

Introduction

A survey of available multi-media and interactive videodisc research, reviews is presented. Conclusions are offered that: 1) multiple media, including videodisc technology, are *not* the factors that influence learning; 2) the measured learning gains in studies of the instructional uses of multiple media are mostly likely due to instructional methods (such as interactivity) that can be used with a variety of single and multiple media; 3) the aspects of dual coding theory which formed the basis for early multi-media studies have not been supported by subsequent research; and 4) future multi-media and interactive videodisc research should focus on the *economic* benefits (cost and learning time advantages) of new technology.

Two tacit assumptions, the *additive* assumption and the *multiplicative* assumption, seem to govern past and present enthusiasms for the use of multiple media in instruction and training:

1) *The Additive Assumption* : Instructional media, if used properly, make valuable contributions to learning and therefore instruction presented in two or more media produce more learning than instruction presented by only one medium because the learning benefits of each of the combines media are additive;

2) *The Multiplicative Assumption* : Multi-media benefits are sometimes multiplicative, that is, greater than the sum of the benefits of individual media.

Multiple Media Research and Theory

These two assumptions have a good bit of face validity and represent the intuitive beliefs of many instructional media specialists. Yet there are many instances in the history of education where controlled research studies produced evidence for counter-intuitive conclusions. The goal of this paper is to examine the research evidence for each of these two tacit and intuitive assumptions and any theories that support the use of multiple media in instruction. While there have been a number of recent research reviews that examine research on the first assumption (for example, Mielke, 1968; Schramm, 1977; Levie & Dickie, 1972; Clark, 1983; 1985; Clark &

Sugrue, 1989; Clark & Salomon, 1986) there have been few systematic research attempts to examine the second assumption and no dominant theory to guide research that multi-media combinations provide valuable learning benefits.

Research Support for Instructional Use of Multi-Media

The discussion begins with an examination of the first tacit assumption.

Does available research support the claim of additive learning benefits from different media?

It is important to explain at the beginning of this discussion that if we have evidence for unique learning benefits from any media, then we could have additive learning benefits from a number of combined media. However, if existing research does not indicate that different media provide different learning benefits, then we could not assume that combinations of media provide different learning benefits, then we could not assume that combinations of media would produce additive benefit. Therefore, the best place to start a review of the additive assumption is in the research that compares the relative learning benefits of different media.

After at least seventy years of empirical research on the media comparison question in a number of nations, it is still not possible to report agreement among all researchers on the answer. Many of the arguments about summary conclusions from the media comparison studies seem to have one primary origin - they stem from conflicts over the intuitive belief by a few researchers and many professional educators that each teaching medium makes *unique* contributions to learning. For example, some researchers expect that instructional uses of computers contribute something unique to academic achievement which is not possible with television, teachers or textbooks - or that video disk instruction may foster unique cognitive skills that are not available from television or books. These advocates of a "strong" media theory suggest that certain media produce unique cognitive effects when used for instruction and therefore some media produce more of some types of learning for certain students and subject matter. The extension of this argument - that combinations of media produce benefits to learning that are the sum of their separate benefits - is the basis of the additive assumption held by those who promote the use of multiple media. Advocates of a "weak" media theory, on the other hand, claim that media do not have any psychological influence over learning but that media may positively influence the "economics" (speed and cost) of learning. At the center of the conflict between these two approaches to media use in education are issues of research design. This is the case in the debate that surrounds media comparison studies.

Additive Media Comparison Studies

In the 1970's skepticism about media comparison studies, still being conducted in apparently large numbers, began to grow. At that time, the evidence began to favor a "weak media" theory. A number of comprehensive reviews concluded that there was no good evidence that any medium produced more learning or motivation than any other medium. Levie and Dickie (1973) noted that most overall media comparison studies to date had been fruitless and suggested that most learning objectives could be attained through "instruction presented by any of a variety of different media" (p. 859). This observation was echoed by Schramm (1977), according to whom "learning seems to be affected more by what is delivered than by the delivery system" (p.273). More recent analyses indicate that media comparison studies, regardless of the media employed, tend to result in "no significant difference" conclusions (Clark and Salomon, 1986). Clark (1983, 1985) has claimed that the active ingredient in studies which find one medium superior to another, is usually some uncontrolled aspect of the instructional method (e.g. programmed instruction) rather than the medium.

Meta-analytic Studies of Media Comparisons

During the past decade, more effort has been made to analyze and refocus the results of existing comparison studies. The statistical technique called meta-analysis has proved to be a most useful approach to summarizing instructional media (and other kinds of educational) research. The current meta-analyses of media comparison studies provide evidence that any reported significant differences in performance have been due to confounding in the treatments employed in the studies. A recent series of meta-analyses of media research was conducted by James Kulik and his colleagues at the University of Michigan (Clark, 1985, contains citations for most of these meta-analyses). Generally, meta-analyses allow for a more precise estimate of treatment effect sizes than was possible a few years ago. Meta-analytic procedures yield effect size estimates that are converted to percentage of standard deviation gains on final examination scores due to the more powerful treatment, if any. Most of the meta-analytic surveys of media research demonstrate a typical learning advantage for "newer" media of about one-half a standard deviation on final examination performance, compared with "conventional" (i.e., teacher presented) treatments. In the case of computer-based instruction studies in college environments, for example, this advantage translates as an increase from the 50th to the 66th percentile on final examinations in a variety of courses. This is an impressive accomplishment if one accepts it at face value. Closer inspection of these reviews, however, reveals that most of the large effect sizes attributed to computers in these studies are actually due to poorly designed studies and confounding (Clark, 1983; 1985). These weak effect sizes seem to support the "weak" media theory.

Additive Media Research Design Problems

According to Clark (1983), the most common sources of confounding in media research seem to be the uncontrolled effects of (a) instructional method or content differences between treatments that are compared, and (b) a novelty effect for newer media, which tends to disappear over time. Evidence for each of these controlled effects can be found in the meta analyses. The positive effect for newer media more or less disappears when the same instructor produces all treatments in a study (Clark, 1985). Different teams of instructional designers or different teachers probably give different content and instructional methods to the treatments that are compared. However, if the effect for media tends to disappear when the same instructor or team designs contrasting treatments, we have reason to believe that the lack of difference is due to greater control of non-medium variables. Clark and Salomon (1986) cited a number of researchers in the past who have reminded us that when examining the effect of different media, only the media being compared can be different. All other aspects of the mediated treatments, including the subject matter content and method of instruction, must be identical in the two or more media being compared. In meta-analyses of college level computerized versus conventional courses, an effect size of one-half a standard deviation results when different faculty designed the compared course. Clark (1983) found that this effect reduces to about one-tenth of a standard deviation advantage when one considers only studies in which one instructor plans and teaches both experimental and control courses.

Novelty in Additive Media Experiments

A second, though probably less important source of confounding in media comparison studies, is the increased effort and attention research subjects tend to give to media that are novel to them. The increased attention paid by students sometimes results in increased effort or persistence which yield achievement gains. If they are due to a novelty effect, these gains tend to diminish as students become more familiar with the new medium. This was the case in reviews of computer-assisted instruction at the secondary school level (grades 6 to 12). An average computer effect size of three-tenths of a standard deviation (i.e., a rise in examination scores from the 50th to the 63th percentile) for computer courses tend to dissipate significantly in longer duration studies. In studies lasting four weeks or less, computer effects were one-half a standard deviation. This reduced to three-tenths of a standard deviation in studies lasting five to eight weeks and further reduced to the familiar and weak two-tenths of a standard deviation computer effect after eight weeks of data collection. Effects of two-tenths or less account for less than 1 percent of the variance in a comparison. The Kuliks (cf. Clark, 1983; 1985 for citations) report a similar phenomenon in their review of visual-based instruction (e.g., film, television, pictures). Although the reduction in effect size for longer duration studies approached significance (about .065 alpha), there were a number of comparisons of methods mixed with different visual media, which makes interpretation difficult (cf. Clark & Salomon, 1986). In their review of computer use in college, the Kuliks did not find any evidence of this novelty effect. In their comparison of studies of one or two hours duration with those which held weekly sessions for an entire semester, the effect sizes were roughly the same. It is possible that computers are less novel experiences for college subjects than for secondary school students.

Conclusions About Additive Research Evidence for Different Learning Benefits From Different Media

So, to repeat the question that began this part of the discussion, "does available research support the claim of different learning benefits from different media?", the answer seems to be - not yet. There is compelling research evidence that learning benefits found in media comparison research over the past seventy years may not be attributed to media per se. One of the problems with research is that it tends to be most clear about those things that fail to produce learning and less intelligible about what actually does cause measured learning gains. As a result of more recent studies it is becoming less and less valid to suggest that any given medium provides a learning benefit that is in any essential way different than those potentially available from another medium. While there is not complete agreement among researchers on this conclusion, the burden of future research evidence seems to be placed on the strong media theories. As a consequence of the lack of evidence for specific effects from specific media, there seems to be little support available in this area for the additive use of multiple media. Thus, the discussion moves on to the second question, the multiplicative assumption.

The Multiplicative Assumption

Does available research support the claim that when two or more media are combined, their learning benefits are greater than (multiples of) any of the combined media used alone?

Implicit in the multiplicative research assumption is the expectation that media in combination may produce learning benefits that are not possible from any of the separate media. This finding is common in science. Even in educational research we sometimes find that individual variables, by themselves, have little impact on learning. However when separate variables are combined, they sometimes interact to produce strong and important effects. This is, for example, the basis for the entire area of "aptitude-treatment interaction" research (refer to Clark, 1982). Thus, we must also examine the possibility that multiple media combinations may be more than the sum of their separate media.

While there are many studies that compare the learning advantage of one medium versus another medium, few studies have compared the multiplicative effects of many media in combination versus any of the combined media used alone to teach the same subject matter.

Interactive Videodisc Studies as Examples of Multiplicative Research

The only current example of multiplicative studies is to be found in the experiments that have been conducted on interactive videodisc (computer control of videodisc access) compared with either computers alone or other single media. Bosco (1986) reviewed 28 of these comparison studies and found results that are similar to those reported by Clark (1983, 1985) for single media comparison studies. When learning was assessed as an outcome, results of were mixed. Some studies showed advantages for the multi-media interactive video, some for the single comparison media (most often computers or television) and some comparisons resulted in "no significant differences". One suspects the familiar lack of control of instructional method and curriculum content (Clark, 1983) between the different media. A similar conclusion was reached by Hannafin (1985) in his review of a number of studies of computer-controlled interactive video. He suggests that learning is influenced by the cognitive effects of instructional methods, not by the choice of media. He implies that the same teaching method can be used in a number of "specific instructional technologies" (media). He states:

> While interactive video technology itself may offer interesting potential, it seems unlikely that interactive video differs from allied technology from either learning or cognitive perspectives. Technologically-independent research in learning and processing provides empirically-based techniques and methods likely to facilitate learning. Similarly, studies designed to examine the ways in which the mental activities of the learner are supported to improve learning offer insights into effective lesson design and activity independent of specific instructional technologies. It seems improbable that these principles will be redefined as a consequence of interactive video technology. (p. 236)

Also similar to the results reported in the single media comparisons, the interactive video studies show "attitude" and training time advantages under some conditions. Subjects seem to report liking the interactive video better than the single media comparisons conditions. However, this attitude advantage might be an example of the novelty effect described by Clark (1983, 1985) since most of these studies represents a relatively brief exposure to the multi media condition.

Another problem with these studies tends to be a lack of control of the informational content of the lessons presented in the different treatments (Clark, 1985). What sometimes happens is that the research team attempts to duplicate an existing, single-medium instructional program on a multi-media system. During the duplication process, information required by the test and available in the original lesson is, by accident, not transferred to the multi-media version. In this case, we would expect to find evidence that the more complete single-media version results in greater learning. Examples of studies where this control problem can be found are described by Clark (1985) and Clark & Salomon (1986).

Conclusions About The Learning Benefits Of Multiple Versus Single Media

Available research does *not* support the claim that when two or more media are combined, their learning benefits are not greater than when they are used alone. While there are relatively fewer studies in this area, their results seem to follow the same pattern as the single media comparison studies.

Why have the media comparison studies resulted in such a negative and ambiguous results? The primary difficulty with the studies may stem from a lack of control of the instructional method or technique used to teach the tested learning content. So, for example, in a study on the use of the interactive video disk versus a non-interactive televised presentation of the lesson, the superior learning from video disk will be attributed to its "multiple" media capacity. Yet, it would be difficult to rule out the strong possibility that the variable which produced a learning gain was not media, but the method variable many of us refer to as "interactivity".

Interactivity: A Medium or A Method Variable?

Interactivity is variously defined (refer to Hannifin, 1985) but common to most definitions are the qualities of providing corrective and informational feedback based on student responses during instruction. Floyd defines interactivity as an instructional context where "...the sequence and selection of messages are determined by the user's response to the material." (1982, p.2).

While practitioners might argue that these qualities are the inherent features of the interactive video disk technology, it is possible to provide interactivity in other media. For example, all of these instructional variables could be presented by computer-based instruction and by live instructors. Hannifin (1985) describes experiments were interactivity was successfully presented to learners by various, single media. These experiments provide evidence for the claim that instructional methods such as interactivity can be provided with a variety of single and multiple media to produce similar learning benefits.

When studies that do not control instructional methods are reported, they tend so show evidence in favor of the multi-media treatment when the results are actually due to powerful instructional methods that are only used in the multi-media condition. This is most likely the case with the recent large scale meta-analysis of forty-seven North American interactive videodisc studies reported by Fletcher (1990). In the introduction to the report, Fletcher acknowledges the validity of Clark's (1983) argument in a statement that media such as videodisc "...do not guarantee [learning] impact, but the functionalities they support and their applications do." (p. II-1) Functionalities is a construct that is similar to instructional methods. Interactivity is a "functionality" of instruction with videodisc *and* other media, including human beings. Nevertheless, Fletcher, in his summary of the review permits the reader to slip back into the strong media argument when he concludes that "Interactive videodisc instruction was more effective than conventional approaches to instruction...and...computer-based instruction...but there was little in the reviewed studies to indicate how interactive videodisc instruction achieves its success." (pp. IV-1,4) Since meta-analytic reviews seldom examine experimental control for methods or functionalities, the conclusions they reach tend to be as confounded as the studies they review. Well-designed studies that control for methods by having the same method available in all media treatments, generally show "no significant differences" on learning outcomes (Clark & Salomon, 1986).

Conclusions About Interactivity and Other Methods

While it is impossible to reach a definitive conclusion, the best evidence seems to support the claim that various instructional methods (such as interactivity) are responsible for the measured achievement gains when multiple media treatments are compared with more "conventional" single media treatments. This result has been found with each successive wave of new media and technology for at least the past seven decades of educational research. Why then do we continue to repeat the same conceptual and design error? It is likely that part of the problem is our tendency to base research questions on problems that have financial or popular support but no theoretical justification.

Multiple Media Research and Theory

The Theoretical Origins of Multi-Media Research

Aside from obvious research design problems, the main obstacle to multi-media and learning studies is that they are conducted without the benefit of any theory about *why* one would expect differences in the first place. Perhaps the only theoretical basis for the interest in multi-media instruction stems from the Dual Coding Theory (DCT) suggested by Pavio over two decades ago (see Pavio, 1985). The first mention of the multi-media concept is reputed to be found in the popular media text by Brown, Lewis and Harcleroad (1959, 1972). Jim Brown, the first author of the text, reported (Brown, Personal Communication, 1980) that his idea of using many media at the same time for instruction stemmed, in large part, from the Pavio theory. In the 1960's Pavio and others noticed that when learners in memory experiments were exposed to both words and pictures of items to be remembered, they often obtained significantly higher recall scores than if they received only words or only pictures. Brown and others generalized this finding and reasoned that instruction using both word media and picture media together would enhance learning more than instruction using either word or picture media alone.

The exact connection between the Dual Coding Theory (DCT) and multi media is not as clear as we might prefer. One might think, for example, that a single medium such as a book or television program would have the capacity to present both words and pictures - and therefore achieve the benefit without the complication of multiple media. Nevertheless, it is useful to briefly examine the current status of the theory since its history parallels the development of the multi-media movement.

Dual Coding Theory and Multi-Media Instruction

Dual Coding Theory proposes that there are at least two separate cognitive coding functions that specialize in the organization and transformation of visual and verbal information (see Pavio, 1986). According to DCT, visual information is organized such that different parts of an imagined object are simultaneously available for further processing. Any remembered scene may be mentally scanned from a "fixation point" according to the remembered relative position of objects in a mental image. In contrast, verbal information seems to be recalled, processed, and used sequentially. Verbal information can, therefore, only be mentally reorganized in sequence - by, for example, changing word order or inserting word strings in remembered sequences. Visual images, on the other hand, can be modified in a great variety of Spatial context and sensory dimensions (for example, by rotation, size, and color). We could, for example, imagine a movie running backwards (because visual information is free of sequential constraints) but we would have difficulty remembering the sentences in a novel backwards.

If DCT is correct, it is reasonable to assume that when we learn information in visual and verbal forms, each form is stored in a separate cognitive system. Early on, DCT proponents claimed that two storage systems for the same information accounted for the superior recall of information taken in by words and pictures. Since recall required that we locate some item in memory, items with two processing locations might be remembered better than items with one location.

Evidence for Dual Coding Theory

After more than two decades of research, many elements of DCT are still controversial. However, there does seem to be general agreement that the theory does *not* support the use of words and pictures for instruction. Whatever produced the early memory advantage of the word plus picture conditions, it was most likely not the words and pictures. Space limitations prevent a thorough discussion of this literature but see Anderson (1985) for a succinct treatment of the issues. As of now, most researchers in this area accept that early memory gains in word and picture conditions were due to features such as the concreteness and familiarity of the items presented in the experiments. There is also evidence that multiple codings of words and pictures resulted in more contexts for remembering. However, it seems that the visual and verbal forms of the instruction did not influence eventual memory activation. The "visualness" or "verbalness" of information mostly likely does not significantly influence its cognitive processing. A popular current theory suggest that cognitive processing may favor a distinction between *spatial* (not visual) and *sequential* (not verbal) information in any modality or medium (Anderson, 1985). Thus, when words, or pictures, or sounds are placed in some relative position to each other in some space, they are processed differently than when they are ordered sequentially. Thus, there appears to be no compelling evidence in the DCT research record to support the sue of multiple media or different benefits for words and pictures in instruction.

Future Directions

The long history of research on the media comparison question, including recent interest in interactive multi-media learning environments suggest a number of future directions:

1. Do not continue multi-media research and application based on expected learning benefits.

There is a lack of evidence for the dual coding basis for multi-media theory and questionable results from empirical studies. This conclusion suggests that we should cease inventing in multi-media studies and applications based on presumed *learning* gains. Future research in this area should not be supported unless there is a clear theoretical reason to expect learning gains due to any characteristic exclusive to a certain mix of media. When interactive videodisc instruction programs are produced and evaluated, Reeves's (1986) evaluation models may prove useful for examining the confounding found in past studies and teasing out important effects.

   2.   Focus "learning from instruction" research resources and studies on the effects of instructional *methods* for different types of students.

There is clear but often ignored evidence that the positive learning results attributed to interactive videodisc technology is, in fact, due to the learning benefits of *interactivity* rather than the technology that provided the interactivity (Fletcher, 1990). There is also tantalizing evidence that this benefit is greater for some students than for others (Surgrue, 1990) and that interactivity may result in decreased learning for yet other students (Clark, 1982). Most likely the number of instructional methods available to support learning from instruction will be found to be as large as the number of distinct cognitive processes that underlie the learning process. Other such methods are implicit in all recent discussions of "metacognitive processes" such as *monitoring* of learning progress; the *connecting* of new with familiar information in memory; and the *selecting* of important elements in instructional materials while ignoring less important elements (Corno & Mandinach, 1984; Clark, 1990). Once we have located a cognitive process that must be supported for certain students, we can cast around for the least expensive and most convenient medium (or mix of media) to present it to students.

   3.   Focus multi-media research on *economic* questions such as the cost of delivering instruction and the speed with which media permit the achievement of present learning or performance standards.

Fletcher's (1990) meta analysis of interactive videodisc studies found some solid evidence for cost and speed or learning gains in some situations. Some of these gains were likely to be due to interactivity, some to the videodisc technology and some to a combination of both. One possible problem with these studies is that they tend to be designed and conducted by people who have a vested interest in finding economic benefits to justify large financial investments in costly training technology. Clark & Sugrue (1989) have suggested that the strategies and reviews of Levin (1986) and, Levin, Glass & Meister (1985) are models for future economic research in this area. Learning benefits are most likely to be found in instructional methods that support the cognitive processing necessary for achievement. But the cost of delivering those methods in various media and the time it takes learners to achieve specified achievement levels may be determined, in large part, by the choice of delivery media and the management of those media.

References

1. Anderson, J.R.: Cognitive Psychology and Its Implications. 2nd ed. New York: W.H. Freeman 1985
2. Bosco, J.: An analysis of the evaluations of interactive video. Educational Technology, 26(5), pp. 7-17
3. Brown, J.W., Lewis, L.B., and Harcleroad, F.F.: Instructional Media and Methods. 1st ed. New York: McGraw Hill 1959
4. Clark, R.E.: Antagonism between achievement and enjoyment in ATI studies. Educational Psychologist, 17(2), 1982
5. Clark, R.E.: Reconsidering research on learning from media. Review of Educational Research, 53(4), pp. 445-460 (1983)
6. Clark, R.E.: Confounding in educational computing research. Journal of Educational Computing Research, 1(2), pp. 29-42 (1985)
7. Clark, R.E., and Salomon, G.: Media in teaching. In Wittrock, M. (ed.). Handbook of Research on Teaching. 3rd ed. New York: Macmillan 1986
8. Clark, R. E., and Sugrue, B.M.: North American disputes about research on learning from media. Biennial meeting of the European Association for Research on Learning and Instruction. Madrid, Spain. 1989
9. Corno, L., and Mandinach, E.B.: The role of cognitive engagement in classroom learning and motivation. Educational Psychologist, 18(2), pp. 88-108 (1983)
10. Fletcher, J.F.: Effectiveness and cost of interactive videodisc instruction in defense training and education. Report No. 81-1502. Alexandria, VA: Institute for Defense Analyses 1990
11. Hosie, P.: Adopting interactive videodisc technology for education. Educational Technology, 27(7), pp. 5-10 (1987)
12. Hannafin, M.J.: Empirical issues in the study of computer-assisted interactive video. Educational Communications and Technology, 33(4), pp. 235-247 (1985)
13. Levie, W.H., and Dickie, K.: The analysis and application of media. In R.M. W, Travers (ed.). Second Handbook of Research on Teaching. Chicago: Rand McNally 1973
14. Levin, I. M.: Cost-effectiveness of computer-assisted instruction: Some insights. Report No. 86, Stanford, CA: Stanford Education Policy Institute. School of Education, Stanford University. September 13 1986
15. Mielke, K.W.: Questioning the questions of ETV research. Educational Broadcasting, 2, pp. 6-15 (1968)
16. Reeves, T.C.: Research and evaluation models for the study of interactive video. Journal of Computer-Based Instruction, 13(4), pp. 102-106 (1986)
17. Schramm, W.: Big media, little media. Beverly Hills, CA: Sage Publications 1977
18. Sugrue, B.M.: A cognitive media selection model applied to the instructional use of computers. Paper presented at the annual meeting of the American Educational Research Association. Boston,MA. 1990

A Design Method for Classroom Instruction in the Multimedia Environment

Haruo Nishinosono

Kyoto University of Education, 1 Fujinomori Fushimi, Kyoto, Japan. Tel. 81-75-641-9281. Fax. 81-75-641-9274

Technology and Experiences in Instructional Design

Worldwide trends towards the introduction of New Information Technology (NIT) in schools reflect the widespread aspiration that it will prove a powerful agent in improving the present insufficient standards of education. In spite of the cost of investment in such NIT facilities, however, in practice they do not guarantee the expected improvement of conventional teaching. Resistance to these innovations is supposed to stem from the conservative attitudes of teachers and their adherence to their familiar teaching styles. We should not, however, blame teachers for this reluctance to change. As teacher education is currently constructed, it does not provide an adequate methodology which involves student interaction or an in-service teaching relationship in a way which would help teachers design instruction to fit the new classroom equipped with NIT. In the conventional methods of instructional design, we ask teachers to prepare a lesson plan which describes educational aims, instructional objectives and proposed activities for each class. An understanding of the actual learning processes involved, the various types of learning environments, the specificity of these to individual students are all often neglected. The integration of new methods, consistent with new ideas, is an obvious necessity. The recent change in the conceptual framework needs to be accompanied by changing teacher skills and changing instructional ideas, including multimedia.

Technology develops very quickly, while the teacher changes his/her perception of, and competence in teaching, very slowly. A theoretical approach in educational technology could enable us to harmonize these two levels and integrate them. As things now are, teachers feel uneasy about their teaching ability while researchers tend to develop instructional theory in line solely with technological developments. For example 'Expert System' as applied to instructional design present an area in which computer technology can be applied to teaching, as does 'Multimedia Technology'.

The adoption of a scientific framework, and a scientific approach to knowledge, as a way of achieving coherence and order, is expected of teachers. In the classroom, however, teachers work on the basis of experience and feel some difficulty in adopting scientific and technological ideas. With this in mind, instructional technology should be based on empirical knowledge and that which can be demonstrated in the classroom. This can be elaborated on later with the assistance of other researchers and teachers.

Design and Technology

In conventional teacher training, the importance of educational philosophy and psychology are emphasized. A knowledge of educational psychology is expected to be applicable to the instructional and other problems of everyday life. The reality of schools can differ substantially from this ideal. True instruction is not solely a result of the philosophy and beliefs of the teachers. Despite the long history of educational philosophy and psychology, students still seem to be primarily influenced by television and other media. Teachers have to become more objective in evaluating instructional ideas and also more competent and thoughtful in making decisions about these ideas in what is an increasingly complicated educational environment.

Developments in computer technology have enhanced our abilities to make rational decisions on instructional strategies and to deal with complicated materials and data about our daily teaching activities. We can easily edit and modify instructional document including not only numerical data but also text, symbols and pictures. These material can be in the form of printed matter, audio-visual media and computer software. Designing such material involves the dynamic process of making our ideas concrete so that we can implement in the real world. In this process, we have to take into consideration a range of factors which can influence the learning and instructional environment. Instructional design for effective teaching also has to consider such factors as the actual physical surroundings in which learning will take place. Computer technology offers powerful tools to help us deal with this range of issues in an objective manner.

In my recent study, three stages in research development are identified:
(1) The research program or paradigm
(2) Models
(3) Cases or examples

In the research program, the following items are studied as part of in-service teacher education.
A) The educational value system, which is especially relevant for education in an information society.
B) Judgemental statements on teaching in a multimedia instructional environment.
C) Competency of instructional design encompassing developments in information technologies and various constraints present in the educational situation.
D) How instructions can be carried out using information technology.

Teachers were encouraged to explore their own values in education, formulate their judgemental statements, and design and implement their instructional ideas. As a way of establishing a base of knowledge about how teachers teach, they are encouraged to explicitly state the judgmental propositions which they have used in designing their instruction.

Three models for an objective description of the instructional plan are proposed here; that is the Learning Process Model, the Information Relation Model and the Learning Space Model.

(1) The Learning Process Model:

In traditional methods of writing lesson plans, the attention of the teacher is focussed on the description of educational intentions, the expected outcomes in terms of behavioral objectives, and the process of teaching activities in the classroom. In the self-learning environment, teachers are expected to be facilitators or promoters of learning, not elicitors of expected answers from pupils. In this context, clear and prescient ideas about the learning process are indispensable in preparing material which fits the learning patterns and information needs of learners.

In the conventional lesson plan, the language of daily life is adopted to describe the teacher's intentions. This methods is easily learned and can be utilized quickly by beginners, however experienced teachers find it confusing to try to tie themselves down to this method especially as a vehicle to describe their actual lessons to other professional teachers. Computer technology provides us with a powerful way of editing texts and symbols. The relationship of the conceptual framework of teachers to the learning process is illustrated by the following figure. This takes into account not only the instructional strategies of the teacher, the perception of the teacher, and their educational goals but also instructional resources, various media and even the computer display. See figure 1.

The process model was originally designed horizontally incorporating the time element, but was later modified into a vertical one consciously imitating a computer display with its roll up/roll down functions. This illustrates the various elements of ordinary classroom teaching and the factors which need to be taken into account in considering instructional design and implementation. In conventional teaching, teachers tend to be information providers and to teach directly, as represented on the lefthand side of the diagram. The teacher's role will shift gradually from being an information provider to being a learning manager of learning. That is the teacher will be gradually released from the role of information presenter and become a promoter of learning, relying on media to convey information to the learners.

Classroom teaching is carried out everyday in every classroom in every country of the world. Teachers are expected to formulate their ideas and make their own individual decisions about teaching. The possibilities of exchanging their ideas and experiences about teaching with other teachers are very limited. There are no real opportunities at an appropriate, professional level for international exchange skill-enhancement in the teaching profession. A skill-enhancement program for instructional design was projected at the beginning of this research project to assist teachers in designing their lesson plans, using the symbol system for science teaching. Pictorial tools which could be used to describe the teaching/learning process was developed and employed at the experimental level. At that time, there was no adequate way to deal flexibly with the wealth of symbols which are used or generated. Magnetic sheets and small pieces of iron plates were used in an effort to describe the teaching/learning process and its media configuration. (See Nishinosono, 1978 for details).

In a computer display, the roll-up/roll-down function is used to enhance our screen vision. The temporal sequence of the learning process can be represented in a top to bottom screen display which corresponds to the sequence classroom instruction from the beginning to the end. Each learning activity can be described in ordinary language. In our experiment, the symbols which are developed specifically for instructional design in science education were used to help student teachers in articulating their ideas about the learning process which they hoped would take place in their actual teaching practice.

(2) The Information Relation Model:

In conventional instruction, information relevant to that instruction is delivered by teachers and is expected to be received efficiently by learners. This framework is a major hindrance to introducing innovation in instruction. Currently there is no professional way to precisely describe the learning environment as it actually is from the perspectives of information allocation and structure. Two ideas are essential in describing the information environment. One is the relation and structure of information being conveyed, closely related to the actual subject matter itself. The other is the configuration and physical placement of various information media relevant to the learning environment. Recent innovations in computer technology have made the description of these structures and configurations easier.

(3) Learning Space Model:

Two models need to be incorporated in instructional design; physical space and psychological space. Physical space is, literally, the arrangement of equipment in a given area and its configuration into a learning environment. This can be represented using the symbols of desks, tables, OHP, equipment etc.

On the other hand, psychological space can be the formation of the group, the interface between learners and equipment, or relations which exist between teachers and learners.

Psychological space can be represented by the use of arrows, lines, boxes, circles and various symbols of access between the teacher and the learner or group of learners. This model has an obvious relationship to the Information Relation Model.

Development of a Computer Language

Macintosh technology has provided us with powerful tools to handle multimedia materials. WIMPS (windows, icons, mouse and pull-down screen) methods have released us from the complicated and time-consuming manipulation of MS-DOS and other programming languages. Even children can easily operate computers and deal with the information made available. Novice teachers in computer technology routinely use newly developed software, for instance word-processing, spreadsheet, database and window applications. When using these technologies, teachers have to make decisions about using data and materials, managing them, and giving them a structure which aids effective instruction.

In WIMPS methods, however, this process of decision-making cannot be easily expressed in language and it is difficult to express the basis for their judgments and decisions to other teachers. To begin to articulate a flexible description of this process, a computer language which can be used easily by teachers who may be ignorant of technology is needed and we are developing a language named "Mind", originally developed form the "Forth" language, to achieve this but entirely in Japanese. My research is devoted to studying the process of decision-making by teachers and to helping teachers express this process and the experiences which lead to it in a precise manner. Judgments and statements based upon them are not (and cannot be) capable of 'proof' in the strictly scientific sense used in empirical manners. An example of such statement would be the following.

"In instructing students in the method and the significance of information gathering, an efficient method for the fourth grade of elementary level is to create a scenario of drama based on their own experiences, to act it out, and then to encourage them to analyze it by themselves."

This statement was made by an elementary school teacher. It is composed of two parts. The first part ends with 'the elementary level', the second part is the rest of the statement. The first part explains the educational goal and the prerequisites and conditions for instruction. The second part outlines the technics and activities required to reach this goal under the given conditions. Of course, there may be alternative strategies to achieve this goal. This kind of judgment/statement can be stored in a computer to be studied later by instructional researchers. If the various conditions are more rigorously clarified, such judgments/statements will be more reliable and useful to subsequent teachers. In reality, it is very difficult for teachers to formulate such rigorous statements without prior training. They lack the conceptual framework needed to express their technical judgment in such a precise manner. To facilitate this process, a computer system which will enable teachers to express their judgments is being developed utilizing a programming language in Japanese.

Description and Analysis of the Learning Process

A judgment of teaching techniques need to be evaluated empirically. Objective observations of classroom teaching is indispensable in evaluating and justifying particular statements in specific classes conducted by specific teachers at specific times. The process of making judgments and decisions about solving technical problems relies on identifying factors and actions relevant to the goal. In this context, there is no need to generalize our assumptions about instructional design. Our aim of evaluation involves observing and analyzing specific instruction. My goal is to develop a method of analysis which can be applied to instruction in an ordinary classroom situation. (See details of this work in Nishinosono et al. 1989). Learning from real-life cases or examples is the best way of evaluating the range of strategies and actions taken in the classroom.

Present Stage of Development:

Currently research on these methods is at the stage of implementing symbol manipulation in computer program design and in experimental trials of formulating judgments/statements put forward by experienced teachers. When sufficient numbers of such judgments/statements have been collected, computer specialist will help us to analyze the coherency of these statements. The primary purpose of this research is to provide working teachers with concrete assistance in designing learning-oriented instruction for a variety of learning environments, to help them create a framework and appropriate tools to express their individual experiences and judgments about instruction, and hopefully to suggest a way in which they can exchange ideas at the national and the international levels.

References

1. Nishinosono, H., Hino E., and Fujita T.: Two symbol systems for designing instructional processes. In Educational Technology Research, Vol. 2(1). Tokyo 1978.
2. Nishinosono, H., Masuda, H., and Karasawa, H.: Structurally describing instructional process and a method of analysis using partially-defined sequences. In Educational Technology Research, Vol. 12(1). Tokyo 1989
3. Selected symbols standardized by IEC-TC3 (1973)

Graphical symbols for use on equipment

5187	Teacher, supervisor
5188	Student operator
5189	Group of students, of operators
5190	All students, operators
5210	Speak
5211	Listen
5163	Recording on an information carrier
5164	Reading or reproduction from an information carrier
5165	Erasing from an information carrier
5166	Recording on an information carrier, Monitoring input data during writing
5167	Recording on an information carrier, Monitoring input data after writing
5168	Monitoring output data during read-out
5169	Recording lock
5048	Colour (Qualifying symbol)
5049	Television
5050	Colour television
5051	Television monitor
5052	Colour television monitor
5053	Television receiver
5054	Colour television receiver
5093	Tape recorder
5094	Magnetic-tape stereo sound recorder
5095	Recording on tape
5096	Play-back or reading from tape
5097	Erasing from tape
5098	Recording, Monitoring at the input during recording on tape
5099	Recording, Monitoring from tape after recording on tape
5100	Monitoring during play-back or reading from tape
5116	Television camera
5117	Colour television camera
5118	Video tape recorder
5119	Colour video tape recorder
5120	Video recording
5121	Colour video recording
5122	Video play-back
5123	Colour video play-back
5077	Headphone
5078	Stereophonic headphone
5079	Headset
5080	Loudspeaker
5081	Loudspeaker/microphone
5082	Microphone
5085	Music
5182	Sound; audio

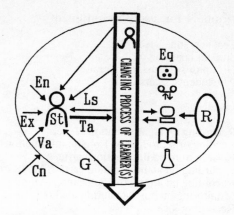

St: teacher's perspective on teaching learning process and instructional strategy.
Ta: instructional tactics or teachers behavior
R: instructional resources and information
Eq: equipment including audio-visual, science experiments and other practice facilities.
Va: value system or philosophical view of teacher.
G: predetermined educational goal or perspectives of learners' changes during the lesson.
Ls: learners' traits or states perceived by the teacher.
En: given instructional environment.
Ex: individual experiences of the teacher.
Cn: various constraints.

Figure 1.   The process model

Multimedia Learning Environment: An Educational Challenge

Harold Haugen

P.O. Box 8119, Dep. 0032. Oslo 1, Norway. Tel. 47-2-347-582 or 47-54-90288. Fax. 2-34-9541
Stord College of Education 5414 Rommetveit, Norway

Education, Computers and Media, the Norwegian Approach

Education dates back for thousands of years, organized schools for hundreds, computers and electronic media only for decades, and we are still looking for new ways to apply them for the best results in learning. *Learning* remains the key objective, whatever media or technologies educationalists, researchers and developers use as tools for transfer of facts/data, knowledge and understanding. The information age calls for new methods and strategies to select and organize information before transforming it into knowledge and wisdom.

The new information technology, NIT, offers a growing number of possibilities, including computers with advanced software, video disks, compact disks, electronic transmission, digitized sound, etc. Traditional education and training systems are not able to keep up with this development. Special measures must be taken to upgrade schools, teachers, instructors, curricula, courses, equipment, etc. Like in many other countries, the Norwegian Government decided that we needed a *Programme of Action* for computers in education (1984-1988). This had its main activities directed towards primary/secondary schools and vocational training. It was succeeded by a more general *National Programme of Action* for information technology in industry, administration and education (1987-90).

A main objective of both these programmes was the principle to look at technology as a tool, not as a goal in itself. It was important to find new methods and applications that would make education and training more rewarding and efficient. An initial obstacle was the lack of adequate software.

After a few rounds of traditional programming exercises the question of software development was addressed more systematically by the governmental task force, the Datasecretariat. A set of *software development tools* was initiated. From 1985 till 1988 the

Mosaikk	- for prototyping and creation of user interfaces
SimTek	- for building, running and revising dynamic simulation models
GrafTrix	- as a graphical, portable tool kit for programmers in Turbo Pascal
Director	- for creation of and working with adventure stories, interactive literature

- came into being. They have been continuously upgraded to new standards and versions, and now claim to reduce development time and costs by as much as 50 - 80% for educational software packages. This gain in efficiency and cost effectiveness - while still keeping flexibility and all possibilities open - have also caught the interest of other users of software, like industry, military forces, organizations, oil companies etc.

When the application of interactive video and other media came around to schools, *Mosaikk* was already there to handle all the different modules, like databases, video, CD-ROM, sound chips and so on. Prototypes and demonstrations could be produced within hours, while more serious applications required weeks or months. It was still, however, way below normal development costs based on traditional means. Now more tools of similar kinds have come into existence, opening possibilities to choose and pick.

While technical and programming hurdles are still present - and probably always will be - the real challenge is now shifted to pedagogy and educational applications of all these possibilities in the world of multimedia. *Interactivity* seems to be a key word. This can to a large extent be obtained by careful combinations of computer technology and programming with elements from media technology, being careful not to overdo the tempting effects of sound, motion, graphics, colours etc. The message itself is easily washed away by the waves of impressive gimmicks.

Presenting a situation through different media

By means of a computer program a situation may be described through text, graphics, animation, picture/photos, movie, sound. Reality may be shown through video or film, while details can be explained through computer graphics. Phenomenons normally not observed by the human eye may be visualized through manipulation of time, size, speed, graphics and artificial animation, e.g. the flow of ions in the process of electrolysis or the infection of T-cells in human blood by AIDS-virus. Illustrating these processes through "simple" video or film, limits the presentation to pre-set sequences and leaves out possibilities of interactivity. It is a notable difference between *interactive video* and *interrupted video*.

Working on an optical storage of pictures through a computer programme makes it easy to lay your own "tracks" or sequence of presentation, making it possible to revers, to choose new sequences, make different combinations etc. at any time. Thus leaving the whole material in an open structure, including animated sequences or parallel sound tracks, the instructor or student may be offered the control of attaching it to other instructional material, e.g. computer assisted learning in a wider sense. The student may be offered the role of a visitor into a specific situation, or of an active decision maker in business or politics. Well known examples are visits to art galleries, business administration, traffic education or flight simulator.

Instruction

The introduction of an electronic/optical instructor in the learning environment has turned out very successful in the training of operators at industrial plants and other situations where specific skills are to be learnt. In connection with a computer simulation of certain operations, the actions by the trainee are recorded continuously (by the computer), and at certain combinations of decisions or actions, a supervisor pops up on the screen, pre-recorded on "live video", asking questions, warning against specific dangers or perhaps stopping the whole process from further destructive actions. Another possibility is to have the instructor of supervisor on call, so that the trainee may call him - on the screen - in situations where help is wanted. The program must then be made to present relevant information in the specific situation where the trainee asks for advise.

The interruption by a computerised supervisor may also be varied in stages, e.g. with a simple sound or text warning at the first mistake, next time the instructor points out the specific mistake and perhaps the third time he may demonstrate the whole operation, indicating clearly where a mistake should be avoided. These latter demonstrations may be shown as principal, graphical animations, as still pictures/photos or by live video recordings.

Simulation

Work on *system dynamics* and *computer simulations* as new educational methods has been going on for 20 - 30 years. The methods have been developed at university level (MIT a.o.) since the 1960'ies, and are being applied in business, industry, politics and strategic planning in order to extend the capacity of human minds to handle problems involving large, complex systems. When several factors, parameters or variables are interrelated through a network of causes and effects ("casual loops"), our minds are too limiting to cope with the real systems. Systematic work to make up simplified -or even complex - models that can be played with and tested out on modern computers, may help decision makers to reach better understanding and insight before conclusions are drawn and decisions are taken.

Pre-defined and rigid systems, e.f. in physics or chemistry, where all relations are known and can be described by well defined mathematical equations, may fairly simply be represented by computerized models. This has been done for years, and is used to illustrate and help understanding of for instance nuclear fission, chemical reactions or a simple lever balance.

More complex systems with less well defined relations between variables, like international economy, pollution of a lake, spreading of AIDS, or world wide terrorism, requires more Trainingraining and skills to transform into reasonable reliable models on a computer. Methods for this are also being developed through the theories and tools of system dynamics. The main challenge turns out to be sufficient facts and knowledge about the real system to make up a representative model.

Application of system dynamics and computer simulations of dynamic systems is now gradually finding its way into teaching and training, often introduced as a new educational method (ref. H. Haugen: System Dynamics as an Educational Method, Computers in Education, Elsevier Science Publishers B.V. (North-Holland), IFIP 1990). Different projects on this matter are presently running in several parts of the world, e.g. in the Nordic countries. Reports so far are promising - also from industry, oil companies etc. Great interest has been expressed by the Norwegian military forces.

Simulations may very well be run on computers with only alpha-numeric entering of data and presentations of results. User friendliness is largely increased however, when graphical interfaces and presentations are included. Even better it becomes when several media are made available, e.g. live or animated sequences of actions or illustrations can be attached to certain situations in the simulation. This is being tried out in connection with pollution projects ("Algae invasion of the Norwegian Fiords"), in programmes for safety instruction of workers at oil platforms in the North Sea, and as an extra possibility to a simulation of fish breeding.

Experiences are so far very limited on the latter ways of applying multimedia as part of computer assisted instruction. Reactions are positive, however, and require further development of educational methods in this direction. (A first prototype of a cooperative project with the Norwegian Army, on the construction/mounting of bridges, may be demonstrated at the seminar in June.)

Hypertext

Normally a text is static, sequential and two-dimensional. *Hypertext* introduces a third dimension, i.e. one may be marking or clicking at a certain word, go *into* or behind the text to find a closer explanation. This has become a well known technique in modern software, particularly in Macintosh and Windows oriented software packages. This third dimension is not necessarily only a single layer of extra text to explain difficult words or expressions. It may be extended and branched more or less indefinitely, and may also be used for "jumping" to other parts of the text or programme.

The hyper-concept may of course be applied to call in abstracts and sequences from other media in an integrated information technology system. With ample supplies of pictures, sound etc. on resources like CD-ROM, LASERVISION, electronic databases through telecommunication, it is possible to offer a new concept of *multimedia encyclopedia*, or an electronically integrated text book. The best ways to exploit these possibilities are still to be found, but the potential seems to be far beyond present experiences.

The concept may also be accessed from a regular, printed text book, where for instance bar codes and a light pen can open the doors to different parts of multimedia. Or vice versa, a message on the screen or from a loudspeaker may point to a certain page or paragraph in the printed text. Technically the possibilities for a complete integration of media are there already. But neither teachers nor researchers are yet prepared to use it regularly in the classroom or auditorium.

Editing

Traditionally text book authors - or occasionally subject teachers - are editing the content and form of topics to be taught. So far this has also been the normal way for computerized learning material, software packages etc. A new trend is the use of so-called *open software*, where the student - possibly in cooperation with other students or the teacher - creates their own content and structure of the material. E.g. this may be a natural, advanced stage in work with system dynamics and simulations where models are to be constructed, changed, re-programmed etc.

With several media available, the challenge to edit your own learning material becomes a new and challenging possibility. It requires experience and skills, and above all it takes flexible hardware and software to simplify the manipulation of media. Most likely the challenge will be limited to teachers/instructors and perhaps to advanced learners and graduate students. Nevertheless, whoever is editing this kind of material, is himself bound to learn a lot about the matter to be taught - and about media technology.

User activity and user experience

These are key words in development of computer assisted learning material, where interactivity and variation are main advantages over traditional texts and pictures. The use of multimedia must not alter this, and care must be taken to avoid concentration on the presentation media and technology more than on the content and learner activity. The user will often judge the material as "good" or "interesting" just because of the new, technical gimmicks. Very often the creator or editor of the material is also trapped into this pitfall. Being afraid that the user will skip some of the gimmicks in order to reach the learning objectives in a more straight forward way, she tends to lay very rigid tracks through a complex collection of material. Thus no real choices may be left for the user.

To obtain intended, long lasting and positive learning effects, will it be essential to keep the interest of the learner, either by exiting elements in the form of games, by unexpected events, or most relevantly by presenting the content itself in a mind catching manner. Use of multimedia effects may be a good help for this purpose. But again one must be aware that every element should have a clear function in the learning process, not just an input to keep the learner's attention. In the latter case it will be more of a distraction than an aid to understand or memorize the subject content. Multimedia may add a new dimension to the programme, but should never be introduced in a way that leads the learner astray.

Tools for creating learning environments

A skilled programmer will always be able to connect her computer programme to different media by means of more or less standardized programming languages. Whether she chooses binary coding, assembler languages or a standard programming language like C, PASCAL, etc., it will always require lots of specialized knowledge; it is normally not a task for the average teacher or media worker. And it takes a lot of time - and money to hire specialists.

Eventually, when the programme is ready for use, it will be very difficult to alter, change or upgrade. And an equal job has to be put in to make a new, similar programme with a different content. Some routines and procedures may be transferred and re-used. But most of the job has to be done all over again.

This is where the Norwegian Ministry of Education - as previously mentioned - has invested in more permanent and standard tools for software development - including the use of multimedia. Several tools are available on MS-DOS computers. The latest addition to our family of tools, is the WINIX TOOLKIT, made for computers able to run MS-WINDOWS 3.0. It applies all the standard tools available under Windows, including standard software like Excel, Word etc., and have already built up libraries to handle video, CD-ROM, sound chips, extra cards mixing computer graphics and video on the screen. As new requirements and wishes are posed by users, new libraries are added.

The purpose and advantage of WINIX TOOLKIT is that editing and composing integrated multimedia learning material, is greatly simplified - both for experienced programmers and for less technologically trained people. Software packages that normally takes months or years to make, can be developed within days or weeks. Particularly valuable is the possibility to create a prototype of a suggested programme within a few hours. This simplifies and helps the discussions between differently skilled persons who set out to develop a project together.

The tools do not eliminate the need for skilled programmers. The programmers may, however, work at a different level and at a different speed than would otherwise be possible. More efforts can be put into finding the best solutions to pedagogic, didactic, perceptive and subject oriented questions, less effort into programming and the technical side of a project. It takes far less training to master the tools - to a certain level - than it would take to master a traditional programming language for persons of other specializations, like teachers, generals or engineers. Also maintenance, upgrading and re-programming are highly simplified when the programme is initially created in one of the standard tools.

Several other tools are now available for the same purpose - to combine computer programmes with multimedia technology. All of them have their pros and cons. The reason why most Norwegian educational software is now developed within the WINIX concept, is that it is linked to a communication package, simplifying and opening for a broader use of distance education - or *distributed education* . Other reasons being the cost of the packages and the fact that it is created with educators as its main target group.

Conclusion

Multimedia opens for new dimensions and possibilities within training, instruction and education. It is important to note that new media should only be applied for specific learning purposes, not for gimmicks or distraction of the learner. To get the full benefit out of technology the setting must include suitable tools for handling and integrating them in a sensible and pedagogic way. Taking all this into account, the potential of new learning environments seem to be very wide and promising. Sufficient experience and educational foundations are still lacking, and should be obtained through projects involving different parts of society, like schools, industry, public administration, military forces, adult education etc.

2. Interface Design:
Issues and New Conceptual Models

Interactivity and Intelligent Advisory Strategies in a Multimedia Learning Environment: Human Factors, Design Issues and Technical Considerations

Max Giardina

Université de Montréal Études et administration, Pavillon Marie-Victorin, 90 Vincent D'Indy, Canada H2C 3J7. Tel. (514) 343 5670. Fax. (514) 343 2283

Introduction

Multimedia environments offer us a new perception of the state of changes in and the integration of technological environments which can increase our ability to process information in the field of education. Moreover, they are compelling us to change our idea of knowledge. This change is reflected in the obvious convergence of different types of access, communication and information exchanges. A number of related fields such as publishing, television, the mass media in general and the nascent data processing sector are overlapping more and more, altering each others' characteristics, and spawning hybrid environments which make it possible to obtain information in new ways.

The situation created by new environments which give different powers to individuals, particularly with regard to access to and the handling of information, is becoming increasingly prevalent in the field of education. This is true of individuals possessing a certain knowledge and individuals wishing to acquire such knowledge. Static equilibrium, in which roles are permanently shared, is shifting to a dynamic equilibrium, where roles change depending on the situation and individual needs. How can we define and explain new situations for which the appropriate words and definitions have yet to be enunciated?

Representing a particular content draws us to new types of knowledge transactions occurring between the environment and the learner. Control and initiative oscillate between the environment and the individual according to the latter's decisions, which in turn are conditioned by the adaptability and flexibility of the environment in relation to individual differences. Interactivity, as defined in a survey of the literature and applied to a wide array of situations, is the basic concept which readily adapts to all manner of situations precisely because it still appears to be vague and used in a polysemic manner when account is taken of the features of the technology used.

In our study we have endeavoured to shift interactivity from a confused state, one which is still too closely tied to a technocentric design in which it appears to be defined to an excessive degree in relation to the technical characteristics of the environment used, in order to define it using the complex design of a reasoning dimension based on coaching strategies which take into consideration the modeling of the knowledge transmitted and enable the learner to gain access to and control such knowledge. In this way, the concept of interactivity acquires a new dimension by focusing particularly on each individual's strategies during learning. This encourages the exchange of the relevant information and knowledge between the interactive environment and the individual. An interactive multimedia environment is rendered operational by identifying a new conceptual framework in which interactivity is defined using elements directly related to the technological environment used, complex design, the learners' actions and decisions, and adjustments tailored to individual differences.

The development of a complex, concrete object enabled us to observe its impact and analyse the reactions of learners in this new learning situation, especially with respect to the flexibility and adaptability of the intervention. In this interactive environment, observations centre first and foremost on the learning process rather than the product. Because we wish to shift the emphasis in the concept of interactivity toward a cognitive dimension, we must foster the inter-exchange of qualitative information which is not merely the verification of an outcome but a significant observation of the process the learner goes through to attain this outcome. To this end, we introduced into this interactive environment a reasoning dimension which makes it possible to monitor the learner throughout the learning process in order to better comprehend his decisions and, as a result, enable the interactive environment to better adapt to the learner. In this study, we examine how such an interactive environment can satisfy the need to personalize training. We therefore analyse various questions related to conception ad development, and to the attitude of potential users.

The new interactive multimedia learning environment

The examination and integration of different media and technological means with a view to developing virtual, multi-access, multi-creation learning systems offers an undeniable, growing educational potential. At the same time, they demand a review and readaptation of various teaching strategies whose design and application in relation to more effective learning demand a great deal more research. A number of research projects have already revealed that the variety of visual and aural stimuli used in a learning situation based on interactive technological media may considerably boost learning (Clark, 1984). Moreover, learning in an interactive environment appears not only to enhance short-term retention but long-term retention as well. The new technological environment demands the renewed articulation and organization of visual, aural and textual information (Faiola and De Bloois, 1988), to ensure its educational effectiveness (Eastwod, 1978; De Bloois, 1982). The link between computers and optical or analog memories establishes the bases of what Streibel (1984) calls an information extraction and spotting system (Merrill and Bennion, 1979; Merrill, 1981). This combination brings together the interaction and information storage capacity of computers and the realism of video and audio for learning purposes (Streibel, 1981; Bennion, 1982). It displays the features of traditional computer-assisted teaching, involving the typical information-question-answer sequence and connection to other information, and the features of audiovisual equipment, involving other kinds of stimuli. Such combinations have spawned what are now being dubbed complex interactive multimedia learning environment or programs (Bork et al., 1977; De Bloois, 1982, Giardina, Duchastel and Marton, 1987). One possibility of this new type of environment is that is has the potential to become a learning tool which can adapt to different situations and more specific learning needs (Schneider, 1975; Siegel, Schubien and Merrill, 1981). These new environments offer the possibility of randomly accessing visual or aural information using procedures based on a diagnostic or prescriptive order developed in a computer program. Moreover, the learner or the program may control access, thereby making available a broad, multimedia database (Romiszowski, 1986). At the same time, in this type of environment, the computer system displays a capacity to acquire and manage certain facets of each student's development, with a view to analysing such information and reacting to facilitate learning. This is the beginning of what Romiszowski (1986) has defined as moderately intelligent coaching that the interactive environment offers the learner at a particular time during learning:

> Modern, computer-controlled interactive video, on the other hand, opens up the possibilities of totally learn-directed control (as in the case of searching a database of 'audiovisual encyclopedia') and also of cybernetic control (as when a computer is used to create a database about the learners and offer an 'intelligent' learner-guidance service). Perhaps, it is in the adoption of one or other of these two forms of control, as opposed to descriptive, pre-programmed, control algorithms, that the really innovative aspects of modern interactive video systems may be found. (p. 396)

One important matter that arises is the more or less explicit control that an interactive system should be able to exercise. In our view, different types of control should be integrated into interactive learning systems; they should be tailored to the various kinds of knowledge modeled within the system. Prescriptive control would, for example, make it possible to diversify information or learning activities. Control centred on the learner would help reveal the latter's learning profile; control which adapts itself interactively would enhance the system's flexibility.

It is perhaps the potential for integrating one or more of these levels of control which will make it possible to move toward truly interactive learning environments (Romiszowski, 1986; Merrill, 1988). When a new technology appears in the field of education, there is a tendency to use it in the same manner as the technology is replacing (Tennyson, 1980, 1983). The new technology demands the application of new learning theories which must be tailored to the process of interactively accessing and processing a given content. Multimedia environments presuppose a novel way of processing information (Cohen, 1984, 1985) which is less structured and linear than books or videotapes, by giving access to a great deal more, different information. It is the profound nature of this new interactive learning environment which would be developed through an innovative educational approach. In turn, this could affect how a student learns to develop new learning strategies with a view to facilitating the acquisition, retention, extraction and processing of information. Recent studies have pinpointed a number of educational applications for interactive systems (Hosie, 1987), based on the assumption that interactive learning environments are especially effective with regard to the acquisition of procedural and mechanical abilities (Priestman, 1984). Military human resources laboratories recently pointed out the sound educational potential of interactive environments when they are used for simulations (Meyer, 1984). Indeed, military training services have installed over 50 000 interactive systems in conjunction with their training service (*Screen Digest*, 1986). Other noteworthy applications, which bear witness to the growing role being played by interactive environments, are to be found at Ford, General Motors and Sears (Hosie, 1987), which are now using them to train sales staff. The importance of interactive videodisc systems has also been stressed with regard to simulating communications equipment when communications operators are trained (Young and Tosti, 1984). At the same time, interactive systems have made inroads in management and administration training programs, where their efficiency and profitability have been noted (Ferrier, 1982). The Groupe de recherche sur l'apprentissage interactif (G.R.A.IN.) at Université Laval has for several years been developing and testing a number of interactive learning prototypes using computer-controlled videodiscs and applied to different fields of study (Marton, 1989).

Despite these encouraging signs, the design of multimedia learning environments is still more intuitive than scientific. Already, certain systematic problems are apparent, e.g. a lack of cohesion which would facilitate the efficient integration of information into a coherent cognitive structure. The interactive educational message is not designed sequentially but is based on exploration dictated by the learner's needs or interests. Thus, it is not designed according to an optimal learning sequence and, as a result, may lead to some dispersal of cognitive energy. It is becoming increasingly important to elaborate an intelligent tutorial dimension, based on broad or specific structures and using indicators engendered by learners' actions through an interface which assists in processing information at different levels. Clear studies and precise research must illuminate the true nature of these interactive environments (Hannafin, 1985; Hannafin and Phillips, 1988). Differences and implications must be examined, not so much in relation to technology as at the conceptual level, i.e. to establish whether information is processed for each individual. This will ensure continuity in relation to earlier educational applications of new technologies, from which multimedia applications are derived, with a view to observing and analysing this new technology and examining the role it should play in learning situations (Clark, 1984).

A key concept: Physical interactivity and cognitive interactivity

Interactivity designates, first and foremost (Bennion, 1978) the mechanical link or the ability to search for images on the videodisc using a computer (Currier, 1983); Daynes and Holder, 1984). Moreover, interactivity describes a new educational design made possible by the articulation of different components of such systems (Levin, 1983; Gayesky, 1985). It is obvious that the integration of this new environment alters the nature of the dialogue between learners and machines in learning situations. For this reason, strategies must be adapted to receive, assimilate and communicate information to achieve satisfactory interaction (Faiola and De Bloois, 1988). While the concept of interactivity is a complex one, we note that the style of interaction in most applications is still simple and fairly undeveloped (Bork, 1984). Often, the learner is confined to a multi-choice approach, which is occasionally carefully disguised, and is unable to interact with the information he receives nor carry on a dialogue with the system when he needs to do so.

As Lelu (1985) has stated with respect to interactivity: "[...] The success of a vague concept is undoubtedly due to the ease with which it can adapt to all situations; however, it escapes any attempt to closely scrutinize it [...]". Interactivity means, by and large, the ability of two people to communicate instantaneously by telephone (voice) or video (voice and picture). The concept of interactivity applied to a technological environment should go beyond the stage of choices left to the learner among an array of possibilities pre-defined by the program designer. While we are aware that the University of Nebraska has defined various levels of interactivity (Hart, 1984; Priestman, 1984) related primarily to different functions of the system's technological features, we would like to add the power and control that an individual should exercise over the learning environment. Interactivity also means a way of accessing images and sound (Dubreuil, 1983): something is communicated to the machine, which carries out our orders. Moreover, the technological environment no longer limits itself to executing commands but also informs the user about the operation under way. Interactivity thus becomes a bidirectional relationship in which the machine is aware of what is being done and what it is doing. By further pursuing this manner of perceiving interactivity, we should be able to truly transform and act upon the information put at our disposal. Another facet of intractivity is its immediacy, the brief waiting time between a response and the system's reaction. The learner must be able to find his way through this artificial universe defined in advance by the designer. The indicators displayed to the learner to enable him to gain access to information in the appropriate place, e.g. a detail in an image, rather than seeking the information by name (Bolt, 1979) further amplify the concept of interactivity through the creation of methods of exchange, and more transparent, user-friendly interfaces (Bolt, 1979) further amplify the concept of interactivity through the creation of methods of exchange, and more transparent, user-friendly interfaces (Bolt, 1984; Lippman, 1984; Negroponte 1970). Interactivity is the factor which should enable the learner to manipulate or transform the objects which the designer has defined in a given interactive learning situation. Each learner can thus proceed at his own pace and create his own history within a given learning situation. The learner is part of the definition of interactivity as he is asked to become actively involved in the learning process. Interactivity continues to manage the spatial and physical dimensions of a content which cannot be considered globally but in segments or by levels of deepening knowledge. What we see on the screen is not the whole, but only a part of the whole, and the sophistication of the tools provided to eliminate barriers on the screen may arouse curiosity and discovery.

The individual, an integral factor in the concept of interactivity

According to the concept of interactivity, designers must ensure that the user or learner feels satisfied at each stage of his development: he must experience a genuine relationship based on congenial interaction with the mediatized environment.

The interactivity sought should re-create or simulate situations such as inter-personal dialogue. This is a basic requirement for the designer as his design must be learner-centred. The learner is the end-user of information, but the point of departure for interaction and inter-exchange.

With the individual as centre of the system, the concept of interactivity and, consequently, the means used to implement it, materialize through their multi-sensorial dimensions: the system's reaction or response time following a decision or request made by the learner; and the processing of information according to the learner's immediate needs, which may engender the right or wrong reflection and enhance motivation or sustain participation. The channels used to gain access to this communication must be easy to use when attempts are made to construct or, better still, simulate quasi-human interaction. In this perspective, peripherals are the points of sensory contact closest to the user; they must be naturally perceived in order for concentration on the act of physical tactile, visual or aural exchange to occur readily at the cognitive level. To achieve this type of interactivity, the designer must shift from a mechanical interactivity which uses and redevelops various technical features (Tarrant, Kelly and Wakley, 1988), to a conception based on the needs of the individual in a learning situation. The interactivity sought thus becomes a combination of the best teacher, the best facilitator, the best manager, and the best friend that the designer has ever had or imagined (Hon, 1987).

Interactivity is perceived as an all-encompasing concept which visualizes the dynamism of varied exchanges between the individual and the interactive system. Possible inter-exchanges of information are defined more specifically by the nascent transaction concept suggesting a cycle of information exchanges intended to generate a meaning. As a result, interactivity can be defined as a series of transactions occurring at different, specific times in a multimedia learning process, at once under the control of the system and the individual to accomplish an information cycle which may be more or less significant depending upon the context in which it is activated. Under the circumstances, interactivity means that technology serves human communication focusing on learning. Such communication is to be found in new tools capable of solving problems in a human fashion. The responsibility of an interactive environment and the designer who develops it is to combine as best as he can human experiences related to a specific situation and make them operational in a technological environment likely to stimulate the user, facilitate the creation or use of new "tools", and exchange or transform knowledge with a view to generating new knowledge. Notions such as "lively", "intriguing", "fascinating" or "instructive" do not appear to belong in the lexicon of multimedia systems and, in particular, the development of computer-based systems. The absence of this dimension, which could be deemed the level of "personality" of new interactive environments, reflects the weakness of the concept of interactivity inherent in these situations.

In this respect, we wish to point out that an interactive learning situation is not created and does not exist solely to serve as an easily handled technological tool, but to be perceived as a constantly changing state, depending on the learner's interests and needs. In order to achieve a more refined concept of interactivity, the interactive environment must be able, through an exchange with the individual, to learn to better pinpoint needs under different circumstances, with a view, ultimately, to adjusting the exchange of information. To this end, the emerging field of artificial intelligence offers us the means of developing interactivity in its noblest sense through the "expression" of this intelligence in communications and information processing, or in the type of more or less appropriate questioning, with a view to making an interactive multimedia system capable of "modeling" its intervention according to individual needs. Particular attention must be paid to personalized learning when interactive learning environments are developed, as the level of exchange and dialogue is amplified therein between individuals and machines. Kulik (Kulik et al., 1980) emphasizes that often, in mediatized learning situations, a particular learning framework is imposed on individuals, based on the erroneous notion that the designer-expert is in the best position to prescribe effective teaching. To the contrary, this type of learning framework imposed as the only alternative for the learner has been extensively criticized in mediatized learning situations because it does not take into account individual differences, encourage learners to assume responsibility for learning, or promote individual autonomy (Merrill, Schneider and Fletcher, 1980; Tennyson, 1984). The ability of new interactive learning environments to take into consideration individual differences and learning needs must surely not be overlooked or underestimated (Hannafin and Phillips, 1988).

In this perspective, the individualization of learning in interactive environments should be achieved through the development of a flexible design which is sensitive to various forms of communication and information exchanges between individuals and machines. It should also be sensitive to the changing needs of learners; the system should also adapt itself to the learner's needs (Goetzfried and Hannafin, 1985; Ross et al., 1984; Tennyson and Bultrey, 1980).

A new type of exchange between individuals and machines leading to more cognitive navigation

We have noted in the research and comments of various authors that a number of dimensions appear to be rediscovered when they regain paramount importance in learning environments. The integration of a new technology can play a vital role in broadening the power of inter-exchange between individuals and machines. Such integration must be bolstered quantitatively by allowing for more extensive communication and more rapid decision-making between user and machine in a limited time. In another perspective, an attempt must be made to achieve reciprocity, i.e. to develop an exchange of information and knowledge between users and the technological environment which is more qualitative and therefore more significant for each individual. This exchange is carried on concretely through the visual organization of information and the control which shifts from the user to the interactive system, and vice versa. At the outset, it is external signs and gestures which count in the course of this interaction between the learner and the technological environment. The further we advance in either direction while seeking to flexibly structure content, using different levels of adaptation, types of powers invested in the learner, and different types of decisions, the more complex interaction becomes. Indeed, interaction becomes more intimate, as the level of exchange is more profound, and more revealing of the machine's limitations in relation to the individual with regard to knowledge, the power to process information, differentiation, and presentation to the learner of this information. Such interaction also reveals the learner's limitations, his acceptance of the technological environment, the assimilation and manipulation of this "finite world" in which the learner navigates in order to learn. Exchanges between the individual and the machine may now be more significant but control over the means used to make such exchanges more significant become more complex as the machine must adopt the user's procedural method. The importance of individual internal learning processes is gaining increasingly widespread recognition (Resnick, 1981). It is through this contact between the learner and the environment that we should study to what extent interactive learning situations affect individuals. If the learning environment is able to adapt information and teaching activities to each learner's abilities, the satisfaction engendered by the student's feeling of involvement in learning when he achieves positive results may alter these internal processes (McEwing and Roth, 1985). However, before we can understand the mental operations a learner engages in, it is hard to conceive the learning situations which precisely respond to the learner's internal processes. It is harder still to imagine situations which can affect a learner's mental activities. Some studies maintain that learning can be positively affected if the student is aware of what he needs to learn. The same studies reveal that advice given to a learner in an individualized learning situation based on an ongoing assessment of his progress can affect his internal learning processes by improving learning. The learner's cognitive processes play a fundamental role and are related above all to the processing of and search for information. The ability to navigate in and explore an environment rich in information encourages the search for and sifting through information, and the integration and observation from various standpoints of a concept by stimulating the understanding of a phenomenon through multiple, graphic, visual, aural or written representations. What we have are the underpinnings of a strategy based on the "advice" that may or may not be given to a learner while he is learning (Tennyson and Buttrey, 1980; Tennyson, 1980, 1981; Johansen and Tennyson, 1983; Ross, 1984). Thus, there exists a continuum in the interaction between the learner and the interactive environment, which varies depending on needs and particular phases of the process. This is what Merrill (Merrill, 1980; Merrill, Bass and Dills, 1984) identified as the conscious processing by the learner of information.

		Student model	
		Expert	
		Coach	Supervise
			Guide
Declarative			
knowledge		Explore	Learner
		Demonstrate	
Procedural		Explain	
Knowledge		Predict	
		Diagnose	

Complex intelligent tutorial model

The quality of the interaction and, consequently, the potential for more effective learning depend on the representation and modeling of the content and the strategies involved in "processing" this content, not on the "intelligent" technical features of an environment. The model we have elaborated in our research to render operational an intelligent interactive learning prototype is an application adapted to this general model.

The BIOMEC system: An intelligent coach

The challenge of designing and making operational an intelligent dimension within a multimedia interactive system is a daunting one involving decisions respecting the type of knowledge to be integrated, and strategies and controls pertaining to the processing of such knowledge. A given qualitative model of a phenomenon may be appropriate to a beginner, but a more sophisticated, complete model of the same phenomenon might be more relevant to an advanced learner. BIOMEC is an interactive multimedia system which helps users acquire the abilities necessary to apply a problem-solving process to learn human biomechanics at the undergraduate level. The starting point when the system was designed and learning needs were pinpointed was the elaboration of activities and resources related to learning. Technology changes and becomes more complex, thus altering the various contexts of individual lives, whether during work, studies or leisure. As a result, there is an increasingly obvious need to differentiate learning activities with a view to responding to training or upgrading needs which are not necessarily the same for each individual. In this perspective, the quality of exchanges at the cognitive level engendered by interaction between individuals and machines has increased. For this reason, there is a greater need for learning and assistance while new learning is taking place, both of which can be controlled by intelligent interactive environments (Duchastel, 1988). It is the level of reasoning inherent in the system which becomes a priority. The BIOMEC system enabled us to apply a number of theoretical principles tied to the design of a coach in order to observe the latter's impact on learners.

Since the first studies devoted to problem-solving and information processing (Newell and Simon, 1963), various theoretical paradigms have emerged based on intelligent environments (Hayes, Roth and Thorndyke, 1985), focusing on the representation of human knowledge within a computer system. Among them, the paradigm referring to the coaching function in an intelligent environment, with a view to representing and manipulating expertise related to a specific content, in order to assist, guide or make suggestions to the learner in a specific context, becomes important and appears to offer a broad potential for consultation.

The use of an intelligent interface also becomes an important factor governing communication with the learner, depending on his needs and interests. The paradigm referring to an intelligent tutorial component appears to be able to partially re-create the optimal situation of a tutor with a learner in a context where learning and teaching are bidirectional (Roberts and Park, 1983).

The design and development of the coaching dimension, which integrates the modeling of various of the learner's cognitive processes, and the representation in a specific field of an expert's knowledge, implies the possibility of exchanging information of different types and at different levels between the learner and the system. They make up a systematic approach which has enabled us to integrate different kinds of expertise (Park, 1987).

The model derived from the artificial intelligence paradigm which we have emphasized in this research, is illustrated in the figure below. This model reveals the cognitive dimension of interactivity that we have in mind, generated by various levels and kinds of knowledge and the relationships between them.

Cognitive dimension of interactivity

Naturally, we cannot overlook the fact that the design and development of a complete intelligent system is an arduous, complex task and that a number of studies stress how attention can be focused on developing a system integrating into a single module the components we have just pinpointed and constituting a concrete application of all of these theoretical principles (Barr and Feigenbaun, 1982).

Particular emphasis is placed on the modeling of a learning process which can represent the state of a learner's knowledge at every stage of his development (Park, 1988). In this way, the learner can be redirected through the diagnosis of mistakes related to a false and ambiguous representation of the content (Anderson, Boyle and Reiser, 1985). BIOMEC can intervene at different levels of the learning process. It models the learner's actions on overall cognitive development. It can intervene with respect to the modeling of a sub-problem which the learner takes into consideration or can react more specifically with regard to a limited operation or in response to a particular mistake. This is possible because the various levels of representation of knowledge can be linked by a broad inferential process initiated by the learner. The reaction is qualitative, not quantitative (Clancey, 1986).

EXPERT MODULE

Knowledge base in the
field considered

TUTORIAL MODEL   INTERFACE MODULE

Problem-solver geared
Knowledge base related to   to specific performance   Menu and communications
teaching strategies   criteria   dialogue

Diagnostic rules   STUDENT MODEL
                                                         Learner input analyser

Prescriptive rules   Mistakes
                             Incomprehension   Level of visualization
                             Learning need

                             State of knowledge
                             History of performance

                             Individual differences

Along with Brown, we maintain that learning (Brown, 1983) occurs in reaction to non-predetermined learning strategies, whose structure is not centred on a hierarchical organization, accompanied by established courses of development based on essential prerequisites related to the body of notions to be acquired (Merrill, Reigeluth, 1980). The learner must be able to consider a question, analyse it, break it down and divide it into sub-questions, according to his own development. In this way, not all of the learner's decisions are corrected. Rather, all of the decisions reached to achieve a given result are considered. The student is not so much pushed into reaching decisions according to a preordained program as he is drawn by ways of doing things and experimenting which is appropriate at specific, significant stages in the learning process (Merrill, 1983). BIOMEC makes it possible for the student to interact with a broad situation, structured in a non-hierarchical fashion, in which each component of knowledge is defined using other components in the overall structure (Duchastel, 1986, 1990), in the form of facts, procedural attachments and production rules. This gives the learner the ability to control learning using a dialogue-based approach of the shared-initiative variety (Carbonell, 1970), in which he can interrupt the dialogue at any time and redirect interaction as he sees fit.

The coach is designed to discreetly observe the student's actions, single out weaknesses and intervene to redirect his efforts (Burton and Brown, 1982; Brown, 1983; Duchastel, 1988; Wegner, 1987; Merrill, 1988).

Educational principles of the coaching system

Traditionally, knowledge is represented according to various pre-organized diagrams related to a field of expertise, in the manner in which the expert in the field proceeds. The underlying tutorial strategy is often rudimentary and seeks to draw the student back to the sub-ensembles of such expertise, according to pre-established development patterns. The coach usually intervenes when the student answers, whether correctly or incorrectly.

This strategy does not respect the learner's cognitive development, nor make it possible to pinpoint elements of analogy, generalization, problem-solving or refinement pertaining to information which occur during learning (Goldstein, 1982).

To ensure that BIOMEC reflects the student's progress, it is suggested that knowledge be given a procedural representation based on an archetypical model of the learner. This situation evokes the concept of "learning by doing", which may enable students to reflect on their ways of thinking and the learning strategies they use, by attempting to solve a problem by dividing it into sub-problems, retracing various steps, and examining decisions reached by the learner or using the tutor. Two categories were used:

(1)   Learning through discovery

Learning through discovery focuses on the links between the various micro-situations possible and the path of the learner's different discoveries in each of them.

Discovery of micro-parts

This led us to develop a reactive learning environment in which the student can:

• identify hypotheses;
• ascertain the consequences of such hypotheses;
• analyse data;

- find counter-examples;
- experiment.

(2) Apprenticeship

In this instance, to prevent the student from overlooking his own mistakes, a coach should be present to constantly assess the student's decisions, with a view to guiding him and revealing the consequences of his mistakes.

The coach is a dynamic component that establishes a link between the field of expertise represented in a procedural manner and the model of the student's changing knowledge. The coaching concept is important in an interactive environment where the student must apply a range of abilities to accomplish a particular task. The most realistic context should boost motivation.

Our coach operates on the expertise model linked to the content processed, with a view to solving the learner's problems. It uses tutorial strategies which react at different levels of specificity to compare the student's decisions with those of the expert and intervene at the appropriate time. The coach's intervention must not curtail the student's interest in the learning activity (Brown, 1983).

Diagnostic strategies are the backbone of coaching; they help model the learner's behaviour and adapt the interactive environment to each learner's needs. In this perspective, the notions of learning and utilization, or training and utilization more closely resemble each other (Kearsley, 1985). The diversity of learning needs and changes in communications and information processing techniques overshadow the fact of learning in favour of learning by application (Duchastel, 1988), through rediscovery of the importance of learning by doing (Dewey, 1920). On-the-spot learning offers great potential; Anderson (1986) stresses the advantage of acquiring an ability in a context which is significant to the learner's immediate interests and needs.

Under the circumstances, the coach still has an educational role to play, bearing in mind the learner's decisions and gestures, so that the latter serve as a point of departure when the learner redirects or reviews the learning process (Burton and Brown, 1979b; Wenger, 1987).

Anderson has been working for several years to elaborate an adaptive theory respecting the acquisition of mental processes (Anderson, 1983). His interest focuses on the transfer and observation of theoretical principles pertaining to a concrete application. Anderson (1984) mentions the almost indissociable link between cognitive psychology and the paradigm of intelligent tutorial systems as, if we are to understand certain facets of cognition, we must observe the learning capacities they generate. Thus, interactive environments that integrate cognitive dimensions such as STI can become, by virtue of their flexibility and adaptability, highly attractive observation and development tools. Cognitive processes can be represented and modeled in interactive environments in the form of production rules which can represent both the system's and the learner's knowledge, in relation to an immediate goal to be achieved (Anderson et al., 1984; Saners and Farrel, 1982; Park, 1988). In an interactive environment, the basic learning model under consideration must take into account the fact that knowledge can initially be acquired declaratively through teaching and, subsequently, be transformed into procedures in an application. Such knowledge compilation is modeled in two forms: procedures and the composition of rules (Wenger, 1987). Third, the interactive environment must have the technical capacity to deal with both components in relation to the knowledge in question, to achieve very precise objectives which help the learner acquire other knowledge.

To summarize, the design of a coach must take into account a number of principles related to the representation of the declarative and procedural knowledge inherent in the content being processed. It must reflect the learner's cognitive development by allowing him to explore and discover, but under guidance. Moreover, based on discreet observation, the design must be capable of intervening more or less explicitly in response to the learner's weaknesses. To operate and maintain a minimum of flexibility, this facet of the coach must have at its disposal a model of expertise pertaining to the task to be accomplished; it must possess a number of tutorial intervention strategies, diagnostic strategies to detect weaknesses and, above all, it must have at its disposal a model of changes in the state of the earner's knowledge.

Conclusion

If the notion of interactivity has, until now, been of limited value, it is perhaps because it was too closely identified with the technological features of the "tool" used or was overly centred on the designer rather than the learner. A review of recent research on interactive learning enables us to pinpoint a number of important concepts which we can use to construct a new conceptual framework within which the concept of interactivity can move toward a dimension focusing more closely on the learner, through more immediate control of the processing of visual, aural or written information, such that the interactive environment then becomes capable of adapting to each learner, based on an evolving model built around ongoing interaction. Designing a multimedia learning system entails articulating various components, such as the information and interaction facets. At present, attempts are being made to broaden this structure by adding other dimensions such as modeling of the student, the integration of educational strategies, and the integration of intelligent intervention strategies. Drawing these various dimensions closer together lies within the realm of the representation of knowledge. Such integration demands a different design which takes into account the structuring of various kinds of knowledge, the learner's relative knowledge, factual and procedural knowledge in the field dealt with, the expert's knowledge, educational knowledge making possible varied tutorial intervention, and the knowledge which links the various kinds and levels of transactions within the system.

The development and implementation of this conceptual framework within an interactive learning environment has enabled us to illustrate the theoretical principles arising above all from paradigms pertaining to information processing and artificial intelligence. This development has taken shape in an interactive multimedia environment equipped with a coach where the exchange of information between the learner and this environment becomes significant and personalized. The intelligent facet of interactivity is aimed at encouraging the acquisition of problem-solving skills and strategies. The value of the learner's acquisitions depends on the degree of interactivity possible in the interactive environment. The coach enables the system to obtain a more "intimate" knowledgeof what the learner is doing and, based on this model and in relation to the content dealt with, it can offer advice when various actions are to be encouraged or proscribed.

References

1. Anderson, J.R., et al.: Cognitive principles in the design of computer tutors. Proceeding of the Sixth Cognitive Science Society. Boulder, Colorado, 1984
2. Anderson, J.R., Boyle, C.R., and Reiser, B.j.: Intelligent Tutoring Systems. Science, Vol. 228, No. 4698, pp. 456-462 (1985)
3. Arnold, J.R., Boyle, C.R., Farrell, R., and Reiser, B.j.: Cognitive principles in the design of computer tutors. P. Morris (ed.). Modelling Cognition, Wiley, 1986
4. Arnold, R.C.: Indicom project evaluation of CAI mathematic achievement. Pontiac, Ohio, 1970
5. Baker, D.: New techniques and approaches to integrating multi-media information in a videodisc program. Conference Proceedings, 1985, Videodisc, UPMCAL DISC and CD-ROM Conference and Exposition, Philadelphia.
6. Barker, P.: The many faces of human-machine interaction. British Journal of Educational Technology, Vol. 17, No. 1, pp. 74-80 (1986a)
7. Barker, P.: Multimedia Cal. computer education. British Journal of Education Technology, Vol. 17, No. 1, pp. 20-33 (1986b)
8. Barker, P.: A practical introduction to authoring for computer-assisted instruction. Part 8: Multi-media CAI. British Journal of Educational Technology, Vol. 18, No. 1, pp. 35-39 (1987)
9. Bennion, J.: Authoring interactive video courseware. De Bloois (ed.). Videodisc/microcomputer Courseware Design. Englewood Cliffs, NJ: Educational Technology Press, 1982
10. Bennion, J.: Student learning strategies on the TICCIT CAI system at BYU. Dissertation Abstract International Computer Sciences, Vol. 39/08-B, pp. 3919, (1978)
11. Bitter, G.G.: Effect of computer applications on achievement in college introductory calculus course. Unpublished doctoral dissertation, University of Denver, 1970
12. Bitzer, M.D., and Bitzer, D.L.: Teaching nursing by computer: an evaluative study. Computer in Biology and Medicine, Vol. 3, No.3, pp. 187-204 (1973)
13. Bolt, R.A.: Spatial Data Management. Cambridge, MA: MIT, 1979
14. Bolt, R.A.: The human interface: where people and computers meet. Belmont, CA: Lifetime Learning Publications, 1984
15. Bonner, J.: Computer Courseware: Frame-based or intelligent? Educational Technology, Vol. 27, No. 3, pp. 30-33. March 1987
16. Bork, A. et al.: Conference on intelligent videodisc systems. Brief Informal Summary. Irvine: University of California, 14 pp. December 1977
17. Bork, A. et al.: Computers and the future: education. Computer Education, Vol. 8, No. 1, pp.1-9 (1984)
18. Bork, A. et al.: Interactive learning. American Journal of Physics, Vol. 47, pp. 5-10 (1979)
19. Bork, A. et al.: Learning with computers. Bedford, MA: Digital Press. 1981
20. Bork, A. et al.: Personal Computers for Education. New York: Harper and Row. 1985
21. Bork, A. et al.: Physics in the Irvine Educational Technology Center. Computers and Education, Vol. 4, pp. 37-57 (1984)
22. Bork, A. et al.: Visions: future for learning and technology. Education Technology Center Information and Computer Science. Irvine: University of California. September 1986

23. Burton, R.R., and Brown, J.S.: An investigation of computer coaching for informal learning activities. Intelligent Tutoring Systems. D.Sleeman & Brown. New York: Academic Press, pp. 51-78 (1982)

24. Burton, R.R., and Brown, J.S.: An investigation of computer coaching for informal learning activities. INT-JRNL of Man-Machine Studies, Vol. 11, pp. 5-24 (1979)

25. Charp, S.: Effectiveness of computers in instruction: viewpoints. Teaching and Learning, Vol. 57, No. 2, pp. 28-32 (1981)

26. Clark, R.: The role of the videodisc in education and training. Media in Education and Development, pp. 190-192 (1984)

27. Clément, F.: Affective considerations in computer-based education. Educational Technology, Vol. 21 No. 19, pp. 190-192(1984)

28. Cohen, V.B.: A reexamination of feedback in computer-based instruction: implications for instructional design. Educational Technology, Vol. 25, No. 1, pp. 33-37 (1985)

29. Cohen, V.B.: Interactive features in the design of videodisc material. Educational Technology, Vol. 24, No. 1. (1984)

30. Collins, A.: Process in acquiring knowledge. In Schooling and the Acquisition of Knowledge. (Anderson, R.C., Spiro, R.J., and Montague, W.E. eds.). Hillsdale, NJ: Lawrence Erlbaum Associates. 1977

31. Collins, A.: Component models of physical systems. Proceedings of the 7th Cognitive Society Conference. Irvine, CA, pp. 80-89 (1985)

32. Collins, A., and Stevens, A.l.: Goals and strategies of inquiry teachers. In Advances in Instructional Psychology.(Glaser, R. ed.). Hillsdale, NJ: Lawrence Erlbaum Associates, Vol. 2 (1982)

33. Collins, A., and Brown, J.S.: The new apprenticeship: teaching students the craft of reading, writing and mathematics. In Cognition and Instruction: Issues and Agendas. (Resnick, L.B. ed.). Hillsdale, NJ: Lawrence Erlbaum Associates 1986

34. Collins, A., and Brown, J.S.: The computer as a tool for learning through reflection. In Learning Issues for Intelligent Tutoring Systems. (Mandl, H. and Lesgold, A.M. eds.). New York: Springer-Verlag 1988

35. Currier, R.L.: Interactive videodisc learning systems: A new tool for educational create visual lesson. High Technology, Vol. 3, No. 11, pp. 51-59 (1983)

36. Daynes, R. and Holder, S.: Controlling videodiscs with Micros. Bytem 1984

37. Daynes, R.: Experimenting with videodisc. Instructional Innovator, Vol. 27, No. 2, pp. 24-25 (1982)

38. De Bloois, M.: Videodisc/Micro-Computer Courseware Design. Englewood Cliffs, NJ: Educational Technology Publications 1982

39. Depover, C.: L'ordinateur média d'enseignement : un cadre conceptuel. Brussels: De Boeck-Wesmael 1987

40. Depover, C.: Un cadre conceptuel pour un enseignement adaptif médiatisé par ordinateur. Mise au point de deux dispositifs d'évaluation formative extemporanée. Doctoral thesis, Faculté de psycho-pédagogie, Université de Mons, Belgium 1985

41. Dubreil, B.: Le vidéodisque pédagogique. Sonsvision, pp. 35-37 (1983)

42. Duchastel, P.: Design principle for intelligent systems in training. Université Laval: LIAE, Faculté des Sciences de l'éducation 1988

43. Eastwood, L.: Motivations and deterrents to educational use of "intelligent videodisc systems". Journal of Educational Technology Systems, Vol. 7, No. 4, pp. 303-305 (1978)

44. England, G.E.: A study of computer-assisted budgeting among the developmentally handicapped. Unpublished doctoral dissertation, University of Calgary 1979

45. Faiola, T., and De Bloois, M.: Designing a visual factor-based screen display interface: The new role of graphist technology. Educational Technology, Vol. 28, No. 8, pp. 12-20. August 1988

46. Farrel, R., et al.: Interactive student modelling in a computer-based Lisp Tutor. Proceedings of the Sixth Cognitive Science Society Conference. Boulder, Colorado, pp. 152-155 (1984)

47. Fletcher, J., and Atkinson, R.: Evaluation of the Stanford CAI programs in initial reading. Journal of Educational Psychology, Vol. 63, pp. 507-602 (1972)

48. Fletcher, J.: Intelligent instructional systems in training. In Application in Artificial Intelligence. (Andriole, J.J. ed.). Princeton, NJ: Petroncelli Books, 1985

49. Fowler, B.: The effectiveness of computer-controlled videodisc-based training. Dissertation Abstracts International, Vol. 42/01-A, p.60 (1980)

50. Frizot, D.: Future shock of today's education. Introduction of a computer in a French secondary school. In Microcomputer in Secondary Education. (Tagg, E.D. ed). Amsterdam: North-Holland Publishing Company 1980

51. Gagné, R.M., and Dick, W.: Instructional psychology. Annual Review of Psychology, Vol. 34, pp. 261-295 (1983)

52. Gayesky, D.M.: Interactive video: integrating design "levels" and hardware "levels". Journal of Educational Technology Systems, Vol. 13, No. 3, pp. 145-151 (1985)

53. Gendele, J.F., and Gendele, J.G.: Interactive videodisc and its implications in education. Technological Horizons in Education, Vol. 12, No. 1, pp. 33-37 (1984)

54. Giardina, M. and Marton, Ph.: Références bibliographiques sur l'apprentissage interactif par vidéodisque et ordinateur. Université Laval: Département de technologie de l'enseignement 1987

55. Giardina, M.; Duchastel, P., and Marton, Ph.: Vidéodisque et EIAO : une technologie en émergence. COGNITIVA 1987, Paris, La Villete. May 18-22 1987
56. Goetzfried, L., and Hannafin, M.J.: The effects of embedded CAI instructional control strategies on the learning and application of mathematics rules. American Educational Research Journal, Vol. 22, pp. 273-278 (1985)
57. Gross, D., and Griffin, N.: Implementation and evaluation of a computer-assisted course in musical aural skills. AEDS Journal Spring, pp. 143-150 (1982)
58. Hannafin, M.J., and Phillips, T.: Perspectives in the design of interactive video: Beyond tape versus disc. Journal of Research and Development in Education, Vol. 21, No. 1, pp. 44-60 (1988)
59. Hannafin, M.J.: Empirical issues in the study of computer assisted interactive video. Educational communication and technology: A journal of theory, research and development. 33(4), pp. 235-247. Winter 1987
60. Hart, A.: Interactive video. Media in education and development. pp. 207-208. December 1984
61. Hassel, J.: An annotated bibliography summarizing and analyzing recorded research on the topic of computer assisted instruction and its effects on reading comprehension. Exit Project, Indiana University at South Bend, 1987
62. Hawkings, C.A.: The performance and promise of evaluation in computer-based learning. Computer and Education, Vol. 13, pp. 273-280 (1979)
63. Hon, D.: Parameters for the design of interactive programs. In CD-I and Interactive Technology (Lambert, S. and Sallist, J. eds.). Indianapolis: Howard W. Sams and Company 1987
64. Hoisie, P.: Adopting interactive videodisc technology for education. Educational Technology, 27(7), Uly, pp. 5-10 (1987)
65. Johansen, K.J., and Tennyson, R.D.: Effect of adaptive advisement on perception in learner controlled, computer-based instruction use a rule-learning task. Educational Communications and Technology Journal, Vol. 31, No. 4, pp. 226-236 (1983)
66. Johnson, W., and Soloway, E.: Proust: Knowledge-based program debugging. Proceedings of the 7th International Software Engineering Conference. Orlando, Florida, pp. 369-380 (1985)
67. Kulik, C.C., et al.: Computer-based instruction: what 200 evaluations say. Paper presented at the Annual Convention of the Association for Educational Communications and Technology. Atlanta. February 26-March 1, 1987
68. Kulik, J.: Effects of computer-based teaching on secondary school students. Journal of Educational Psychology, Vol. 75, No. 1, pp. 19-26 (1983)
69. Kulik, J.A., et al.: Effectiveness of computer-based education in elementary schools. Computer in Human Behavior, Vol. 1, pp. 59-74 (1985)
70. Kulik, J.L., Kulik, C.C., and Bangert-Drowns, R.L.: Effectiveness of computer-based education in elementary schools. Computer in Human Behavior, Vol. 1, pp. 59-74 (1985)
71. Lelu, A.: L'interactivité. Science et vie, les choc des média, No. 152, pp. 106-111 (1985)
72. Levin, W.: Interactive video: the state of the art teaching machine. The Computing Teacher, pp. 11-17 (1983)
73. Lippman, A.: Imaging and Interactivity. Proceedings of the 15th Joint Conference on Image Technology, pp. 17-19 (1984)
74. Marinick and Gerlach, S.: Designing interactive, responsive instruction: A set of procedures. Educational Technology, Vol. 26, No. 11. November 1986
75. Martin, J.B.: A practical voice input system. In Computers and Communications: Implications for Education. (Seidel, R.J., and Rubin, M.C. eds.). New York: Academic Press 1975
76. Marton, Ph.: La programmation télévisuelle : une première évaluation de l'application dans l'enseignement. Didasco, Vol. 1. Quebec. Fall 1983
77. Marton, Ph.: Bilan des recherches sur l'apprentissage interactif (1983-1989). Groupe de recherche sur l'apprentissage interactif (GRAIN). Université Laval: Département de Technologie de l'enseignement 1989
78. Martorella, P.: Interactive video systems in the classroom. Social Education, Vol. 97, No. 5, pp. 325-327 (1982)
79. McEwing, R.A., and Roth, G.: Individualized learning with computer-based instruction. Educational Technology, Vol. 25, No. 5, pp. 30-32 (1985)
80. Merrill, M.D.: Learner control in CBL. Computers in Education, Vol. 4, pp. 77-95 (1980)
81. Merrill, M.D.: Component display theory. in Instructional Design Theories and Models: An Overview. (Reigeluth, C. ed.). Hillsdale, NJ: Lawrence Erlbaum Associates 1983
82. Merrill, M.D.: What is learner control? In Instructional Development: The State of the Art, II. (Bass, R.K., and Dills, C.R. eds.). Dubugue, IA: Kendall/Hunt 1984
83. Merrill, M.D.: Where is the authoring in authoring systems? Journal of Computer-Based Instruction, Vol. 12, No. 4, pp. 90-96 (1985)
84. Merrill, M.D.: Prescriptions for an authoring system? Journal of Computer-Based Instruction, Vol. 14, No. 1 (1987)

85. Merrill, M.D.: The role of tutorial and experiential models in intelligent tutoring systems. Educational Technology, Vol. 28, No. 7, pp. 7-13. July 1988

86. Merrill, M.D.: Schneider, E.W., and Fletcher, K.A.: "TICCIT." Instructional Design Library, Vol. 40. Englewood Cliffs, NJ: Educational Technology Publications 1980

87. Merrill, M.D.: Schneider, E.W., and Fletcher, K.A.: "TICCIT." Instructional Design Library, Vol. 40. Englewood Cliffs, NJ: Educational Technology Publications 1983

88. Merrill, P.F., and Bennion, J.: Videodisc technology in education: The current scene. NSPI Journal, Vol. 10, pp. 18-26. November 1979

89. Merrill, P.F.: Education and training applications of videodisc technology. In Videodiscs: The Technology, the Applications and the Future. (Siegel, E., Schubin, M., and Merrill, P.F. eds.). New York: Van Nostrand Reinhold, pp. 69-101 (1981)

90. Meyer, R.: Borrow this new military technology and help win the war for kids' minds. American School Board Journal, Vol. 71, No. 6, pp. 23-28 (1984)

91. Negroponte, N.: The Architecture Machine. Cambridge, MA: MIT Press 1972

92. Pagliaro, L.A.: CAI in pharmacology: student academic performance and instructional interactions. Journal of Computer-Based Instruction, Vol. 9, No. 4, pp. 131-144 (1983)

93. Papert, S., Mindstorms, children, computers and powerful ideas. New York: Basic Books 1980

94. Park, O., and Tennyson, R.D.: Computer-based instructional systems for adaptive education: A review. Contemporary Education Review, Vol. 2, pp. 121-135 (1983)

95. Priestman, T.: Interactive video and its applications. Media in Education and Development, pp. 182-186. December 1984

96. Reiser, R.A.: Reducing student procrastination in a personalized system of instruction course. Educational Communications and Technology Journal, Vol. 32, No. 1, pp. 41-49 (1984)

97. Ross, S.M., et al. Matching the lesson to the student: Alternative adaptive design for individualized learning systems. Journal of Computer-Based Instruction, Vol. 32, No. 1, pp. 41-49 (1984

98. Russel, A.: From videotape to videodisc: From passive to active instruction. Journal of Chemical Education, Vol. 61, No. 10, pp. 866-868 (1984)

99. Sandals, L.H.: Computer-assisted learning with the developmentally handicapped. Unpublished doctoral dissertation, University of Calgary 1973

100. Schneider, E.W.: Application of videodisc technology to individualized instruction. In Computers and Communication: Implications for Education (Seidel, R.J., ed.). New York: Academic Press 1975

101. Screen Digest, p. 38. February 1986

102. Self, J.: Bypassing the intractable problem of student modelling. In Proceedings of ITS-88. Montréal: PUM, pp. 18-24 (1988)

103. Siegel, E., Schubien, M., and Merrill, P.F.: Videodiscs: The Technology, the Applications and the Future. New York: Van Nostrand Reinhold, 1981

104. Stevens, S.M.: Surrogate laboratory experiments: interactive computer/videodisc lessons and their effects on students' understanding of science. Dissertation Abstracts International, Vol. 45/09-A, p. 2827 (1984)

105. Strain, A.R.: Computer-assisted instruction in social arithmetic for the retarded. Unpublished master's thesis. University of Calgary 1974

106. Streibel, M.J.: Dialog design and instructional systems design for an intelligent videodisc system. Videodisc and Optical Disk, Vol. 4, No. 3. June 1984

107. Streibel, M.J.: How to design an intelligent videodisc system: visual principles and dialog-design. Paper presented at the International Visual Literacy Conference. Lexington, Kentucky. November 2 1981

108. Suppes, P., and Morningstar, M.: Computer-Assisted Instruction at Stanford, 1966-68: Data, Models and Evaluation of the Arithmetic Programs. New York: Academic Press 1972

109. Tarrant, N., Nelly, L., and Wakley, J.: Project Management Guidelines to Instructional Interactive Videodisc Production. Educational Technology, Vol. 28, No. 1, pp. 7-18. January 1988

110. Tennyson, R.D., and Bultrey, T.: Advisement and management strategies as design variables in computer-assisted instruction. Educational Communications and Technology Journal, Vol. 28, pp. 169-176 (1980)

111. Tennyson, R.D.: Instructional control strategies and content structure as design variables in concept acquisition using computer based instruction. Journal of Educational Psychology, 72, pp. 525-532 (1980)

112. Tennyson, R.D.: Use of adaptive information for advisement in learning concepts and rules using computer assisted instruction. American Educational Research Journal, 18, pp. 425-438 (1981)

113. Tennyson, R.D., et al.: Artificial intelligence methods in computer-based instructional design. Journal of Instructional Development. Vol. 7, No. 3, pp. 17-22 (1984)

114. Wenger, E.: Artificial intelligence and tutoring systems: computational and cognitive approaches to the communication of knowledge. Los Altos, CA: Morgan Kaufmann Publishers 1987

115. Wiser, M.: The differentiation of heat and temperature: An evaluation of the effect of microcomputer teaching on students' misconceptions. Technical Report. Washington: Office of Educational Research and Improvement 1986

116. Young, J., and Tosti, D.: The Effectiveness of Interactive Videodisc in Training. U.S. Army Technical Report, Georgia. 1984

Integrating HyperMedia into Intelligent Tutoring

Philippe C. Duchastel

EDS 555 Newking St. P.O. Box 7019, Troy, Michigan 48007, USA. Tel. (313) 696 2164. Fax. (313) 696 2325

HyperMedia and Intelligent Tutoring

The merging of hypermedia and intelligent tutoring can occur through two approaches:
- integrating intelligent tutoring into hypermedia;
- integrating hypermedia into intelligent tutoring.

The former involves enhancing a basic hypermedia system with features that provide more structured browsing or tutoring, ranging from the traditional to the AI-based approaches (Barden, 1989; Jonassen, 1990). The second approach is the one explored here. I will be examining some of the possibilities of integrating hypermedia into intelligent tutoring, and some of the problems that are likely to be encountered. I will be using the GEO geographical tutor (Duchastel, 1989) and the OPTICLAB optics workbench (Duchastel et al., 1988) to illustrate some of the views expressed in this discussion.

As information resources, intelligent tutoring systems (ITSs) are quite different from hypermedia systems (HMSs), principally because of the ITS emphasis on representation of knowledge. ITSs are artificial intelligence (AI) systems, whereas HMSs are not. The crucial distinction between them lies in how they treat information.

ITSs structure information into a knowledge base, whereas HMSs keep information unstructured and use it as data. The structured information of ITSs involve semantic relations (see Figure 1) constituting a knowledge web that can be manipulated and interpreted by simple goal-directed rules. The information is thus computationable, which gives it the power ascribed in general terms to AI technology.

The information contained in HMSs is termed unstructured because it lacks internal semantic meaning (Duchastel, 1986). Even though there are a multitude of connections between information elements within a HMS (that, after all, being the defining characteristic of hypermedia), the connections are merely pointers and generally do not embody semantic relationships (see McAleese, 1990, for a very interesting exception). The rich information contained and displayed in HMSs (see Figure 2), in part because of this very richness, and in part because of the lack of semantic relations, can only be interpreted by very complex rules, which make use of much additional knowledge. What this means essentially is that the interpretation must be performed by a human, and that the information is not computationable, and thus not open to the power of AI technology.

The contrast just presented between ITSs and HMSs deals with their treatment of information either as knowledge (which is computational) or as display data (which is non-computational). This leads to another contrast, this time in terms of pedagogical style. ITSs provide highly adaptive orientation to the learning session. Their computational ability to interpret the student's actions and responses in terms of a knowledge model of the student provides them with this intelligent adaptiveness. It additionally enables them to give the student much more leeway in the interactive instructional transaction, thus allowing greater learner control than traditional CAI while nevertheless keeping track of the unfolding of the learning session. This allows ITSs, at all times, to be ready to intervene in order to orient the session according to the tutorial rules they contain. ITSs are fundamentally teaching systems.

HMSs, on the other hand, are learning systems (Duchastel, 1990): they do not tutor, but they are terrific learning resources. HMSs provide full learner control, and indeed, they rely on the student's intelligence and curiosity to make them educationally useful. Thus, they do not contain any pedagogical expertise (as an ITS does). Their main virtue lies in containing interesting information.

The contrast just presented lay the foundation for considering the emergence of hybrid systems which can combine the virtues of both ITSs and HMSs. The central component of such hybrid systems will be the student model.

Student Modelling for HyperMedia

Student modelling is aimed at deriving and maintaining an explicit picture (a computational representation) of the student's competence in a given domain: what the student knows, does not yet know, and knows incorrectly. To derive this model of the student, a system has to follow the student's interaction with the tasks being undertaken and with the information being presented. The system then derives from this monitoring an interpretation of where the student is situated in relation to the domain knowledge represented in the system. The student model is what an ITS adapts to, it is the basis for all tutoring.

In the hypermedia area, the availability of a student model within an HMS would in principle enable the system to tailor itself to the particular characteristics or interests of the student and to the perceived needs of the moment. This intelligent adaptation of an HMS would not aim to be directive, as an ITS often is, but would instead involve a selective orientation of the information made available or a tailoring of the HMS interface, all with the aim of letting the student make well-informed and wise decisions about where to proceed. One interesting illustration of this (Nielsen, 1990) is the potential for dynamically differentiating between anchors (buttons) in a frame, adjusting their prominence according to estimated relevance to the student, as determined by an examination of the student model.

As indicated above, the process of student modelling involves capturing the flow of interaction during a session, and interpreting that flow for adaptive purposes. In an HMS, a trace of the student's browsing can easily be captured (Macleod, 1990). However, it is the interpretation of this trace that is difficult for a system to perform.

Interpretation involves transforming students actions into a representation of levels and types of knowledge possessed by the student. A representation of student knowledge, in turn, is overlayed on a formal representation of the knowledge possessed by the system. Some representation of knowledge is therefore essential.

A knowledge base paralleling and characterizing the display information in an HMS is needed. In a local application, this connection between knowledge and the hypermedia display information can be wired-in programmatically; in a more generic system, which would allow for ease of upgrade and for change of knowledge base, the knowledge-information connection must be more explicit and declarative.

Knowledge elements within a knowledge base are fine-grain characterizations of whatever is being represented. Display information in an HMS is often at a much larger grain of description (see Figure 3) in which the elements are themselves composites of many more elementary elements, although the latter are not explicitly represented as distinct elements. Connecting the fine-grain knowledge elements with the large-grain display information elements is therefore not without problems. One possibility is to chunk the hypermedia information into what can be expected to be meaningful elements of interest and then to tag the chunks with knowledge elements. This can be done not only with textual descriptions, but also, and perhaps even more importantly, with the alternate media in an HMS, such as images and sounds (Giardina et al. 1988).

This enhancement would enable an HMS to use the knowledge tags as handles for symbolic manipulation, and in particular for establishing dynamically what information elements are appropriate for tasks which the student is trying to perform. Student tasking is at the core of teaching, and must be considered in the design of a hybrid hypermedia-based intelligent tutoring system (HMITS). As will be seen next, the information technologies that are now emerging in the world of practical application tend to emphasize different views of tutoring, with strong implications for an HMITS.

Views of Tutoring

Hypermedia is a non-pedagogical technology, one which is open to learning through browsing, but which must count on the student's own intelligence for learning guidance. Didactics, on the other hand, and all technology that supports didactics, are essentially goal-directed processes that aim to achieve a result that is focused (a point also made by Nguyen-Xuan, 1990). Enter learning objectives, the essential core of any teaching system.

As I opined elsewhere (Duchastel, 1990), the philosophy behind teaching is essentially at odds with the free access philosophy of hypermedia. Teaching and browsing actually pull the student in opposite directions. It is this conflict (also discussed by Spath, 1990) that I want to further explore here.

An important problem with many teaching systems is their inflexibility in affective terms. Their emphasis is on cognitive adaptation, on providing the student with the proper cognitive elements of knowledge that are needed at a particular time in the learning session. The more a system is geared to individualizing instruction, the more adaptive it can be in these terms.

In contrast, HMSs do not adapt cognitively to the student; this is their week point. However, they are very strong in learner control, and thus affectively efficient. What we see in the contrast between HMSs and teaching systems is a trade-off along the cognitive-affective dimension. Each type of system emphasizes one pole of the dimension to the detriment of the other.

Adaptation is the essence of what is known as pedagogical knowledge (the tutorial rules of an ITS), which in turn can be characterized mainly as curricular knowledge. Indeed, pedagogical knowledge involves knowing the structure of knowledge, both generic structural knowledge applicable broadly and specific domain knowledge that constitutes the particularities to be taught. Pedagogical knowledge also involves knowing common problems (misconceptions) that can be expected in particular learning situations.

An interesting aside to this is the thought that dealing with misconceptions is necessary either because learning took place erroneously by itself of because the teaching that occurred was itself deficient, probably not making enough use of contrast and analogy teaching strategies.

Applying this curricular knowledge in practice involves constantly adapting to the student's needs through a cycle of testing and remediation/presentation. What this amounts to is keeping the student at the edge of her learning frontier (Goldstein, 1982), that is, beyond what she already knows, but not too far beyond that the knowledge becomes unintelligible. In conceptual terms, the material presented must be new (so as to learnable), but nevertheless fit within a familiar cognitive structure and thus remain meaningful. In affective terms, it must be challenging (so as to be interesting), but also not overly difficult so as to detract from persistence.

Applying curricular knowledge thus becomes a process of tasking the student at the appropriate level. This is what an ITS constantly does (and that all teaching is meant to do). HMSs, though, do not themselves task the student with anything; they merely provide the student with access to information (with browsing capability). An HMITS (HyperMedia Intelligent Tutoring System) would then have as its technical aim to "provoke the student into browsing!"

Towards a Student-Centered Didactic Model

Tutoring involves guiding the learner along a certain course, even if that course is open to re-direction along the way; and hypermedia involves making available many different routes for the student to take according to current interest. We are therefore faced with suggesting a course to the student without being too directive about it. This involves a fine act of judgement in order to balance the needs for guidance and for learner freedom of open exploration.

The general thesis underlying this approach is not foreign to ITSs, for their very power at interpreting student needs has permitted them to be flexible in terms of control and actually give the student much more control than is traditionally possible in computer-assisted instructional systems (Duchastel, 1986). So ITSs are powerful and HMSs are alluring. It is this very feature of HMSs that performs the task of keeping the learner involved in exploring what is available for learning. Interest becomes the driving force. The problem for the student is knowing where to go, deciding what path would be the most interesting to pursue.

At the core of hypermedia is the navigation issue. Various aspects of navigation come into play in any HMS: interest pulls in many different directions, while at the same time lack of context (what is described as the homogeneity problem - all text is similar, especially as it is displayed on the small screen on the CRT - Nielsen, 1990) can leave one stranded deep in a section on the information set without an overall view of where one is situated. As a problem, navigation is an instructional issue, in that one way of guiding the learner lies in providing context as and when needed. Indeed, situating the learner in cognitive space is one of the key tasks of an important contemporary theory of instruction, elaboration theory (Reigeluth and Stein, 1983).

Hypermedia destroysspatial context by enabling all information to be juxtaposed in any which way the user wishes (Landow, 1990). This is very beneficial from one point of view: it enables the juxtaposition and highlighting of various points of view, such that an object or event can be analysed from different perspectives (Spiro, 199). A radio, for instance, can be seen as a set of electronic circuits, as an instrument for listening or for broadcasting, as a design in the modern world, and so on.

Various means of restoring spatial context or of overcoming disorientation, however, can be devised. In addition to the traditional ones such as overview diagrams, these can include large screens for the multi-juxtapositioning of information elements, the use of color to indicate depth of search, or depth bars for the same purpose, along with the possibility of always zooming back out. The student model can also be used to good avail here if the information elements in the system are categorized in some appropriate fashion, in which case an 'orientation agent' could possibly help situate the user or reposition the interaction at an appropriate point.

As can be well realized, the important didactic approach here is a suggestive one. It provides the user with the information of a context nature that will enable quick orientation and re-situating if necessary. The important feature of this soft approach is that decision authority for the evolution of the session is invested in the learner, and not, as is traditionally the case in instruction, with the teacher or author.

Conclusions

The design of hypermedia systems involves the design of various fundamental components, such as the information model and the interaction model (Jonassen & Grabinger, 1990). What we see the need for now in seeking to extent the hypermedia paradigm further is the design of yet other components, particularly the student model and a didactic model (Mandl, 1990).

The basic distinction between the ITS world and the HMS world lies in knowledge representation. The design of more intelligent HMSs thus involves structuring knowledge of various kinds: first, knowledge of the student (a student model) that can help interpret student needs; second, knowledge of the inter-relationships between the display elements within the HMS; and third, soft didactic knowledge that can interrelate the two.

It was argued that tutoring involves establishing a workable balance between cognitive and affective needs, a balance that is delicate and extremely important in the conative and affective needs, a balance that is delicate and extremely important in the conative domain of learning. An HMITS is a hybrid system that must maintain the best of the ITS world and the best of the HMS world, even though each emphasizes a distinct tutorial view. The aim of such system becomes provocation into browsing.

In the end, the system must basically work together with the student in a symbiotic relationship aimed at fulfilling epistemic needs that keep changing as the interaction evolves. In that basic sense, any computer-based learning system is foremost an interactive environment with its own constraints and possibilities. Our task, then, is very much to both elucidate the grammar of that environment (as Alves de Oliveira & Costa Pereira, 1990, have proposed) and to invent and test new syntactical approaches to the design of that environment (as Nielsen, 1990, is doing). This task is made all the easier as interest grows in hypermedia systems (Jonassen & Mandl, 1990), and in particular in intelligent environments and in their interaction with outside aims such as learning and instruction.

References

1. Alves de Oliveira, A., and Costa Pereira, D.: Psychopedagogic aspects of hypermedia courseware. In Jonassen, D., and Mandl, H. (eds.). Designing Hypermedia for Learning. NATO ASI Series F, Vol. 67. Berlin: Springer-Verlag 1990
2. Barden, R.: Developing a hypercard-based intelligent training system. ETTI, 26, pp. 361-367 (1989)
3. Duchastel, P.: Computer text access. Computers & Education, 10, pp. 403-409 (1986)

4. Duchastel, P., Imbeau, J., and the STI Group.: On interacting with information: OPTICLAB. International Journal of Educational Research, 12, pp. 811-820 (1988)
5. Duchastel, P.: Knowledge-based instructional gaming: GEO. Journal of Educational Technology Systems, 12, pp. 189-203 (1989)
6. Duchastel, P.: Formal and informal learning with HyperMedia. In Jonassen, D., and Mandl, H. (eds.). Designing Hypermedia for Learning. NATO ASI Series F, Vol. 67. Berlin: Springer-Verlag 1990
7. Giardina, M., Marton, P., Duchastel, P., and Doublait, S.: BIOMEC: Modélisation et développement d'un module d'apprentissage intelligent utilisant le vidéodisque interactif. Proceedings of the International Conference on Intelligent Tutoring Systems, pp. 448-453. Montreal, Canada 1988
8. Goldstein, I.: The genetic graph: A representation for the evolution of procedural knowledge. In Sleeman, D., and Brown, J.S. Intelligent Tutoring Systems. New York: Academic Press 1982
9. Jonassen, D.: Adding intelligence to hypertext with expert systems and adding usability to expert systems with hypertext. 1990
10. Jonassen, D., and Grabinger, S.: Problems and issues in designing hypertext/hypermedia for learning. In Jonassen, D., and Mandl, H. (eds.). Designing Hypermedia for Learning. NATO ASI Series F, Vol. 67. Berlin: Springer-Verlag 1990
11. Jonassen, D., and Mandl, H. (eds.). Designing Hypermedia for Learning. NATO ASI Series F, Vol. 67. Berlin: Springer-Verlag 1990
12. Landow, G.: Popular fallacies about hypertext. In D. Jonassen, and H. Mandl (eds.). Designing Hypermedia for Learning. NATO ASI Series F, Vol. 67. Berlin: Springer-Verlag 1990
13. Macleod, M.: Tools for monitoring and analysing the use of hypermedia courseware. 1990
14. Mandl, H.: Basic pedagogic-didactic dimensions for evaluation of computer-based systems on open learning. 1990
15. McAleese, R.: Concepts as hypertext nodes: The ability to learn while navigating through hypertext nets. In Jonassen, D., and Mandl, H. (eds.). Designing Hypermedia for Learning. NATO ASI Series F, Vol. 67. Berlin: Springer-Verlag 1990
16. Nielsen, J.: The art of navigating through hypertext. Communications of the ACM, 33, pp. 296-310 (1990)
17. Nguyen-Xuan, A.: Effects of prior knowledge on learning to use a command device. 1990
18. Reigeluth, C., and Stein, F.: The elaboration theory of instruction. In Reigeluth, C. (ed.). Instructional Design Theories and Models: An Overview of their Current Status. Hillsdale, NJ: Erlbaum 1983
19. Spath, P.: Design considerations in hypermedia tutorials. 1990
20. Spiro, R.: Towards a general theory of hypertext: Nonlinear instruction for the development of cognitive flexibility in ill-structured domains. 1990

** Let's talk about Western Canada.
Fine. What is the capital of British-Columbia?

** Vancouver.
No, the capital of British-Columbia is Victoria.
Where, is Victoria situated?

** Let's discuss Banff.
I do not know Banff. Is Banff the name of a place?

** Yes. It is a town.
Where is Banff located?

** In the Rocky Mountains.
Is Banff in British-Columbia or in Alberta?

** In B.C.
What is the population of Banff?

** 5000.
What other towns are near Banff?

** Tell me about Victoria.
Victoria is situated on Vancouver Island. It is the second largest city in British-Columbia. What else would you like to know?

** What is its population?
...

Figure 1.   Part of the knowledge base of the GEO intelligent tutoring system

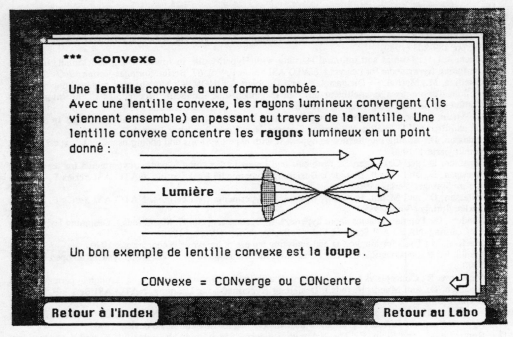

Figure 2. Hypertext display from the OPTICLAB prototype

What is the capital of Ontario?
** Toronto

What is its population?
** Where is Kingston

I do not know. What is Kingston?
** A city

O.K. In what province is Kingston?
** Ontario

O.K. Do you know its size?
** No. Let's talk about Alberta.

Fine. What are its major cities?
** Calgary

Yes, and another one?
** _

Edmonton. Which one is the capital?
.
.
.

Figure 3. Graphic display from the GEO tutor

Instructional Transaction Theory: Resource Me

Ann Marie Canfield, Scott Schwab, M. David Merrill, Zhongmin Li and Mark K. J

Department of Instructional Technology, Utah State University, Logan, UT 84321, USA

Introduction

The need for corporate, military and industrial computer-based training (CB) continues to rise. As a result, courseware developers and managers are confronted with the time-consuming aspect of the CBT development process (Faiola, 1989). Programming, debugging, and testing courseware is such a time-consuming aspect that efficient courseware development is an immediate concern (MacKnight and Balagopalan, 1988-89). The time required to develop one hour of computer-based training has been estimated to take anywhere from 200 to over 6000 labor hours (Carter, 1990; Lippert, 1989). These numbers make it difficult and expensive to produce current and timely CBT.

Transaction Theory is a relatively new and innovative approach to courseware authoring developed at Utah State University under the Second Generation Instructional Design (ID2) Research Program. This approach involves providing subject matter experts with tools to aid them in the design and delivery of effective, reusable and easily modifiable courseware. Transaction shells provide a novice designer with the ability to produce effective computer-based instruction (CBI) while dramatically decreasing the development time.

Transaction Theory provides a basis for generating a comprehensive library of transactions appropriate to courseware delivery (Merrill, Li and Jones, 1990). Within these transactions graphic mediations can take on any form of media which can be accessed by the computer. Still graphics, videodisc, CD-ROM, simulations and the many other media forms that are available can be incorporated into a transaction shell. Parameters for representation to the transactions enable the utilization of multimedia forms.

Transaction Theory

An *instructional transaction* is defined as a mutual, dynamic, real-time give and take between the instructional system and the student in which there is an exchange of information. It is the complete sequence of presentations and reactions necessary for the student to acquire a specific type of instructional goal. It requires active mental effort by the student. A *transaction shell* is the structure of a transaction identifying the interactions, parameters, and knowledge representation needed for a given class or family of transactions. When a transaction shell is instantiated with a particular subject matter and with particular values for its parameters, it is called a *transaction instance*.

An ID2 system achieves design efficiency in part by having available to the designer prepared instructional units or transaction shells which have already been coded and which can be easily adapted and included in a course under development. Both a transaction shell and a transaction instance are pieces of computer code which when executed causes a given transaction to take place. Transaction instances are domain independent, in that they are each designed to instruct a particular type of content, but are not tied to any given content domain. For example, a shell designed to instruct the steps in an activity "knows" it must be configured with that "type" of content. However, the shell is independent of the content having to come from a single domain, such as tax preparation. The steps to fix a broken modem will work just as efficiently as the steps in filing a tax return in a shell designed to teach step activities.

Transaction instances are in effect the structure of instruction. They are customizable, both at design and run-time by setting the instructional parameters. Once a transaction has been selected or prescribed, it must then be configured and authored. Configuration involves setting the parameters, modifying the strategy, and attaching the content. Authoring involves attaching domain specific instructional materials to the instructional structure set up by the transaction.

For example, in concept learning by compare/contrast, the transaction would contain all the elements to generate examples, practice, and assessment items for concept learning. However, it would require that images of the different concepts, with the defining attributes indicated, be provided by the designer. Each transaction instance knows what domain specific data it requires, and will guide the designer in preparing and entering that data.

Each transaction instance has default values for each of its parameters, including its strategy elements. While most practical instruction will require the modification of these parameters, the acceptance of default values allows the rapid prototyping of instruction incorporating the content and instructional strategies identified. This rapid prototyping allows the designer to get a feel for the structure and look of the finished course while still early enough in the design process to easily change design decisions. The effects of making different design choices can also be easily compared.

Transaction Classes

Instructional transactions can be grouped into a limited number of classes. The nature of the interactions for a given class of transaction depends on the type of knowledge structure(s) that the transaction seeks to promote and the learner performance enabled by the transaction. We assume that different knowledge structures require different types of instructional transactions. We also assume that different transactions promote the acquisition of different types of learner performance.

We have identified three primary classes of transactions: *component* transactions, *abstraction* transactions, and *association* transactions corresponding to the three forms of elaboration in the knowledge representation. The knowledge frames required for a given transaction are called a *transaction frame* set. The transaction frame set for a component transaction is a single knowledge frame and the components which comprise this frame. The transaction frame set for an abstraction transactions is at least a class frame and two or more instance frames from an abstraction hierarchy. The transaction frame set for an association transaction is two or more associated frames from the Elaborated Frame Network.

Knowledge Representation and Elaborations

In previous papers a knowledge representation system has been proposed as a means to organizing and representing content in a knowledge base. This scheme proposes an *Elaborated Frame Network* consisting of three types of knowledge frames: *entities, activities and processes.* We also suggested that these frames could be elaborated in three ways: *component, abstraction and associations* elaborations (Jones, Li, and Merrill, 1990). Components consists of parts of an entity, steps of an activity, and events of a process. Abstraction specifies instance, class and superclass relationships for entity, activity or process frames. Associations link frames together on the basis of shared components.

Transaction Parameters

Each transaction shell is characterized by a set of parameters which enables the shell to be customized for particular learner populations, tasks, and learning environments. Transaction shells, by implementing parameters which can be changed at design or run time, can be configured in many ways to represent a complete range of instructional interactions. Several instructional functions are necessary in order for an instructional transaction to successfully interact with a learner. All instructional transactions, regardless of the type of knowledge or skill taught, must be capable of performing these functions. The specific parameters that are necessary for a given type of transaction to accomplish these functions will differ from one class of transaction to another. In fact, the difference in the way these functions are accomplished by different classes of transactions is one of the characteristics that distinguish one class of transactions from another.

Each function is accomplished via several *methods* that are specific computer programs that enable the function to be accomplished. These methods require values on a number of instructional *parameters*. These parameter values determine exactly how a given method is applied in a given transaction instance. The interactions enabled by a given transaction can exhibit a considerable variance depending on the values assigned to the parameters which constrain its methods. Instructional design via instructional transaction shells consists of selecting parameter values appropriate for a given learner population and particular learning task. These parameter values then enable the methods of each function to carry out this function in a way consistent with the requirements of a given learning situation.

All instructional transactions must include the following functions: *knowledge selection knowledge sequence, instructional management* and *instructional enactment* The remainder of this paper will be focused on the Knowledge selection parameters required for a transaction shell. The discussion will further be limited to the knowledge mediation parameters associated with knowledge selection.

Knowledge Selection Parameters

From all knowledge associated with a given transaction instance, the knowledge selection function determines that part which will be taught during a particular enactment of the transaction. The knowledge selection function is accomplished via three methods: *knowledge partitioning, knowledge portrayal,* and *knowledge amplification. Knowledge partitioning* parameters select from the knowledge available to the transaction that knowledge which will be taught, and while making this selection divide the knowledge into mind-size pieces or segments. *Knowledge portrayal* parameters select from the various mediations available in the resource data base those representations that will be used by the current transaction. *Knowledge Amplification* parameters select form the available ancillary knowledge that which will be included in a particular enactment of the transaction.

Associated with each of the knowledge frames for a given instance of a transaction is a *resource data base* containing the mediated representation which will be presented to the student by the transaction. Each of the frames in the knowledge base may include a large number of components: parts, steps, or events. Each of these knowledge frames may be implemented by several different mediations in the instructional resource data base.

A primary advantage of learning from an instructional situation is that the learner can be brought into contact with a much wider scope of knowledge via the mediation of this knowledge than would be possible if the learner was required to learn only form real work or on-the-job. Not only can a wider scope of knowledge be presented but this knowledge can be mediated in ways that enable it to be more effectively learned than learning it form its naturally occuring state.

The *knowledge portrayal* method selects from the various mediation available in the resource data base those knowledge mediations that will be used by the current enactment of the transaction.

Knowledge Portrayal Parameters

Parameters in the transaction shells which refer to the resource data base enable the easy retrieval of the information. The mediations are cataloged with specific values from the parameters. When a transaction shell is instantiated, a parameter value is indicated.

Mediations are accessed from the data base which match the parameters of the shell and the mediation is configured in the transaction shell. Parameters for knowledge mediations may include:

Type [physical, functional]

The same information can be represented in an number of ways. A functional view represents the components of the entity, activity or process in a way that shows how it works rather than how it looks. A physical view represents the components of the entity, activity of process in a way that shows how it looks as well as how it works.

Mode [language, symbolic, literal]

Representing mode refers to the means used for the representation rather than to a particular delivery system. Literal representation provides information in ways that can be sensed by one or more of the senses: sight, hearing, touch, smell and taste. The corresponding representations are visual (still and motion), auditory, tactile, olfactory and taste. Adequate transactions for many subject areas may be seriously limited by delivery systems with limited representational capabilities. However, the capabilities of instructional delivery systems continues to expand with vendors announcing increased capabilities with increasing frequency. True multi-media systems, integrating digital representation of motion visual, graphic, text and audio have been or are about to be announced. Futuristic systems include virtual reality involving helmets and gloves which allow remarkable tactile involvement with audio visual representations provide new representation capabilities. Literal representations can vary from these high technology, futuristic virtual-reality simulations to simple line drawings. The challenge for an instructional theory is to be able to proscribe those necessary and sufficient representations for particular instructional tasks. Physical representations usually require some form of literal representation.

Symbolic representation includes notation systems, diagrams, and graphs of all sorts. Symbolic in this context means those representations that go beyond ordinary language to provide increased precision for a particular subject matter area. Symbolic representations include music notation, map symbols, circuit symbols, architectural symbols, math symbols, etc. Functional representations usually require some form of symbolic representation.

Language involves descriptions via words and grammatical structures. Except where language or written expression are the entities involves in the instruction, physical and functional representations in the form of language are usually less adequate than literal or symbolic representations.

Fidelity [low...high]

Fidelity refers to how close the representation resembles the real thing. While there are some rules of thumb that would suggest that more fidelity and more literal representation is better, there are many situations where instruction is enhanced by lower degrees of fidelity and by symbolic and language representations.

Organizing knowledge into a knowledge data base and mediations into a resource data base enables transactions to use and reuse data and mediations. Mediations can be in the form of text, still graphics, simulations, video, etc. A given transaction shell, when asked to find a mediation of a microscope could obtain from the resource data base a graphic image of a microscope. Also from the resource data base, a transaction shell could configure a video segment of a microscope in use or an animated graphic of microscope use. The use of transaction parameters to the mediations allows the mediations to be cataloged and retrieved to be used by any Instructional:Transaction transaction.

Conclusion

The ID2 Research Program at Utah State University is actively working to advance Transaction Theory. We are also developing, for several clients, prototypes and working versions of transaction shells and the appropriate knowledge representations. This paper represents a portion of our current thinking. We invite your comments. Please address inquires concerning this paper to the authors, at the Department of Instructional Technology, Utah State University, Logan, Utah 84322-2830.

References

1. Carter, J.: The ICW decision handbook. Randolph AFB, TX: Headquarters, Air Training Command Technical Report in press as AFP-50-xx (1990)
2. Faiola, T.: Improving courseware development efficiency: The effects of authoring systems on team roles and communication. Educational Technology, Vol. 29(8), pp. 16-19 (1990)
3. Lippert, R.C.: Expert systems: Tutors, tools, and tutees. Journal of Computer-Based Instruction, Vol. 16(1), pp. 11-19 (1990)
4. MacKnight, C.B., and Balagopalan, S.: Authoring systems: Some instructional implications. Journal of Educational Technology Systems, Vol. 30(1), pp. 7-11 (1988-89)
5. Merrill, M.D., Li, Z., and Jones, M.K.: Limitations of first generation instructional design. Educational Technology, Vol. 30(1), pp. 7-11 (1990)
6. Merrill, M.D., Li, Z, and Jones, M.L.: Second generation instructional design (ID2). Educational Technology, Vol. 30(2), pp. 7-14 (1990)

Enhancing the Acceptance and Cultural Validity of Interactive Multi-Media

Diane M. Gayeski

OmniCom Associates, 407 Coddington Road, Ithaca, New York, NY 14850, USA. Tel: (607) 272-7700

Interactive Media - Are They Really Used?

Although studies have shown that interactive multimedia are effective and efficient instructional tools, they have not been adopted as widely nor as successfully as predicted. This presentation will focus on culture as one factor which impacts the effectiveness of interactive media. Several case studies of customized and locally produced multimedia projects are discussed and demonstrated, and a model for participatory development is presented.

Numerous studies have shown that computer-based training and interactive video are effective means of achieving instructional objectives. However, by many accounts, these media have not been adopted as widely or as quickly as had been predicted a decade ago (Eikenberg, 1987; Gayeski, 1989; McLean, 1985). Although more than half of all U.S. organizations with over 50 employees use computer-based instruction (according to a recent *Training Magazine* survey), most of this use involves generic tutorials in computer skills, such as word-processing tutorials. Interactive video use essentially did not expand from 1986 to 1989, with about 15% of U.S. organizations using interactive video to deliver training (Geber, 1990, October). Many organizations have produced or bought one program to test the technology, but few have adopted it as a prevalent educational medium.

For example, in a 1988 survey which revealed the long-range outcomes of 40 major U.S. interactive video projects for education and training, less than half of the respondents continued to use these programs, or endeavored to produce additional programs (Gayeski & Williams, 1989, October). Of particular significance was the finding that instructional programs produced by internal staffs, or by a combination of internal and external personnel were more successful than were programs produced by outside vendors exclusively. This fact is particularly interesting to note given the commonly held belief that slicker programming, generally created by experienced and expensive vendors, is better than simpler programs created in-house.

Even when interactive multimedia is applied, it is often underutilized. According to most researchers in the field, the power of interactive multimedias yet to be exploited: most programs are rather mundane tutorials on using computer software or "electronic flashcards" for educational use (Merrill, 1985). Merrill reflects the disappointment of many researchers in new instructional technologies, and contends that some of these strategies are hold-overs from 1960s programmed instruction, which have been found to be boring and rigid.

As more powerful hardware and software platforms are developed, and as more urgent needs for education and training press upon our nations and corporations, we need to examine the reasons for the apparent failure of multimedia systems to achieve their potential. Although there are a variety of reasons for this apparent failure, one is particularly significant: Because interactive systems are widely perceived to be expensive, they are often not produced on the local level. Yet this technology is presumed to be individualized, and demands personalization and identification of the user with the program to be optimally effective (Gayeski & Williams, 1985). This presents an interesting paradox: how can interactive multimedia be truly individualized yet mass-produced? We must find ways of customizing generic programs and of producing effective programs on the local level.

Culture In Training And Education

"Anyone who takes a moment or two to think about it will quickly conclude that culture involves style, ethos, and values. And as training professionals, we know that culture has everything to do with the way people give and receive information. In short, it has everything to do with the way people learn" (Guptara, 1990). Communication theorist David Berlo (1960) asserts that meanings are in people and maintains that it is difficult or even impossible for individuals of varying backgrounds to precisely share their meanings for events of concepts. In fact, for meanings to remain relatively constant across sources and receivers, the message itself should change, since the interpretation of the message is sure to change. Although culture is recognized as an important aspect of communication, it has been virtually ignored as a variable in interactive multimedia, even though this family of media can support a number of translations, transliterations, and program treatments within a given program.

Most audiences for training and education are becoming increasingly diverse. According to the 1987 Hudson Institute study, U.S. industries are facing a shortage of qualified applicants and a drastic shift in the nature of the traditional labor pool. This fact can be explained by the lower birth rate during the 1960s and 70s, as well as the apparent failure of our school systems to adequately prepare many students for entry-level jobs requiring literacy and numeracy. In order to fill jobs, organizations will need to hire immigrants, ex-convicts, older workers, handicapped individuals, temporary/part time workers, and even more women; they will also need to improve the productivity of the workers they do have (Odiorne, 1990). Only 15% of new entrants to the labor force will be native white males.

In the decades to come, companies will not be just "multi-national", composed of units operating in different countries under the control of one central office. Rather, we are moving towards "transnational" organizations. Transnational organizations strike the "...right balance between a global perspective and local market flexibility..."; they are "...composed of a worldwide network of semi-autonomous locations [and] are considerably harder to coordinate and control. It requires a new approach to leadership, management and cooperation -- not to mention training and human resources development" (Randolph, 1990, p. 48).

Although the dominant U.S. assumption of the "melting pot" has diverted attention from and even suppressed discussions about ethnic and cultural differences, gradually diversity is being acknowledged and even fostered. Today, many organizations such as Digital Equipment, the Bank of Boston, and GTE are instituting training on cultural differences, like the successful "valuing diversity" series (Copeland, 1988). And, as Geber (1990, July) points out, there is an important difference between "valuing" diversity and merely "managing" it as if it were something to be "contained".

Training *about cultural diversity*, however, is quite different than *culturally diverse training*. Techniques that are appropriate and effective in one setting may be unsuitable or even offensive in another. Guptara (1990) writes that in many cultures, games and exercises are for children only; in the Middle East adults learn by "discoursing at length upon the subject at hand". Interactive video, although invented in Japan, is not used in Japanese training, because they work and learn in teams - not individually. The Japanese culture also does not encourage risk-taking. Studies of manufacturing have found vast differences in the ability of different nations in Western Europe to profit from new production technologies depending upon how the culture views technology and the relative status of abstract versus concrete work (d'Iribarne, 1990).

Besides the differences among national cultures, there are also significant variations of culture *within* nations. In his book, *The Nine Nations of North America,* Garreau (1981) posits nine distinct regions and cultures within the United States and Canada. Despite the pervasive homogenizing effects of mass media and nationalized educational systems, there is a clear disparity in dialect, mores, dress, and economy. Some organizations have attempted to address these differences in their mediated communications. For instance, in the early 1980s Pitney-Bowes created a videotape which explained new management policies and was sent out to be viewed within district offices. The beginning and ending segments of this program were identical, but the middle section contained a message from each region's district manager. These regionalized sections differed both in content (various regions were experiencing different economic conditions) as well as in the style, dialect, and dress of the speaker.

Reynolds (1990) cites the example of the Brazilian director of training for Xerox corporation who never uses materials as they arrive, but adapts them to fit local circumstances. While this may be relatively easy to do with print materials, multimedia programs are difficult if not impossible for end-users to modify. "With automated training programs, no local trainer can offer on-the-spot modifications. This type of training includes multimedia self-study packages, computer assisted instruction, and interactive video. In most cases, local subsidiaries or customers lack the technical capability to adapt such materials; the only recourse is to modify the materials before they are sent overseas" (p.75).

OmniCom Associates has faced a number of interesting challenges posed by multi-cultural interactive multimedia projects. For example, in creating a Training:Programs program for the Rabo Bank in the Netherlands, it became clear that a computer program would appear "rude" if it incorporated the common North American practice of having the program address the user by his or her first name. The program instead politely asked the person if the or she preferred to be called "Mr., Miss, or Mrs." and then used that form of address in subsequent interactions. In developing educational programs for medical patients in Japan, we were confronted with the necessity to define the computer as a servant or as a teacher since the way in which the computer would address the user would vary greatly depending upon that assumption.

Reynolds (1990) offers several practical suggestions for developing training which will be delivered to international audiences. He cautions developers to be careful of things like dialect, culturalization (bias towards US culture), dubbing in voices (Americans with British accents), instructional strategies (like using games which are not appropriate for Chinese adults), body language, using different currency and non-Roman character sets, the length of other translations, cliches, and acronyms. The typical informality of many U.S. programs is considered rude or condescending by many other cultures.

The concept of culture has been extended from national or ethnic styles to organizational mores, methods of operation, and belief systems (Deal and Kennedy, 1982). Even within a given country and region, the vocabulary, examples, styles, and actions of individuals vary greatly depending upon the organization in which they work or study. For example, the duties, customer interaction patterns, dress, and work environments of tellers in banks within a three-block radius in my home community of Ithaca, New York, are quite varied. Even though banks are subject to federal regulations and offer similar products, their corporate cultures are quite dissimilar. Moreover, branches of the same bank differ depending upon the city in which they are located and their customer base. Many organizations successfully use humor or novel treatments such as music videos in their training, while others permit only conservative methods.

Since interactive multimedia require users to actively participate in the program, the style of presentation and the response judging algorithms must be sensitive to their vocabulary, beliefs, and everyday surroundings. For example, I once was asked to review a computer-based Training:Computer-basedraining orientation for new employees which used the metaphor of sports events as a way to present instructional modules. As the user learned more information, he or she took part in new athletic endeavors such as races, and tried to "beat the clock" in covering more material. The screens were rather attractive, but used animated figures of male athletes. Since I am neither an athlete nor a male, I was annoyed by the program and quickly tired of the format and content. The image did nothing to promote my identification with the content nor my motivation to learn more about the company. I have also seen users quickly become aggravated by programs which could not intelligently recognize and respond to common regional or local vocabulary or differences in spelling. For example, a CBT program may be programmed to anticipate the correct answer as "check" but would fail to recognize (or even consider incorrect) the perfectly acceptable alternative words "cheque" or "draft".

The use of technology to deliver information and instruction is itself a cultural variable to which we must be sensitive. Many organizations desire to reduce training costs by eliminating traditional classroom training in favor of distributed and electronically delivered instruction. Although the superficial measures of content mastery may be similar for the two approaches, the subtle messages delivered may be quite different. For instance, seminars promote increased human interaction and socialization, fostering a "family" culture. Interactive multimedia do not facilitate interpersonal relationships, but do enhance a "high-tech" culture.

The complexity of specifying content to be included in training courses is also increasing in current organizational environments. Often the processes and products to be taught are in the state of flux. Various experts within an organization or constituencies within a community may have different views about what is "correct". And, as the community of trainees and students becomes more diverse, it is progressively more difficult to communicate the same meanings accurately and efficiently. In other words, we have moved from:

- teaching stable and agreed-upon content by having homogeneous audiences learn deterministic terms and procedures via linear media

to:

- *attempting* to teach fluctuations and debatable content to heterogeneous audiences through abstract models for problem-solving via a rich mix of interactive multimedia.

Although it may seem straightforward to update and customize interactive multimedia, the legal, financial, and technical requirements for doing so may be daunting. There is still considerable debate about the legality of customizing or "repurposing" media, even if unauthorized copies of copyrighted materials are not made. Gaining rights to material is time-consuming and often expensive. The computer-based text and code in interactive multimedia is often unaccessible to the end-user. "Typically, you will not own the code for programs used to develop and deliver automated training, either, making it impossible to translate message and instruction displays (Reynolds, 1990). Since off-the-shelf programs are written using a variety of authoring tools and programming languages, customers would need to not only gain rights to modify the program, but would also need to license the authoring tool used to create it, and then learn to use that tool.

Clearly, traditional methods of delivering uniform content to homogeneous audiences using complex and lengthy development models are obsolete. Can culturally sensitive, effective interactive multimedia be produced by end-user organizations in a cost-effective and timely manner? We offer two case studies of organizations who are doing just this.

Case Studies

Case Study One

Marine Midland Bank, a top-20 U.S. bank, implemented CBT and interactive video starting in 1982. OmniCom Associates trained two of their staff members in CBT authoring and in interactive video design. We selected MS-DIS (IBM-compatible) computers as the standard for delivering CBT, and the Panasonic Interactive Video system, a videotape based integrated system, for delivery of interactive video programming.

Marine Midland licensed our authoring system, I.De.A.S. for three regional training centers and began producing CBT in-house. Typical programs were designed and authored in-house in a 2-3 month time frame. When necessary, OmniCom assisted by reviewing program strategies, and by performing custom programming for unusual routines, such as animation of text or sound effects. CBT is delivered in bank branches and in regional training centers. Some of the CBT programs include a complete teller orientation (accompanied by a print manual), a program on how to use a mainframe account management system, and COMPAS, a computer-based training and reference system on bank products. Tellers and customer representatives can use COMPAS to initially learn about products such as checking and savings accounts, and later as on-the-job aids in recalling procedures by simply typing in a term.

CBT programs are created with different paths for different regions within the Bank, and for different levels of trainee experience. For instance, certain terminology, equipment, and procedures vary depending upon the region and whether the branch is located in an urban or suburban area. Also, the instruction is adapted to trainees who are new in banking, to those who may have worked in other banks, and to those who already have experience within Marine Midland Bank.

Marine Midland also purchased six interactive video playback systems which were placed in training centers and rotated among branch banks. We co-produced four interactive video programs with them; Marine Midland did the research and initial scripting while OmniCom produced the final script, shot and edited the tape, and completed the computer authoring. The topics for these custom programs include how to handle a robbery, how to avoid forgery, professional dress and behavior for bankers, and customer relations. The robbery program contained different branches for different regions since the security procedures and equipment vary.

Marine Midland also used two generic interactive video programs and "re-purposed" some linear video programs by adding computer-generated questions and feedback. Interestingly, even though the generic video programs had high production values, tellers thought the actors and scenes looked contrived and preferred the simpler programs custom produced for Marine Midland.

A typical interactive video program involves a 20-minute trainee experience. The program planning took an average of six months (mostly involved in gaining approval from managers and legal departments on content). Video production was generally accomplished in two weeks, and editing and computer programming took another week. Programs used in-house personnel as actors because they could behave in a credible manner. Subject-matter experts were always present at video taping to approve the scenes as they were being shot. This fact led to the additional unintended benefit of enhancing communication between management (such as the Vice-President for security) and branch personnel. These programs were produced during 1985-87 and cost under $30, 000. each.

Today, CBT is still in use within Marine Midland. In 1987, the bank instituted a branch automation project which has placed PCs on every customer representative's desk, so the delivery hardware has become widely available. Unfortunately, the interactive video hardware systems are no longer being produced, so although it was successful, interactive video production has not been continued. Some of the interactive video programs were re-edited to linear versions to make them more accessible. We have advised the bank to wait for the next hardware standard, which we believe is digital video, to emerge and become affordable. Our authoring system which the bank has licensed, I.De.A.S., can be updated to make use of new hardware when it becomes available.

Case Study Two

Lederle International is a division of American Cyanamid responsible for pharmaceutical marketing. They are present in 100 countries using 30 different languages, and this division trains about 240 sales representatives annually. Traditionally, they have used manuals plus classroom training with native speakers to deliver information on new products as well as general sales and management training. A typical complaint of managers within the various international sales offices was that the training programs were too generic, and that they didn't fit the market.

They explored interactive video for international sales training, but the trial failed for a number of reasons. First, the translation costs were too high, given that scenes would have to be re-shot as well as re-scripted to deal with differences in international styles and medical protocols. Secondly, the hardware was too expensive and complicated to be feasible for the number of dispersed sites. They also tried CBT created by outside vendors. Although the training was effective, Lederle didn't have the license for the authoring system used to create the CBT, so the programs couldn't be translated and adopted for the various markets. It would have been too costly to license the authoring system for each market, and too difficult to train personnel to use the authoring system. They needed to find another way.

We worked with Lederle to develop a standardized hardware platform as well as software systems. They are using IBM PC compatible computers, including laptops. All software is designed to run in an optimal manner on a variety of machines, from powerful desktop computers with VGA displays to the "lowest common denominator machine: one floppy disk drive and CGA (low resolution) graphics. We also designed and programmed a custom authoring system for Lederle, LederLearn. All programs, whether developed by vendors or by in-house staff, will now be created with LederLearn. Their training manager has conducted two workshops on LederLearn which now enable managers to create their own CBT modules reflecting local market conditions, and written in the native language.

One may wonder why, with so many commercial authoring systems on the market, should Lederle create its own?

- 1. Lederle can give copies of LederLearn freely to each market, without the necessity of buying individual copies from a vendor (or violating copyright).
- 2. LederLearn was customized to meet Lederle's needs. It is designed to facilitate translation and creation by non-programmers.
- 3. Lederle has a copy of the source code to LederLearn. This means that the authoring system can't become obsolete; it can be upgraded for new hardware or techniques as needed. The software also can't be "orphaned", as happens to some authoring languages when their vendors go out of business or drop the product.
- 4. Since all programs will be created with LederLearn, they are standardized for ease of use, translation and updating.
- 5. LederLearn creates code in BASIC. This means that programs can be modified easily, and there is no need for run-time modules on playback machines.

LederLearn is menu-driven. Even novices can learn to create CBT in a matter of an hour or so. It supports information, keyword, multiple-choice, text animation, and graphics screens. Programs automatically generate a file of student responses, for later review by designers and/or managers. Built-in utilities allow for easy translation and updating, and even for identifying the graphics standard of the equipment or of a particular graphic. Several programs have now been created in LederLearn, including one on a new cancer treatment. As they are released, Lederle's international markets translate and adapt CBT programs using LederLearn.

Participatory Design and Development

Most current instructional design models are linear and deterministic. They assume that there is one "correct" set of facts, terminology, and procedures, and one "best" way to communicate them. Given contemporary pluralistic audiences and changing information, a more pertinent set of guidelines for instructional development is needed. OmniCom Associates has used the *Participatory Design Model* (Gayeski, 1981; 1991) as the basis for its development of culturally appropriate instructional media. It was initially conceptualized in the context of developing series of educational videotapes on ethnic studies, and has been applied for over fifteen years in a variety of corporate and educational situations.

As figure 1 indicates, this model differs from traditional linear ISD models in several ways: First, although there is an implied logical flow in procedures, the model acknowledges that, in fact, many multimedia projects start somewhere in the middle of the process (e.g., "Let's create an interactive video simulation to teach students lifesaving skills."). Secondly, it assumes that there is no one source of content and strategies, and provides a way to identify and reconcile areas of commonality and areas of diversity (e.g., "Shall we follow the Red Cross or the American Heart Association guidelines for CPR?"). Rather, it advocates design of programs by a team representing a training program's *constituency* -- all of the individuals impacted by that program.

Having more input the content and instructional methods means that the resulting program will be acceptable and appropriate to more groups within an organization. Generally, subject-matter experts have mastery of the content but not of how it's applied or taught in the field. They may not be aware of learners' common misconceptions or of constraints that come into play on the job. Finally, instruction which acknowledges the legitimate diversity of views on a given subject is more authentic. For example, if a training course teaches just one way to assemble a product and the trainee finds out later on the job that there are actually several acceptable ways, the instruction loses credibility. With that as an introduction, here is an explanation of how to use the Participatory Design Model. (See Figure 1.)

- **Step 1** Identify which processes have *already* occurred, and which have been skipped, in order to determine where to start in the design model. In actual practice, the designer may find that some decisions and deliberations have already taken place.
- **Step 2** Analyze the overall need for the program.
- **Step 3** Determine your *constituency*: for whom and/or about whom are you producing the program? The constituency is everybody who has requested the program (the client), has input to the content has requested the program (the client), has input to the content (managers, subject-matter experts, curriculum supervisors, regulators, etc.) and those who will use the program (instructors and learners).
- **Step 4** From a program development team of instructional developers and constituency representatives. The team must include both *subject matter experts* (those who understand the content) and *process experts* (those who understand how the content is actually applied and/or learned and can identify the common performance problems associated with this content).

Take, for example, the development of a multimedia program on avoiding labor union grievances. The development team might include several labor relations specialists, a representative on the union, a communications specialist, a manager who observes the mistakes that new supervisors make which may result in grievances, an instructional designer, a scriptwriter, a video producer / editor, a trainer who has taught courses on the topic, an experienced supervisor who has dealt with grievances, and a newly promoted supervisor who has had no previous experience with this topic.

- **Step 5** Identify existing needs and problems as seen by all members of the program development team.
- **Step 6** Define goals that address the identified problems.
- **Step 7** Explore all viewpoints represented with regard to achieving the goals and designing the program.
- **Step 8** Identify common areas of agreement and areas of diverse opinion within the team.
- **Step 9** Taking into account previous input, determine specific objectives for the program.
- **Step 10** Analyze the setting in which the program will be used. For instance, will people use the program in a formal classroom, on their own time in the company library, as they socialize in the lobby or cafeteria, or in their own homes?
- **Step 11** Determine the program's format of format(s). Which delivery methods will be used, and which strategies will be employed?
- **Step 12** Pool ideas for potential content. Usually there will be more material that can be covered in one program. Screen these ideas by: 1) assessing how they address the objectives; 2) seeking the constituency's reactions or additional suggestions; 3) researching content for accuracy and duplication of other sources, and; 4) determining whether the technical requirements of the delivery method will permit ideas to be implemented. Now a draft module or program segment can be prototyped. This step is repeated for each of several programs in a series or for several segments within a program.
- **Step 13** Have the entire program development team evaluate each module as it develops.
- **Step 14** Produce final modules or programs, using the feedback gained in formative evaluation.
- **Step 15** Assemble the entire training package, which may include several programs or supplementary materials.
- **Step 16** Have the program evaluated: 1) internally by the program development team; 2) by users; 3) by outside experts, such as managers who can assess the long-term performance outcomes of the training.
- **Step 17** Summarize the evaluations from these sources and hand them back to the program development team for possible revisions.

Conclusion

Several important factors which promote culturally appropriate interactive multimedia have emerged from this examination of design and production variables: First, it is important that training programs be produced with a high level of staff involvement; programs produced mostly by outside vendors and with high production budgets have been found to be not as successful as programs produced more modestly with in-house resources. Second, when new media are introduced, it is important that staff are trained in their development and utilization, that the impact on the corporate culture is examined, and that companies retain control of hardware and software so that programs can be maintained and updated to reduce the impact of equipment obsolescence. Finally, multimedia programs must also be carefully designed to meet the local styles, language, and expectations of their audiences.

We recommend the following steps in adopting interactive multimedia:

- 1. Choose a simple, widely supported hardware standard.
- 2. Select an authoring tool based on staff resources and instructional needs.
- 3. Retain control of the authoring tool. Examine the need to license the tool for an entire site or organization. Find out if it is necessary to license run-time modules. Ensure that the tool can be maintained and updated.
- 4. Teach the internal training or curriculum development staff to develop (or at least modify) multimedia programs.
- 5. Develop and enforce standards for programs focusing on instructional strategies and the facilitation of updating and individualizing instruction for regional and corporate cultures.
- 6. Employ a participatory model for design and development of programs.
- 7. Co-produce initial multimedia programs with consultants who can create effective models which fit the local culture.

Interactive video and CBT are potentially very powerful technologies for advancing knowledge, but they often fail because they are not well integrated with the users' culture. Organizations must plan for staff training, careful selection of hardware and software, and custom development of programs which directly relate to their needs and styles. Experience has shown that it is possible and desirable to produce multimedia programs quickly and inexpensively in-house (Gayeski & Williams, 1987). Only then will interactive multimedia be truly "interactive".

References

1. Berlo, D.K.: The process of communication. New York: Holt, Rinehart, and Winston 1960
2. Copeland, Lennie. Learning to manage a multicultural work force. Training, May, pp. 48-56, 1988
3. Deal, T.E., and A.A. Kennedy. Corporate cultures: The rites and rituals of corporate life. Reading. Mass.: Addison-Wesley 1982
4. D'Iribarne, A.: Advanced technological forms which reflect the cultural, economic, educational, geographical and social reality in Europe. In: Cooley, M. (ed.). European competitiveness in the 21st century: Integration of work, culture, and technology. Brussels: FAST Programme 1990
5. Eikenberg, D.: Honeymoon's over for interactive, time to grow up. Backstage, pp. 1,8.38.40, September 4 1987
6. Garreau, J.: The nine nations of North America. New York: Avon Books. Gayeski, D.: When the audience becomes the producer: a model for participatory media design. Educational Technology 21(6), pp. 11-14 (1981)
7. Gayeski, D.: Why information technologies fail. Educational Technology, February 1989
8. Gayeski, D.: Corporate and instructional video. Englewood Cliffs, NJ: Prentice-Hall 1991
9. Gayeski, D., and D.V. Williams.: Interactive Media. Englewood Cliffs, N.J.: Prentice-Hall 1985
10. Gayeski, D., and D.V. Williams.: Getting into interactive video using existing resources. E-ITV, pp. 26-29. June 1989
11. Gayeski, D., and D.V. Williams.: Videodisc and the Teflon factor. The Videodisc Monitor, pp. 22-26. June 1989
12. Gayeski, D., and D.V. Williams.: Where have all the videodisc gone? Data Training, pp. 32-33. October 1989
13. Geber, B.: Managing diversity. Training, pp.23-30. July 1990
14. Geber, B.: Interactive video. Training, p. 64. July 1990
15. Guptara, P.: The art of training abroad. Training and Development Journal, pp. 13-14. November, 1990
16. McLean, L.M.: Seeking information on interactive video: The information sources and strategies used by corporate training developers. (ERIC Document Reproduction Service No. ED259719 (1985)
17. Merrill, M.D.: Where is the authoring in authoring systems? Journal of Computer-Based Instruction pp. 90-96 (1985)
18. Odiorne, G.: Beating the 1990's labor shortage. Training, pp. 32-35. July 1990
19. Randolph, B.: When going global isn't enough. Training, pp.47-51. August 1990
20. Reynolds, A.: Training that travels well. Training and Development Journal, pp. 73-78. September 1990

94

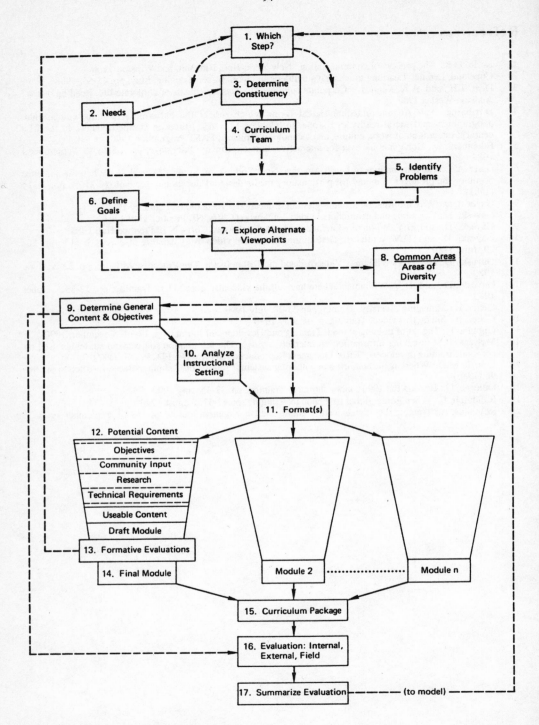

Figure 1. Participatory Design Model

Contextual Browsing Within a Hypermedia Environment

C.P. Tompsett

Centre for Information Based Learning, Kingston Polytechnic, Penrhyn Road, Kingston-Upon-Thames KT1 2EE, United Kingdom. Tel. (44) 81 547 7705 and (44) 81 547 2000. Fax. (44) 81 547 1457. Email. CP.TOMPSETT@UK.AC.KINGSTON

Introduction

An intelligent tutoring system must develop appropriate models of knowledge, learning and teaching to achieve the ideal of a learning environment that teaches all learners, accounting for differences in experience, previous knowledge and preferred learning style. An intermediate target is to create an environment that supports the flexible presentation of knowledge without the inclusion of active tutoring elements. Such systems rely on the learner to control the presentation of information on a multimedia learner workstation while the system must ensure that appropriate material is readily accessible. This model reflects a human centered style of design with strong demands on the user interface.

Learning Environments

A conventional distinction in education is that between teaching and learning. Responsibility for learning is retained by the student and teaching is considered to be the collection of activities carried out by another person that encourage a student to learn effectively. This is a broad set of activities ranging across the whole domain of educational, cognitive and social psychology (if not further). This range will include aspects such as:

  establishing a desire/need to learn
  creating a setting with no distractions
  selecting learning targets relevant to need and ability
  selecting activities that foster development of cognitive structures
  providing materials that illustrate the required view of knowledge
  building on existing skill and knowledge
  responding to individual need during learning activities
  responding to individual answers (correct or incorrect)

All these activities are of course integrated, requiring a complex planning activity occurring at many layers of action and across markedly different timescales. Traditional views of the teaching activity, particularly in training, adopt a directed view of teaching in which the learner is strictly controlled and has little scope to alter the learning environment -i.e. the teacher knows best.

Intelligent Tutoring Systems

The problem is not so simple, however, for intelligent tutoring systems (ITS). Ignoring, for the present, the problems of student and user modelling, the emulation of the teaching activity requires three primary knowledge sources:

knowledge of the domain - structure, content, facts and rules etc.

knowledge of resources - to introduce, test, coach, discuss, demonstrate etc.

knowledge of learning - development of cognitive structures, stages of learning, classification of abilities, complexity of learning tasks etc.

These three knowledge-bases are not interdependent, however. If the student does not study enough examples then he/she is very likely to fail any test the first time round. Similarly, if knowledge within the domain is not apparent within the teaching activities then there will be no potential for the student to learn that particular aspect of the domain. Rather than the three knowledge-bases listed above we in fact require at least one more (figure 1), and three more (figure 2); the latter approach is the simpler of the two to develop.

The production of a 'course' as opposed to the design of an intelligent tutoring system requires that each of these six knowledge sources (three 'models' and three integrations sources) are addressed. The distinction between different methods of producing courseware depend on the extent to which any of these knowledge bases are active, providing flexible response during a learning session, or which are only apparent as a 'pre-compiled' does not necessarily imply that the knowledge has been ignored in the design. For a CBT course we would expect the designer to consider the knowledge that is to be taught, to select a model of learning and to apply knowledge relevant to design of resources. These aspects of knowledge are integrated to produce a single set of resources that 'represent' the knowledge according to the needs of supporting a particular model of learning. Flexibility is programmed specifically to account for whether learning takes place according to the model of how a 'standard' student should 'learn'.

Pre-compiled knowledge

Although this view of CBT suggests that frame-based CBT is fundamentally limited in its potential to support complex learning, several aspects of pre-compilation of knowledge should be considered. Firstly, pre-compilation allows us to consider only the results of applying the knowledge and not the knowledge itself. Therefore we do not need to understand the separate processes underlying the design of the course and the complex interactions between these aspects - we only need to produce decisions that are valid for the design. If we are able to produce a specification of whether learning has occured then we can assess design, derived form established practice, without understanding the formal basis for these designs. Secondly, and along a similar line, we can introduce far more factors into the design of the materials than will be accommodated in a formal model and this applies at many levels. Particular aspects of a restricted group of learners, allowing for age, computer experience, culture and attitude to learning, may all influence the design of frame-based courseware. Similarly many different aspects of design influence the generation of a single frame, from knowledge about presentation of text and supporting graphics to menu design and response analysis. Thirdly the pre-compilation allows for continuity through a particular piece of courseware - maintaining a storyline does not make sense within an intelligent tutoring system (or hypertext environment). Fourthly pre-compilation, although viewed as detrimental to flexibility of learning, may only affect a minority of the students. If the population of students are sufficiently homogeneous in their learning needs and are accommodated successfully most of the time by the courseware, it may be more efficient to supplement such a course with human tutors rather than attempt a more intelligent but complex approach. Fifthly, in respect of the major deficiency in frame-based CBT - its inability to respond interactively once written - this must be set against the disadvantages of generating the frames interactively. In this situation the generic nature of such generated frames ignores many aspects of good teaching. The selection of a few 'paradigm cases' to provide initial models of a problem domain and the ability to use highly specific linguistic phraseology, exploiting the sophistication of natural language and the nuances of meaning (relating to informal knowledge) cannot be captured in formal systems [Ref. 14]. Finally, on a technical note, pre-compilation avoids regeneration of the same frames/decisions on many similar occasions.

Integrating CBT with Intelligent Tutoring

The preview above suggests that, given consistency within the learner group, a limited scope to domain and well-defined learning goals, CBT may provide an effective model for courseware construction. If we are to suggest an advance on this technology it must provide us, at present, with added value without introducing too much complexity in the many areas offered by an Intelligent Tutoring System (ITS).

One suggestion is to combine the success of CBT with the flexibility of knowledge-based generation of courseware, using one of the established training shells now coming on to the market (e.g. ATR Trainer, reported elsewhere in the conference by Robson Rhodes) [Ref. 1]. Following similar suggestions in respect of Interactive Video [Ref. 13], it would be feasible to 'run' such a generative system with a suitably large number of users to establish appropriate sets of frames to provide completion in some sense, could then be recreated to include additional aspects of good CBT design. Such a system would provide both the initial advantages of frame-based CBT for a homogeneous group of learners with the flexibility of generative approaches to accommodate individual learners where the advantages of well focussed instruction outweigh the weaker design of generated frames.

Returning Control to the Learner

The major problems facing ITS design at present stem from a lack of applicable models of human learning. This applies as much to the overall framework of conceptual development as to the intimate modelling of learning and forgetting information. Some advances have been made in terms of defining learner styles, but styles exist only as a set of discrete entities rather than a multi-dimensional set of characteristics. Knowledge of how to match learner characteristics and resource generation without producing two set of resources appears to be a unrealisable in the near future. If an alternative to active control of learning by the system can be found then the application of intelligence to the learning will be more likely succeed.

Open learning concepts reject the constricting approach to teaching and place more responsibility on the learner to control both the choice and pace of learning materials, within a more flexible view of what might be appropriate. This fits ell with a hypermedia approaches where the learner actively selects routes through semi-structured materials. The design task in this situation is to define appropriate routes through a large resource base.

The systems that we are developing at Kingston, which we term 'Information Based Learning', apply knowledge-based structuring techniques to the design of hypermedia systems. These systems are characterized by four features:

1   limited specification of learning goals
2   development of sub-structure to resources
3   identification of resources in terms of purpose and content [Ref. 4]
4   separation of procedural and declarative facets

The first aspect is taken as a pre-requisite for understanding the use of hypermedia materials for learning (as well as for not using CBT). The second and third aspects reflect our contention that totally open hypermedia systems for learning are unrestricted and fail to support effective learning. The fourth point is related to our view that the ability to 'do' and to 'understand' are distinct facets of knowledge and to model the differences and connections we must develop linked representations.

The knowledge-based Engineering Training Project investigated the intelligent knowledge-based learning in the domain of computer controlled milling machines (CNC milling). Information was collected from three major sources. A consultant was engaged by one of the partners to prepare information for inclusion in the knowledge-base although interviews with the expert were not possible during the major phase of knowledge elicitation. The second primary source was interviews with lecturers in the domain relating to one small demonstration and a large industrial application. Further information was collected from manufacturers' product information and textbooks used by students and lecturers. A section of text, as prepared by the consultant and typical for the domain was [Ref. 6]:

1.13.40 Short hole drills (inserted tips)

Short hole drills or throw-away-tip drills (perhaps better-known as U-drills from the trade name of the originator of this type of tool), are the most modern method of originating holes from the solid at rapid metal removal rates and to a reasonable accuracy. They do however demand a machine of good rigidity and a relatively-high spindle power, Typical size ranges are 16 to 80 mm diameter and the flutes may be straight or helical. Internal coolant feed through the body of the drill is usually provided and large quantities of coolant at high pressure (typically 20 bar) are strongly advised.

When drilling from the solid the drill design incorporates two tips, one cutting over the center and the other cutting the periphery of the hole. (However, for holes up to about 20mm diameter, single-tipped drills are available). Tips are commonly of a six-sided design based on a triangular form although some drills use a mixture of square and six-sided tips. Attainable tolerance are in the bands up to about IT 7 or 8. Normal maximum depths of hole are quoted as 2 or 3 times the hole diameter.

Cutting speeds are typically 10 times faster than HSS twist drills (say up to 350 m/min in mild steel) and feed rates are typically in the range 0.1 to 0.3 mm/rev depending on the work material.

For diameters larger than say 70 mm, trepanning versions of this type of tool are available, the maximum diameter of standard sizes being about 250mm.

Hypermedia Structuring

The written material was supplemented with video material, either as stills or as sequences of machining from the industrial application, shot to illustrate practice in the problem domain. Although the assumption was made that the recorded knowledge would be coded in some knowledge representation system (KL-ONE was chosen as a model) [Ref.3] with video as a supplement to the AI representation, we have been reviewing this resource as a typical 'hypertext resource'. For the purposes of this paper we are concerned to review the implications of adopting straightforward hypertext approaches to support learning.

Since the collect text is divided into paragraphs it seems initially appropriate to consider that a hypertext approach would present the material as a set of 'cards' with automatic sequencing between the four cards. This may not accord with views of hypertext such as the Xanadu [Ref. 11], but it is clear that we are seeking to model the presentation of information as opposed to the notions of evidence or authorship as is the case in that system. At present we have a simple structuring of this information as linked cards, one for each paragraph:

This is not the only structuring that was available from the documentation. The text was hierarchically structured with an abstracted level of headings as below:

Section 1   Tooling

1.00.00 Tooling (xref to 1.80.00, 2.00.000,3,41.10)
    1.10.10 Hole originating
        1.11.00 HSS
        1.12.00 HSS-TiN Coated
        1.13.00 Carbide
            1.13.21 Solid twist drills
            1.12.22 Brazed twist drills
            1.13.24 Step drills/counterbores (xref 1.11.31, 1.11.32)
    1.20.00 Hole finishing
    1.30.00 Threading

    ...

Section 2   Machining data
Section 3   Safety
Section 4   Adaptors for tools
Section 5   Attachments and units

Hierarchical Structuring

This structuring provides both an hierarchical organisation to the information and cross-referencing between sections and even across major sections (as in the reference to machines within the short hole drill section). The hierarchy is loosely organized on the basis of: primary function of tooling; cutting edge composition and then internal physical structure to the drill. On the other hand, separation into cutting edge composition is also made at a higher level: (sections 1.40.00 surface machining (HSS) and 1.50.00 surface machining (carbide) and even occurs as a separate section 1.80.00. Within the more global structure, section 2, machining data, incorporates both information about the tools and the material to be machined. Thus each sub-section of section 2 refers implicitly to a matching sub-section of section 1.

The classification into this one hierarchical structure is derived from the linear text presentation rather than the optimum structure of information for browsing or learning that can be provided by hypertext. It would be reasonable therefore to assume that the minimum extra features that would be available within a hypertext representation would include facilities to support both this hierarchical structuring of the information and the cross-referencing. How to name links, either maintained as it is presented here or reproduced in terms of naming links to similar sections -e.g. 'similar functions', or 'other tool types' is not considered at this point.

Cross-referencing

The nature of cross-referencing is very general but two distinct aspects can be identified. In this text, cross-reference performs a distinct function from the implied cross-references in the hierarchical structure. Although for a learner they both provide a reference to suitable information to enhance learning they fulfil distinct functions for someone merely seeking information.

For an information seeker a cross-reference indicates materials that should be examined to support an understanding (here it would support understanding whether a particular machine has these qualities) whereas the hierarchy supports alternative solutions (same function but different tool) within some loosely defined problem space. Indeed it should be noted that as the problem space becomes more confined we would expect that switching to different sections at higher levels will provide responses that are outside the current solution space. This reflects the concept of context to information search- whether the user is interested in any information available or whether the relevant information is only a small proportion of that accessible.

This use of cross-reference here is limited. In the text chosen there is one cross-reference that is indicated in the list of topics which matches with the comment on rigidity and spindle power of the machine. However it would be simplistic to suggest that this is the only cross-referencing that would be supported in a hypertext version. Some more general criterion is required to provide the links between the sources of information. Two general approaches could be considered here. The simplest is the concordance view that allows for search according to linguistic repetition. For the 'cards' suggested above we have:

metal removal rates, accuracy, rigidity, spindle power, size ranges, flutes, internal coolant, high pressure; drilling from the solid, cutting over the centre, periphery, single-tipped drills, Tips, six-sided design, triangular form, square tips, tolerance IT 7 or 8 maximum depths, hole diameter;

Cutting speeds, 10 times faster than HSS twist, 350 m/min in mild steel, feed rates 0.3 mm/rev; trepanning versions etc.

The relatively large number of items that would lead to other information cards, taken with the variety in the kind of reference that is being made, suggest that this straightforward approach is too random in its application. Apart from the sheer size of the total vocabulary, two issues are significant -firstly whether the different links that are possible will lead to distinct items and secondly whether the degree of specificity for each link is clear. For example, the references to tip design could all lead to the same 'card' describing tip insert shapes for hole origination, the current application. Alternatively they might lead to general principles associated with the relationship between chip shape and the detailed relationship between cutting edge and cutting surface that lead to these assumptions.

The second point raises the possibility that a link might take you to more detailed information -from typical speeds to a table of actual speeds for different materials, or to more general aspects relating to speed characteristics of carbide tips in general. In some cases these two aspects of variation may lead to the same target card but for different reasons. These two approaches, however, require different methods to resolve the problem of automatic generation of links. The first requires that we understand how the material has been created in the first place, since if several 'terms' could all link to the same 'next card' this reflects consistency with which various terms are associated. The second raises the issue of why a particular term is being pursued (i.e. why does the user intend to follow this link) since searching for more specific information suggests that a 'context' is being developed, whereas a wider search suggests that the relevance of current information is being placed in a wider context, or being reflected against alternative views in order to determine the range of possibilities.

The second approach to establishing links would emphasize the overall structure of the text on 'cards'. Since the author has made conscious choices of grouping information, it may be important to work only at the card level representation. That is there are only a certain number of cards that should sensibly link to this one, as over fragmentation of the text into spurious terms leads to too many links (and the hyperspace maze problem). To create these links would again require that some consistency within the information is required. Once again, however, we might expect to see aspects of generalization recurring, since it is consistency that is fundamental to the notions of generalization, specialization and contrast [Ref. 7].

Purpose

A further factor of importance in linking text, beyond overt cross-referencing and the intention of the user in pursuing a link, is the intended purpose of the author in creating the text, especially in technical domains. A trivial indication of the importance of this effect is created by reading the four paragraphs outlined above in a random, incorrect order. If we start with the third paragraph all we are given is comparative information between cutting carbide-tipped inserts and HSS (high speed steel twist). This is very particular information which is of little value without further information concerning the preconditions for using such a tool and the range of tasks for which the tool is used. More precisely, there is a distinction between text that provides further discussion about an object or concept and text that provides us with a definition of an object. A further category, outside these two, is created where a reference is made to ideas that lie exclusively outside the rest of the hypertext system. An example from above is the discussion of why these tools are sometimes called U-drills.

This kind of information is problematic in hypertext and even more so in an ITS because it is non-operational. Since there is no cross-linkage with other concepts it cannot be expressed in formal deductive terms and the system is unable to test the ability of a student to apply the knowledge -it can only be restated in the same form. This is a form of 'informal knowledge' [Ref. 14], whose value is not given in terms of linking concepts within a closed problem domain but rather with linking this closed domain with the wider domain of experience and future practice. Within a hypertext system, with flexible routes through the information available to the learner, this information mus either become an isolated piece of text with no links or integrated with some other text with which it occurs, in association with other ideas. As above, the problem changes from what could be done to what the author intended to achieve by including the text.

Where domains are non-technical this category of information is expected to expand considerably. Montage effects, created by juxtaposition of ideas may become more significant than the more formal aspects of cross-reference. In this case the control of linkage relies even more heavily on the intention of the author in associating two pieces of text.

If we extend our notion of hypertext to include hypermedia nodes at which interaction with the student occurs, such as answering questions, running a simulation etc. the notion of purpose becomes both more critical and more evident -since the potential purpose of a node is at least partially defined by its intended teaching purpose [Refs.10, 8]. Although not explored in this paper, it is our contention that combining both formal content and teaching purpose as defining characteristics of a hypermedia node is sufficient to support all hypermedia activity.

Structuring

The model of hypertext that is currently being explored in this domain provides a structure to support the need to generate links, as above, and simultaneously providing a step towards the goal of an ITS. To simplify the ITS paradigm and at the same time retain the open learning metaphor of hypertext, changes are made to the six knowledge source model (figure 2). The knowledge source that has been most fully explored in AI is the domain structure. Knowledge relating to generation of resources has been extensively developed where the teaching function of the resource is well defined. For these reasons (and lack of progress in the general learning knowledge source) we have replaced the learning source with the learner to provide control to the learning sequence.

This emphasizes the open learning aspect, as the system cannot usefully prepare large sequences of learning material. It highlights the need to support a student who wishes to learn and not just browse, which accentuates description of resources in learning terms as well as knowledge content. Inherent in this is the assumption that a student must be able to infer, from general descriptions of resources in terms of domain and purpose, the actual result of selecting that link. If feasible, the system will properly account for the need to support a learner's intention in following a link.

We would also contend that the need to describe teaching activity in terms that can be understood by the learner is a pre-requisite for the generation of an active ITS teaching component -that the techniques and tactics that are manipulated form a comprehensible set for the learner as well as the 'tutor'.

Figure 4 shows the general model of such a system. The resources are represented as a knowledge sources to allow for the generation of learning materials, or extensions such as the intelligent use of video material selected as 'appropriate' in some knowledge-based terms.

The domain source must provide the additional information that is required to support linking between nodes. Two aspects, from the discussion above, need to be considered. These are the natural association between concepts, as reflected by consistent recurrence of the same terms in frames, and the need to support both generalization and specialization.

These characteristics are present in several knowledge representation schemes and form basic structuring aspects of KL-ONE. This system has been chosen for its clarity in associating concepts with roles, defined in terms of role-name, number, allowable fillers and modality (this is similar to slots in frame-based systems). This view naturally links the concepts that occur together, the separate roles, to the context in which this arises, the parent concept. Logical restrictions that link the roles together in terms of relationships are also included with the concept definition. Particularly clear is the difference between the same concept being needed twice in one context and the function (role) played by each one in that context, but also detached from the wider restrictions. The second aspect is provided by a formally defined hierarchical structure for subsets of concepts. These two structures (retained as distinct structures in the current system) allow the context of any hypertext item to be mapped onto the conceptual network and the aspects of generalization and specialization to be maintained in terms of the (multiple) hierarchies.

Two views of this general structure are then of interest. Firstly, as a problem solving environment, the effect of adopting a specialization within one particular context will have resulting consequences for the other roles in the context. This provides an open exploration environment in which the interplay between areas of knowledge become apparent without necessarily seeking to solve any one problem (in addition to supporting problem solving where necessary). Thus making choices about the type of machine being used will produce resulting effects on the type of tooling that could be used (as well as many others). The potential for such a problem solving tool to support continuing education in industry has been discussed as part of the Artisan Project [Ref. 9]. As with any complex domain problems still remain in terms of managing the volume of information that is potentially available and currently we assume that some 'fish-eye' approach to defining the context will be used [Ref. 12].

The second issue is the potential for associating purpose, not just with individual hypertext nodes, but directly with concepts. Certainly there is no difficulty in linking teaching activities, such as coaching, demonstrating, hinting and testing with rule bases (as demonstrated in the ATR Trainer shell [Ref. 1]).

Further it can be argued that other aspects such as definitions, overviews and provision of supportive video should be available globally -that is if it is available for some concepts then users will be confused if there is no logical reason no to provide it for other, apparently similar concepts. This suggest that a refinement to figure 4 would assume that there is a logical knowledge source that determines the potential links to resources with the purpose of the actual resource generated being determined by the learner.

The advantage of this format, is that the structure of the domain provides a unifying map to support browsing. This map is generated from the conceptual network and will be highly interconnected. It is evident that restrictions will have to be placed on the amount of the map that is available, but the implicit hierarchy of concepts (as context) allows access to higher levels of abstraction over the whole domain.

This structure provides a significant reduction in the complexity of links as presented to the learner. The initial domain level will typically have a number of nodes that is an order of magnitude smaller than the hypertext resource structure itself. In terms of the content the specialization/generalization provides a focussing device to the information available. As the context becomes more specialized, the scope of relevant information (as potentially relevant concepts) decreases but the detail within the information increases, since more detailed information becomes available. For example, when the context does not include a specification of the material being cut (as 1.13.40 above) only generalities about the performance characteristics can be stated. As soon as a particular material is brought into the context then the additional detailed information comes 'into focus'.

Supporting Exploration

The system as described should support coherent exploration of a domain by a learner. The potential to monitor both level of detail and conceptual overview as separate components provides access for both serialist and holist styles of learning in terms of spreading access to the entire network. Overt control of where exploration is sensible can be initially performed through introduction of extra concepts as soon as a reference has been encountered. More stringent control could be exercised in terms of the interconnectedness of the network as the learner browses.

Many issues remain for consideration within this model, including the use of icons (already conventional for illustration of several machining concepts) and video as a resource that allows cross-reference rather than simple attachment to demonstrate concepts [Ref. 15]. The limitations of generated frames has already been stated, although the identification of formal and informal aspects of knowledge supports a clear separation of where hand-crafted frames following the combined CBT/ITS model suggested above.

Perhaps the most significant issue for current study is the problem of identifying a set of 'purposes' that are meaningful to both the learner and the teacher. At present we have been considering only a small set of teaching based activities and this must be contrasted with learner based activities, and more generally browsing activity, to ensure that the result of following a link is meaningful to the learner as well.

Conversational Diagnosis

These aspects are under exploration in another project, conducted jointly with Jonathan Briggs and Dr. Nicholas Oates [Ref. 5]. The terms of the project require the use of an IBM standard pc with minimal graphics which restricts the application to hypertext structuring. The project is financed by the Department of Health to provide continuing education for community pharmacists, giving access to new information from the medical community and supporting them in the use of this information in the selection of appropriate therapy and advice for customers. The initial material for the system has been largely taken from text-based materials by one of the 'experts' for the project that were already in existence [Ref. 2].

These materials were of a suitable size to present on screen for the prototype with only small alterations to the amount of information available at any one time. Each piece of text is described at the 'note' level in terms of the general content and, at the sentence level, in terms of the knowledge representation formalism applied above. The project is tightly constrained in terms of both scale and time but also affords a ready demonstration of the potential of knowledge-based approach. In this project the constraints on knowledge-based exploration are developed through specification of a particular patient.

This effect, which we have termed conversational diagnostics (though this is in no way a replacement for a diagnostic system), is designed to reflect a conversation between professional equals. Specification of some characteristics of a particular patient provides information that systematically applies derived hierarchical structuring to the set of available notes. After information on a patient is volunteered the user can return to the browsing environment with some notes now excluded as being irrelevant. In addition some other notes are identified as being particularly important, namely those that refer directly to new deductions. Some additional notes that refer to the procedural aspects of diagnosis have been included to supplement the decision taking process.

Further information on trial with the project will be available at the workshop.

References

1. Tompsett, C.P.: Education training and knowledge-base design. In Expert Systems, November 1988
2. ATR Trainer. Available from ATR, Kingston Polytechnic. Millennium House. Kingston upon Thames. London, KT1 1BL, UK. Described in more detail in: French, P. Automatic generation of student models in a rule-based system. Proc. CAL 1989
3. Roast, C.: Private communications. Dept. of Computer Science, York.
4. Briggs, J.H. and Tompsett, C.P.: Hypertext and knowledge-based systems for education. Proc. 6th ICTE. Orlando 1989
5. Extracted from materials supplied by R. Thorne, AMTRI, a technical consultant for the project to the Engineering Industry Training Board. Any apparent inaccuracy in the material as presented here is due to misinterpretation of this material and is entirely my own fault.
6. Branchman, C.: On the epistemological status of semantic nets. In Associative Networks, (N. Findler, ed.) Academic 1989
7. Nelson, T.: Managing immense storage. Byte, January 1988
8. Goldstein, I.P.: The genetic graph, a representation for the evolution of procedural knowledge. In Intelligent tutoring systems. (Sleeman, D. and Brown, J. eds.). Academic 1982
9. Mayes, J.T., Kibby, M., and Watson, H.: StrathTutor, the development and evaluation of a learning by browsing system on the Macintosh. Computers and Education, Vol. 12
10. HITS, Hypermedia learning system. Logica UK Ltd.
11. Lawrence, G.: Private communication. Delta Project Artisan. Greater London Enterprise, October 1989
12. Remde, J.R., Gomez, L.M., and Landauer, T.K.: Superbook: an automated approach tool for information exploration--hypertext. Proc. of Hypertext 1987, Chapel Hill, N. Carolina 1987
13. Tompsett, C.P.: Knowledge-based support for hypertext. Proc. 5th International Conference on Expert Systems, London 1989
14. Briggs, J., Tompsett, C.P., and Oates, N.: Guiding learners through a medical hypertext database using knowledge based rules. To be presented at PEG 91, Genoa, Italy, May 1991
15. Blenkinsopp, A., and Paxton.: Symptoms in the pharmacy. Blackwell, Oxford 1990

108

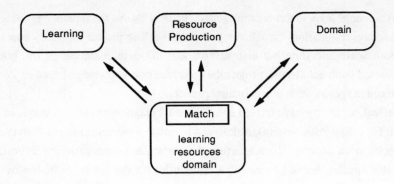

Figure 1.

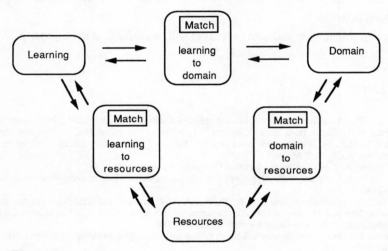

Figure 2.

109

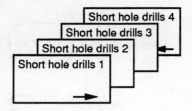

Figure 3.

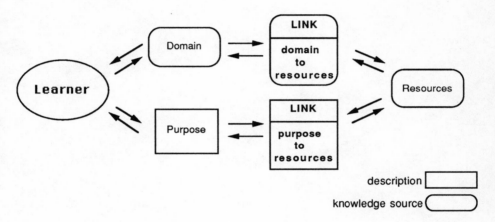

Figure 4.

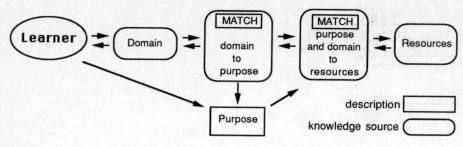

Figure 5.

Hypertext's Contribution to Computer-Mediated Communication: In Search of an Instructional Model

Alexander Romiszowski and E-cheol Chang

Syracuse University. Department of Instructional Design Development and Education, 330 Hunting Hall, Syracuse NY 13244-2340, USA. Tel. (315) 443 3703

Introduction: Hypertext And Its Contribution To CMC

"Collaborative creativity" is one of the tenets of the belief-structure of many Hypertext enthusiasts. Indeed, one particularly fruitful area of application for hypertext systems has turned out to be the collaborative annotation of student papers by both faculty and students is also something that many proponents of hypertext advocate and (occasionally) practice. One of the more long-lived working hypertext environments - Intermedia at Brown University - was specifically designed to support this sort of collaborative educational activity (Yankelovitch et al. 1988; Landow, 1987).

However, current hypertext systems which can support this type of activity effectively are large, purpose-built systems, which are costly and not easily compatible across different computer systems (Meyrowitz, 1986; Delisle et al. 1986).

Our current approach is based on the concept of utilizing, as much as possible, what already exists and is established in significant quantity in the educational marketplace. It should be possible to adapt an existing pc-based hypertext environment so that new messages can not only be stored in appropriate subdivisions of the basic structure one creates, but can also be freely cross referenced to other relevant messages. We are investigating the applicability of some currently available and relatively cheap hypertext applications packages for this purpose.

A recent experiment involved the use of a networked communication space, set up in Hypercard and running on a Macintosh network. Each of the participants in the CMC seminar has a stack of prepared cards, with scrolling text windows, thus giving unlimited writing space, but dividing the text into "chunks", so that each separate issue/topic in the discussion has its own card. These cards can be accessed by all the participants, who can read them, add small annotations and make links to cards in their own stack. As the discussion progresses, a cross-referenced network of documents is created. This is expected to facilitate the review of the discussion by a new participant or by someone who has not logged on for some time. It also ensures that new comments are linked to earlier ones on the same topic, as well as making it very easy to review all the contributions of any one participant.

During October/December 1989, we used several alternative structured communication systems: the hypertext system just described; a file-sharing system in which all participants comment a position paper in the same file, but do so by inserting their comments among other related comments (implemented on existing mainframe computer systems); another mainframe-based system, using two scrolling windows, on a split-screen, so that comments can be typed in as the paper is being read; and a user friendly, Macintosh equivalent of this system.

A later experiment uses the same hypertext communication network as we used before, but as a group collaboration tool to author a joint critique of a given body of research literature. Unlike the earlier study, in which each course participant instigated a discussion on a separate topic, all the students are contributing to the same critical writing exercise. Initial observations suggest that the use of a hypertext environment in this way will be of greater value to the students and will enhance the educational effectiveness of the exercise, more than was the case in our earlier study.

A further line of research and development is investigating the use of long-distance computer mediated communication as feedback support to computer based instruction. We have developed some open-ended or "conversational" hypertext-based CAI packages, utilizing the "STRUCTURAL COMMUNICATION" methodology of courseware authoring. These packages ask a student to analyse a knowledge base on, for example, a business case study, and form a complex multi-faceted solution to the problem or problems posed. This student response generates a complex, multi-component, feedback comment that discusses the divergences that seem to exist between the student's and the author's viewpoint of approach. the student may be satisfied with this comment, or may disagree with the author's interpretation of the discussion so far. The next stage of discussion, in the event of misunderstanding or disagreement, then takes place on a CMC network, linking students to the curse tutors. In this way, those students who wish to initiate queries or comments on the content of the basic package may do so for as many iterations of comment and reply as proves necessary. Initial results of this approach are most promising, both in terms of effectiveness and practicality.

C.M.C.: Instruction or Conversation?

As a theoretical introduction to our discussion, it may be interesting to compare and contrast two paradigms of teaching that we shall refer to as "INSTRUCTION" and "CONVERSATION" (see Fig. 1).

The instructional paradigm is the one within which much of the educational technology movement has developed. This is the approach which designs teaching on the basis of specific pre-defined objectives that specify some post-learning performance and the expected standards to be attained. The teacher's role, apart from delivery of the message, is to match student behaviour against predetermined criteria and to furnish corrective feedback as and when required.

The conversational paradigm differs sharply in many aspects, as the compare/contrast table in Figure 1 seeks to illustrate. The objectives may be the result of an agreement between teacher and learner to explore a topic and may be more concerned with the topic itself, or the exploration process, than with specific predefined outcomes. The role of the teacher is to analyse and evaluate the progress of the discussion, in order to ensure that important aspects of the content and its structure are being adequately addressed and,when necessary, to participate by means of constructive comments that challenge the participants to rethink their positions or restructure their ideas.

Let us now consider Distance Education. In Figure 1, one can see the contrast between the suitability of the most commonly used distance delivery media in relation to the two paradigms of teaching. Classical correspondence course assignments, with automatically marked objective tests, supported by the minimum of postal contact with the tutor, are good examples of the instructional paradigm in action. Audio and video teleconferencing, as most commonly practiced, are examples of the conversational paradigm. Computer-mediated-communication has been placed in the middle, to emphasize that it may be used in both manners: either to deliver computer-based-instruction at a distance; or as computer-based teleconferencing (or, indeed, as some combination of these).

There is no implication in the schema presented in Figure 1 that one paradigm is "good" and the other "bad". On the contrary, most educational and training systems require the use of each of these teaching approaches in different parts of the total course.

Case Study 1: Structuring And Controlling The Computer Mediated Seminar

Over the last two years at Syracuse University, we have been developing a program of research and development which is investigating approaches to the use of CMC as a support medium to campus based courses (Jost et al 1990). Many of these follow the conversational paradigm in general, but do have clear objectives of "general skills" nature in mind. Examples are management decision making skills, consulting skills, task analysis skills, or heuristic design skills as used in management information systems design, and indeed, instructional systems design. Some conventional teaching methods which are particularly successful in such areas include: seminars (to research the relevant knowledge base, share experience and viewpoints); case study exercises (to develop the necessary heuristic skills of applying the knowledge base to real problem solving, under controlled conditions); and project work (to transfer and further develop these skills under real-life conditions). The first two of these methods are largely "conversational," especially as regards to interactions between the participants. Success in the classroom depends on the knowledge and skill of the teacher as a group leader and facilitator. Can these teaching methods be effectively implemented by means of electronic distance education methodologies?

Live audiographic or video teleconferencing would seem to have the closest similarity to the classroom-based seminar or case discussion. Indeed, there are many successful implementations of these methodologies in both educational and training contexts (Chute 1990; Hanrahan 1990). The use of computer-mediated-communication (CMC) has, on the other hand, revealed both advantages (greater, deeper and more participative discussion) when well moderated, and problems (the above mentioned problems of structure and control) with less well moderated. It would seem appropriate to focus attention on how to overcome the problems and therefore make seminar and case methods more effective in CMC environments, and less dependent on the skills and education of the teacher/moderator.

1. Structuring the Initial Paper

One approach to overcoming the "problem of structure" was to create a discussion environment that would automatically cluster all comments on a given issue, or interrelate them in some way, so that a reader accessing the discussion files may quickly and easily gain an overall impression of the conversation so far. The simples approach to doing this was to somehow separate the issues in the original position paper, so that any later comment would be automatically related to that issue. In a mainframe-based electronic mail environment, this can be done by numbering or otherwise identifying the paragraphs of the original paper and requesting that comments on any paragraph are directed to files whose names correspond to the relevant paragraphs. This approach relies quite heavily on the cooperation (and the computer-use skills) of the participants. However, a trial experiment in the summer of 1989 showed that suggesting this simple discipline did much to reduce both the structure and control problems which were observed in earlier attempts at running seminars on electronic mail systems (Romiszowski and Jost, 1990).

2. Structuring the Discussion as a Hypertext

An alternative approach to maintaining structure is to furnish some form of HYPERTEXT environment for group discussion. This was implemented in Hypercard, on a Macintosh computer cluster. The "notecard" metaphor which Hypercard is based on is particularly useful in the present context, as the discipline of writing each issue of a seminar position paper on a separate card, followed by the linking of any comment by a button to that specific card, would automatically create clusters of related information in the growing discussion.

The implementation is illustrated in Figures 2 and 3. Each participating student has an individual "stack of cards" as a workspace. Each student prepares a short seminar paper on some aspect of the topic under study, carefully structuring it so that each issue addressed is placed on a separate card. Figure 2 shows the fifth card of a seminar paper dealing with the topic of expert systems. This card has been chosen as illustration because the student's paragraph is short and is indeed completely visible in the top window of the card. Please note, however, that this is a scrolling window, so we are not unduly restricting the amount of text that the student may use to address a given issue. Below the text window, there are (in this implementation) six icons which act as gateways to the workspaces of the other seminar participants.

Two participants have, at this time, made comments on the issue presented. To see what, for example, "Dills" has said, a reader clicks on that icon and, when requested, types in the card number which appears in the window below the icon (14 in this case). This takes the reader immediately to card 14 of Dills' stack, to read the comment shown (in part) in Figure 3. This comment has aroused a reaction from another participant (the course tutor, it so happens), which has been cross -indexed as to be found on card 3 of the "Romi" stack. The "conversation" may go on to further iterations (e.g. Dills replying to Romi and Maria raising a related issue and so on). All initial comments are linked to a specific card in the position paper, but later, readers may make connections between comments from different clusters, eventually creating a complex network of cards that can be browsed along many different "trails".

3. Clustering Related Comments in a Communal Workspace

Yet another approach, also using Hypercard, is illustrated in Figure 4. Here, a single seminar paper (on the topic of hypertext) is presented, once more subdivided into separate issues, but all the comments on that issue are placed by all participants in the same scrolling comment window on the same card. The figure shows only two comments. By scrolling the window, readers may reveal a further fifteen comments on this single issue, generated by seven participants. Each participant may make a comment on the original paper, or on some other participants' comments, or may reply to these comments. One can add comments to the end of the list, or can insert them at the most appropriate point, as full wordprocessing capability is available in the window. A reader will browse the discussion by scrolling the two windows on a given card, adding comments if desired, and then move to the next card and repeat the process.

This approach was also implemented in an IMB mainframe environment, under CMS. The procedure por arranging the paper and the comment space as two scrolling files on a split screen required the students to learn a series of some half dozen operating system commands and further file manipulation routines. Also the screen design possibilities were more primitive. In terms of access to comments and the structure of the resultant textual records of the seminar discussion, the mainframe and Macintosh versions were, however, identical. Students did indeed find this system to be equally acceptable on either mainframe or personal computer. The initial learning curve to master the mainframe operating system was a passing inconvenience far outweighed by the greater availability of mainframe terminals, which eliminated queuing.

Some Results and Conclusions of Case Study 1

The various methods described above were used systematically on several seminar-type courses during 1989-1990. Observations and tests were made to evaluate the effect of the different approaches on the problems of structure and control, and whether any other problems or advantages were observed. Student surveys were also applied. A full account of these studies is presented elsewhere (Romiszowski and Jost, 1990; Grabowski, 1990; Chang, Corso and Romiszowski, in press). Only some of the highlights of these results are presented here in summary.

1. All the approaches described were successful in considerably diminishing the problems of "structure" and "control". A final "test discussion" across all topics in a one semester long seminar-based course revealed that all students had a similar view of the topics that were discussed and the relationships that existed between the topics. They did not agree, however, on their viewpoints in relation to these topics. This is as should be: the structure of a complex domain was successfully communicated, without necessarily conditioning the participants to one set of opinions (the professor's) on how the domain should be interpreted and used.

2. The hypertext environment was rated as inferior to the split screen environment by most students. This was mainly because of the need to move back and forth between cards that were addressing the same issue, as opposed to seeing the issue and the earlier comments side by side on the screen. This objection may not have been present if a more sophisticated hypertext environment, with windowing capabilities, has been used (e.g. as the Intermedia system used at Brown University -Meyrovitz 1986). However, as the split screen methodology was successful in overcoming the "structure" and "control" problems, and is easier to implement (as well as being more widely available if implemented in the mainframe environments), there is some doubt as to the need for more complex solutions. This conclusion may, of course, only be valid in the case of relatively small groups of participants, as was the case in all our trials.

3. Student preferences were 2 to 1 in favor of computer-based seminar discussions, over face-to-face seminar sessions along more conventional lines. In particular, participants praised the discipline of having to carefully think out a response - "it not only records creative observations which would otherwise be forgotten, but actually encourages the generation of creative insights". They also tended to make a hardcopy printout of the discussion record, sometimes to study it at leisure and plan their own comments "in the comfort of my armchair

before going to the computer to key them in", but also to keep a record for later use. In this latter context, they praised the fact that "related comments are clustered all together rather than scattered about as in an e-mail file" (this was another plus for the split screen systems over the hypertext environment).

4. Prolonged use of the systems over a series of seminars during a whole semester led to an increase in effectiveness on a number of counts. Level of student participation increased, from a few short and rather superficial messages per student at the beginning to a much richer and deeper discussion in later seminars. In particular, the quantity and the quality of participation of certain foreign student groups (who, for reasons of language difficulties or cultural habit, seldom participate actively in small group seminars) would grow to be almost indistinguishable form the American students, and maintain the discussion on task, diminished significantly as students became accustomed to methodology. In one course, moderating messages from the tutor at the beginning of the semester were twice as voluminous as the sum of the student comments. By mid-semester they were less than half the volume of student comments and by late semester they were down to some 10% of student comments. This reduction in moderator interventions was achieved at the same time as the depth, length and quality of student discussion was growing and without any recurrence of the problems of structure and control, that initially led us to commence this research.

It therefore appears that quite simple approaches to the design of a structured conversational environment may be enough to overcome some critical problems associated with less structured approaches to the use of CMC for goal-directed discussion. Furthermore, the use of such structured environments appears to facilitate student participation and student direction of the discussion process. This is important as, in contrast to moderator-based conferencing systems, it opens the possibility of quite intensive use of student-directed group discussion, with little moderator intervention. This extends the practical viability of CMC as a distance education methodology to that very large area of education which requires a conversational approach with respect to learning process, but nevertheless has some relatively precise goals in mind as regards the outcome.

Further research is in progress, extending our inquiry to, on the other hand, other effective group-discussion methods which are yet to be efficiently implemented in CMC environments (for example the case study method) and on the other hand, other approaches to the design of discussion-organization tools and environments that may assist distant learners to interact intellectually, in the "deep processing of complex ideas". The following case study presents some of this initial work.

Case Study 2: The Use of Case Studies in a Distance-Education Environment

Over the last few years, we have been developing a range of case materials that can be used for the teaching of instructional design and development skills. These are shortly to appear in book form (Romiszowski, Mulder and Pieters - in press). This instructional design and development case collection covers a wide range of skills that are used by a practicing instructional designer. One particular skills area of great importance is what we term "front-end analysis". This is the analysis that <u>ought</u> to be performed in order to ensure that a particular training design project starts off on the correct lines.

Several cases have been developed to help our students learn these skills in a practical context. One of these cases will be used here as an example of the general approach we are using. The readers are invited to imagine that they have been called to bid on a project by a local university that has perceived a problem in the area of the skills of its faculty members. You arrive to an initial meeting where you are briefed on the background to this supposed problem. You are asked to design an in service course to "teach our faculty to use audiovisual media".

In the past, the case situation would be developed as a role play exercise in the classroom, a number of typical "stakeholders" in the problem and interested parties being represented by the professor and assistants. The students on the course could interview several faculty members and gather whatever data they felt was necessary in order to better understand the problem and its underlying causes.

In preparing a case like this for publication, we face two problems. First, the data gathering stage of interviewing faculty and other interested parties is a very dynamic student led exercise when performed in the role play context. When this is transformed into written case materials, we have the transcripts of discussions/interviews with a variety of people, which have to be read at length by the student and in this process all the student-directedness of the activity is lost. The second problem is connected with the case discussion. Most published case materials do not actually instrument the discussion but restrict themselves to the case description, the data, and the setting of some problems for discussion. The discussion organization and implementation is up to the leader of the group in the classroom situation. If the case is being studied individually by a reader of the text, then it's really up to the reader to organize it for him or herself. Our interest in some of the case studies we have been developing is to take the instrumentation through to the case discussion stage. To do this, we turned to a methodology called "Structural Communication", first developed in the United Kingdom in the late 60's and early 70's (Egan 1972, 1976; Hodgson 1974). This was an attempt to create a discussion environment for open-ended self study of topics where multiple viewpoints and various possible correct responses were the rule. The methodology was applied in many different contexts during the early 70's including an experimental correspondence course in the Harvard Business

Review, where a Harvard case was discussed by readers responding to a pre-structured "programmed instruction" exercise (Hodgson and Dill 1970 a & b, 1971). Most of these early implementations were in the form of paper text-based self-study exercises, but some used mainframe computers as a delivery medium. With current technology, the Structural Communication methodology presents itself as a powerful and practical approach to the authoring of conversational CAI (Romiszowski, Grabowski and Pusch 1988). It is also one of the few approaches to the design of interactive self-instruction that is based on cognitive, rather than behaviorist, learning theory (Pusch and Slee 1990).

The implementation of such case studies in an electronic format is desirable for at least two reasons. Firstly, this will overcome some of the utilization difficulties that extensive use of such an interactive methodology has when implemented in a paper format. Secondly, electronic implementation of such exercises should enable one to open them up for student generated comment and input in a way that a published and printed version can never do. By the combination of electronic computer mediated communication with the electronic storage of the basic case-study materials, it should be possible to create an exercise which, in the initial stages, presents authors' prepared views and comments and then allows students to comment those comments and actually converse with the author, although that author may be located somewhere at a distance. Current research that we are engaged in at Syracuse University is exploring the viability of this approach. We have developed some computer software that can implement the Structural Communication methodology, in Hypercard on the Macintosh computer and also on mainframe systems that can be networked worldwide if necessary. Ultimately, this software will operate as a "shell" with which authors can create exercises on many topics (Chang, Corso and Romiszowski, in press).

We will use the Macintosh system here as an illustration because of its better visual qualities. For data gathering, we have employed the previously mentioned Hypertext environment, where information about the problem that has posed in the case is stored as a network under student control. By doing this, we are avoiding the degradation of the role-play exercise when presented as printed transcript, because the student is still required to decide what type of information he or she thinks is pertinent and follow this through as a trail from one card to another in the "maze" of information that has been created about the background to the case.

Figure 5 illustrates the problem that has been set and shows how a student can go either to the solution or to the case study sections at will. Figure 6 shows the front card of the case study section which introduces the student to 7 key figures who can be interviewed and also to the resumes of these 7 people (stored in the "who's who" cards indexed along the right and side of the screen). By clicking on the name of a person on the star shaped diagram in the middle of the screen, the student opens a conversation with that person which is presented over a number of cards in a stack. Each of the cards, however, deals with a particular issue, some of these being relevant and others irrelevant to the solution of the problem originally posed.

Figure 7 shows a typical card. The scrolling window in the upper part of this card contains the transcript of a discussion between the analyst and the particular person being interviewed. At the bottom of the card, there are a series of icons that enable this card to be linked to relevant cards in the interview stacks of all the other six available participants in this automated role play. We note that there is relevant information in card 3 of the stack named "Bean" and also in card 7 of the stack named "Egan". The student immediately knows that relevant trails of inquiry can be commenced by clicking onto those stacks. If the student considers the card currently being read as supplying information that is important for the solution of the problem, then this would suggest following trails to other relevant information at that point in order to immediately formulate a position in regards to that aspect of the problem. If on the other hand the student feels that the issue being dealt with on the current card is not very relevant to solving the problem, then a lot of reading can be avoided by not clicking on the subsidiary cards and indeed continuing directly to another card on a different aspect of the problem altogether. This inquiry environment created by a network of information cards is an attempt to give back to the student the control over what questions to ask and what information to follow up.

When the student has gathered as much information as he or she thinks is relevant and has formulated a clear idea of what are the underlying causes of the problem and what solutions may be most appropriate, a click on the button labeled "solution" takes the student to another part of the software which is prefaced by a card entitled "Structural Communication" (see Figure 8). The student can at this point click on other buttons which give some background to structural communication methodology and how to use it as a learning device. One of these cards is shown in Figure 9. The main button, however, that a student should click on is the one labeled "exercise", for a presentation of the response matrix. The response matrix for this particular case is shown in Figure 10. This presents a total of 20 types of solutions that could be applied in some combination to the problem that the case has posed. The student can select any combination of these 20 clicking on the appropriate buttons. The choice made appears at the bottom of the card.

Once the student has responded, the program analyzes this response and presents an index to the comments available plus a suggestion as to which may be appropriate for that particular student to read. This is presented on a card illustrated in Figure 11 which acts as the discussion guide for the remainder of the exercise. The student can now click on any of the icons and go to the related comments. Note that the student is not restricted to clicking on those comments which are diagnosed as being appropriate but can look up any of the comments that are available. However, those that the author considers as appropriate to the way the student handled the problem would be the ones that normally the student would read first. On clicking any one of these, the student will automatically be taken to a comments card like the one illustrated in Figure 12. Here there is a scrolling window in which the author's comment is presented. Figure 12 shows a comment generated by the student NOT including item Q from the response matrix

(Figure 10). Note that there is no physical restriction on the length of this comment. It can be very much more than one screen of text if that is required. Note also that the style of the comment is open ended. It takes the student beyond the exercise in order to reflect more deeply about the implications of the particular position or viewpoint that has been adopted.

Note particularly, however, that the card presents a second scrolling window, entitled "Your Comment", in which the student can type in any message to the author requesting further information, registering disagreement with the author's view or whatever comes to mind. This facility allows a discussion to go a stage beyond the original Structural Communication type of exercise. In the Macintosh implemented version, these comments are stored in their respective cards and can be browsed by the author or indeed by other participating students. In the mainframe implementation of this system, which is planned to be used in distance education contexts, the student comments are automatically E-mailed to the author, or to the course organizer/tutor, wherever he or she may be. The tutor then replies directly on E-mail to the student, thus developing an open discussion on the question that was raised.

Research, Results and Comments on Case Study 2

We are in the process of researching the use of these interactive case studies in a distance-education environment. Our initial study looked at content learning while the next one is looking at the transfer of technical skills and how effectively these skills could be taught.

The audience

The audience chosen for the first study included a college class composed of 90 sophomores, juniors and seniors. The course was an introductory computer course required for each student as part of their college program. The course provided instruction on hardware, software, historical events, and hands-on experience with both personal computers and mainframes. Significant here is the timing of the research study, which was conducted during the last third of the semester. By then the students were comfortable with and proficient in the use of the computer equipment and how to maneuver through software packages. Thus, the learning curve for the equipment use was not a factor in the study.

Equipment

The equipment used was a Vax mainframe with terminal access. A number of terminals were available across 3 geographically separated campuses so terminal access was never a problem in completing the various assignments.

Product

A case involving systems analysis was chosen for this study. No discussion of this topic occurred in class prior to the computer based case study. A pre test of 5 questions was administered to measure what preconceptions existed for defining systems analysis or its component parts. The case analysis involved a company which attempted an in-house restructuring of its information system only to further complicate its existence, the case was rich in factual information as well as conceptual and theoretical ideas that could be further clarified or tested. A two-page introduction to the topic of systems analysis was written and added to the case. This addition substituted for the usual faculty lecture provided in the more traditional mode of teaching.

Once the student had received and read the pre-prepared faculty response, they were provided with an area to respond freely. Thus, there was an opportunity at that point to capture the student's immediate reactions to the faculty's preconceived answer. This consisted of an area where the student could continue the dialogue on a particular question, concept, response matrix item, standard comment received, the software strokes involved or anything else. This was designed to give the student the continued instruction normally accorded in a face-to-face discussion. In this project, it occurred on a continuous, on line mode from a distant terminal.

Post Test

In order to measure the amount of learning that had taken place, a post test was administered in class. The questions were similar to the pre-test administered earlier. The E-mail notes as well as the internal free-form areas were also evaluated.

Outcome

In addition to the increasingly deep discussion of the case itself, the E-mail messages were rich with comments about the various components of the structural communication method, case material and the student preferences for on-line discussion over more conventional classroom-based case discussion. The pre and post test results show that learning did take place. There is no doubt that with the E-mail component, the system is much more interactive than other computer-based products. It is interesting to note that the quantity and the quality of the case-related comments far exceeded what would normally be achieved in a class-based session with its typical time constraints and group dynamic pressures. It is also interesting that, by and large, the participants enjoyed the experience and many of them felt they got more out of it than out of an equivalent class-based session. Finally, we have demonstrated that open-ended subject matter can be effectively taught in a distance education environment, without unduly controlling and conditioning the viewpoints of the participants to a "standard" interpretation of the case.

Advantages

The basic advantages of Computer-Based Instruction (CBI) are well known. It provides for interactive, learner-paced learning that can take place anytime of the day or night. Students can repeat the learning units a number of times. By introducing the E-mail component, the CBI now becomes truly interactive in terms of further discussion or explanation of the topic. The faculty is only a "call" away and neither student nor faculty is constrained by time of call, length of information, or number of contacts.

Because this implementation is mainframe-based, it is conceivable that world-wide coverage could occur. Mainframes are communicating with mainframes all over the world and networks such as Bitnet support thousands of users around the world. With a terminal hookup to a major university or through another channel (such as banking or the utilities), students could be accommodated almost anywhere and, once the hookup is made, interactive computer-mediated distance education is a reality.

Potential Limitations or Problems

Given the operational advantages, simplicity and relative economy or distance learning with the more sophisticated hardware and software now becoming available, the key to its success falls ever more on those who develop and support this instructional mode. Faculty involved in this method need to expend a great deal of time and energy in guaranteeing the success of a project.

In developing the instruction, they need to construct meaningful case descriptions and adequate and descriptive pre-case reading material that is the automated version of their lectures. This needs to be condensed enough to be adequate reading and yet comprehensive enough to provide all the necessary new material to a student in an easy to digest fashion.

The construction of structural communication exercises is also a skilled and time consuming task. It relies on a deep knowledge on the part of the author, not only of the subject area being explored and its structure, but also of the typical misconceptions, alternative viewpoints, or ambiguities that are commonly exhibited by students of the subject. It requires some authoring skills, to write a discussion dialogue, in advance, that feels natural and spontaneous during student interaction.However that is a problem common to all high quality computer based instruction, and one which supports the view that such materials should be prepared by specialists, to be used by many, possibly within some form of distance-education system.

Once available, the materials we are developing continue to demand tutorial support. Perhaps the largest area of instructor control and input is through the E-mail facility. The dialogue is only as good as the continued feedback from the faculty. It is at this point that the greatest time expended takes place - and yet probably the best learning as well. By bouncing off ideas and thought with the faculty member, the students fix in their minds the content being conveyed in the form of a structure. The teacher has the opportunity to evaluate and reshape this structure, if necessary, by personal comments and questions directed to the individual student. For the faculty member this can be tedious and extremely time consuming. The greater the number of students per class, the more the problem compounds. On the other hand, it can also be very rewarding.

Faculty Perspective

From the faculty perspective it was an enjoyable, but challenging assignment to create the project and an enormously time consuming but extremely gratifying experience answering each E-mail message that came through. In addition to the course content that the students apparently did learn very well, we gained a true appreciation of their level of expertise in manipulating the mainframe and sending/receiving the numerous E-mail messages. Students in the class became very computer-literate and software-comfortable, which provided an auxiliary benefit to this case-study method.

Further Developments

Work is now in progress to combine the user interface benefits of the Macintosh with the networking advantages of mainframe computers. The relatively sophisticated Structural Communication exercises are resident on the hard discs of distributed microcomputers, allowing fast and graphically engaging interaction in the initial exercise. Coupling the microcomputer to a videodisc is not reuled out as a further development. Student input is, on the other hand, limited to short text messages, which can be easily handled by currently widely available electronic networks (such as Bitnet or Internet).

Once the computing problems of this system are sorted out, a phase of large-scale experimentation will commence, involving students scattered across several sites, maybe several countries or even continents, collaborating on highly structured seminar or case-study assignments.

In parallel, with this networking system development, we are working on improving the student interface, incorporating what we have learned from our earlier small-scale experiments.

125

References

1. Bates, A.W.: A midway report on the evaluation of DT200 paper presented at the Open University International Conference on Computer Mediated Communication in Distance Education at Milton Keynes, October 7-11 1988
2. Benson, G.M.: Technology enhanced distance education paper presented at the Conference on Distance Education in the North East. Springfield,MA. April 1988
3. Bush, V.: As we may think. Atlantic Monthly, 176(1), 1945
4. Capodagli, J.: Hypertext and hypermedia, a conceptual design and the learner. (In press). Syracuse University occasional publication (being revised for publication in Hypertext form).
5. Chang, E., Corso, M., and Romiszowski, A.J.: Effects of interface variables on learning from computer-mediated seminars and case studies. (In press). IDD&E Working Paper No. 27. Syracuse University School of Education. Syracuse, New York.
6. Chute, A.: Teletraining. Educational and Training Technology International, 27(3), 1990
7. Conklin, J.: Hypertext: an introduction and survey. Computer, 20(9), 1987
8. Davie, L.E.: Facilitation techniques for the tutor in computer mediated communication courses. Paper presented at the Open University International Conference on Computer Mediated Communication in Distance Education. Milton Keynes. October 7-11, 1988
9. Delisle, N.M., and Schwartz, M.D.: NEPTUNE: a Hypertext system for CAD applications. Proceedings of the ACM International Conference on Management of Data. Washington, D.C. 1986
10. Egan, K.: Structural communication: a new contribution to pedagogy. Programmed Learning and Educational Technology, 9(2), pp. 63-78, 1972
11. Egan, K.: Structural Communication. Belmont, CA: Fearon Publishers 1976
12. Eldridge, J.R.: New dimensions in distance learning. Training and Development Journal, pp. 43-47 (1982)
13. Feenberg, A.: Computer conferencing in the humanities. Instructional Science, pp. 169-186 (1987)
14. Grabowski, B.: Social and intellectual exchange through electronic communications in a graduate community. Educational and Training Technology International, 27(3), 1990
15. Hanrahan, L.: Planning for success: College distance education programs. Instructional Developments, 1(2). Syracuse, NY: Syracuse University School of Education 1990
16. Hiltz, S.R., and Turoff, M.: The Network Nation: Human Communication via Computer. Reading, Mass: Addison Wesley 1978
17. Hodgson, A.M.: Structural communication in practice. In Romiszowski, A.J. (ed.). APLET Yearbook of Educational and Instructional Technology. London, UK: Kogan Page 1974-75
18. Hodgson, A.M., and Dill, W.R.: Programmed case: Reprise of the "Missfired Missive". Harvard Business Review, pp. 140-145, Jan/Feb 1971
19. Hodgson, A.M., and Dill, W.R.: Programmed case: The "Missfired Missive". Harvard Business Review, pp. 140-146, Nov/Dec 1970a
20. Hodgson, A.M., and Dill, W.R.: Programmed case: Sequel to the "Missfired Missive". Harvard Business Review, pp. 105-110 (1970b)
21. Jonassen, D.H.: Hypertext/hypermedia. Englewood Cliffs, NJ: Educational Technology Publications 1989
22. Jost, K., Green, T., Florini, B., Grabowski, B., and Romiszowski, A.J.: Computer mediated communication: Developments and innovations. Instructional Developments, 1(1). Syracuse, NY: Syracuse University School of Education 1990
23. Katz, M.M., McSwiney, E., and Stroud, K.: Facilitating collegial exchange among science teachers: an experiment in computer based conferencing. Harvard Graduate School of Education 1987
24. Kaye, A.: Computer conferencing for distance education. A paper presented at the Symposium on Computer Conferencing and Allied Technologies. University of Guelph. Guelph, Ontario, June 1-14 1987
25. Kaye, A.: Distance education: the state of the art. Prospects, 18(1), pp. 43-54 (1988)
26. Kommers, P.A.M.: Conceptual mapping for knowledge exchange by hypertext. Proceedings of the Hypertext '87 Conference. Chapell Hill, North Carolina. 1989
27. Landow, G.: Relationally encoded links and rhetoric of hypertext. Proceedings of the Hypertext '87 Conference. Chapel Hill, North Carolina. 1987
28. Lauzon, A.C., and Moore, G.A.B.: A fourth generation distance education system: Integrating computer assisted learning and computer conferencing. American Journal of Distance Education, 3(1) (1989)
29. Levinson, P.: Connected education: Progress report from the front line of higher learning. Online Journal of Distance Education and Communication. May 1989
30. Mason, R.: The use of computer mediated communication for distance education. A paper presented at the Open University International Conference on Computer Mediated Communication in Distance Education at Milton Keynes. October 7-11, 1989
31. Meyrovitz, N.: Intermedia: the architecture and construction of an object oriented Hypermedia system and applications framework. Proceedings of the 1986 OR:OOPSLA Conference. Portland, OR. 1986

32. Nelson, T.H.: Literary Machines. Edition 87.1. A hypertext publication on hypertext, published by the author. 1987

33. Pusch, W.S., and Slee, E. J.: Structural communication: a forgotten application of cognitive theory to instruction. Insructional Developments, 1(2). Syracuse, NY: Syracuse University School of Education 1990

34. Robertson, G., McCracken, D., and Newel, A.: The ZOG approach to man-machine communication. International Journal of Man-Machine Studies, 1981

35. Romiszowski, A.J.: Information technology in Brazil. In Twining, J. (ed.). World Yearbook of Education 1987: Vocational Education. London, UK: Kogan Page 1987

36. Romiszowski, A.J., and DeHaas, J.: Computer mediated communication for instruction: Using E-mail as a seminar. Educational Technology. October 1989

37. Romiszowski, A.J., and Jost, K.: Computer conferencing and distance learner: problems of structure and control. Proceedings of the 1989 Conference on Distance Education. University of Wisconsin. August 1989

38. Romiszowski, A.J., and Jost, K.: Computer mediated communication: a Hypertext approach to structuring distance seminars. Proceedings of the 1990 International Symposium on Computer Mediated Communication. University of Guelph, Canada 1990

39. Romiszowski, A.J., Mulder, M., and Pieters, J.: Case Studies of Instructional Systems Design and Development. (In press) London, UK: Kogan Page

40. Rosenberg, M., and Banks. V.L.: The EDTECH experience. In Ohler, J. (ed.). Online Journal of Distance Education and Communication. University of Alaska South East. Juneau, Alaska 1989

41. Toner, P.D.: Computer conferencing in formative evaluation: the development and evaluation of a new model of tryout and revision. (Unpublished dissertation). Michigan State University 1983

42. Yankelovitch, N., Haan, B.J., Meyrowitz, N.K., and Drucker, S.M.: INTERMEDIA: The concept and the construction of a seamless information environment. Computer, 21(1), 1988

43. Yankelovitch, N., Meyrowitz, N.K., and Van Dam, A.: Reading and writing the electronic book. Computer, 18(10), 1985

Paradigm:	'Instruction'	'Conversation'
OBJECTIVES: (OUTPUT) (why?)	specific pre-defined products standard	general negotiable processes variable
MESSAGES: (INPUT) (what?) (when?) (who?) (whom?)	designed pre-prepared instructor one-to-many	created on-line participants many-to-many
INTERACTION: (PROCESS) (focus) (analysis) (feedback) (complexity)	behaviors criterion-ref corrective one-layer thick	ideas contents/ structure constructive interwoven layers
DISTANCE EDUCATION: example	Correspondence courses	Teleconferencing Videoconferencing Computer Mediated Communication (CMC)

Figure 1. Two teaching paradigms

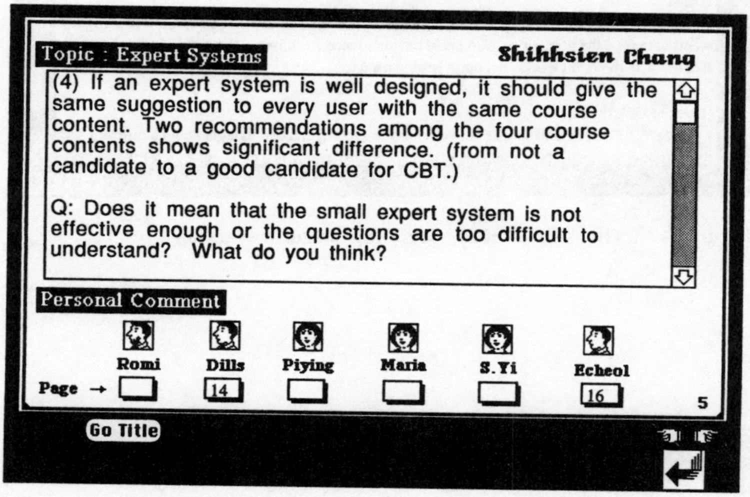

Figure 2. The fifth card in a seminar paper on Expert Systems

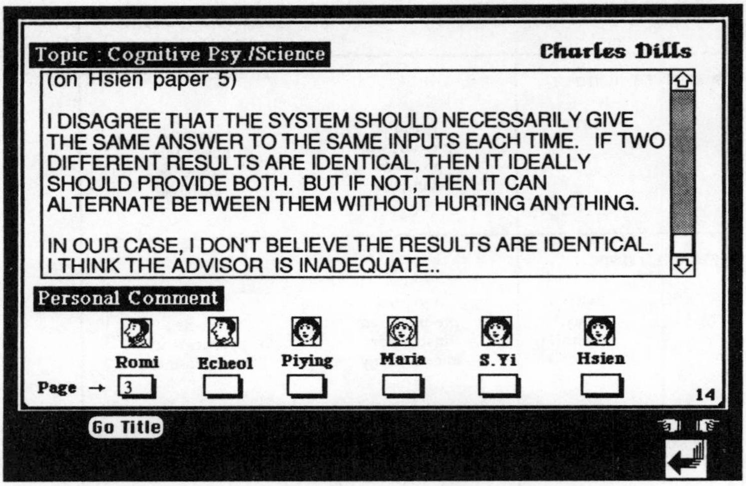

Figure 3. A comment card on the question posed in Fig. 2

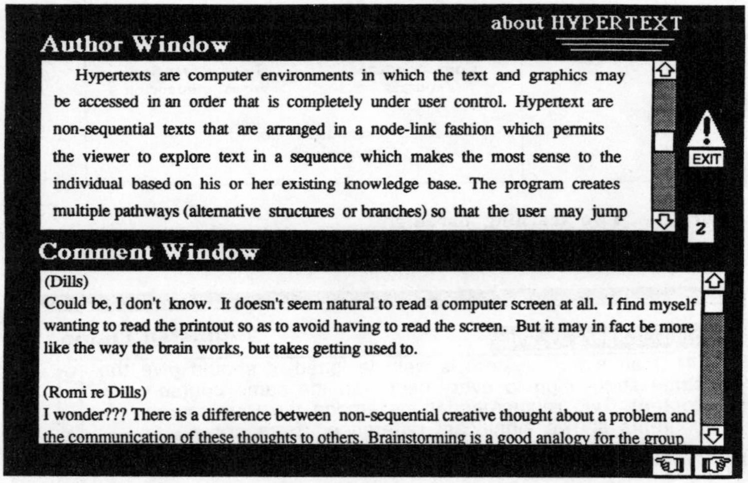

Figure 4. The split-screen, scrolling window version

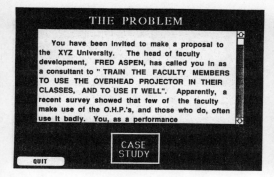

Figure 5. Initial card of the
O.M.P. case study

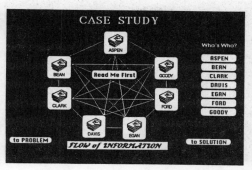

Figure 6. The Hypercard-based
case-study materials

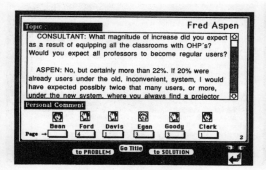

Figure 7. Typical card from
an interview transcript

Figure 8. Home-card of the
case-discussion exercise

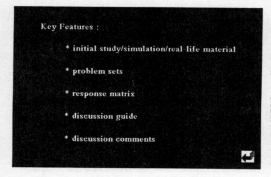

Figure 9. The components of a Structural Communication exercise

Figure 10. The Response Matrix

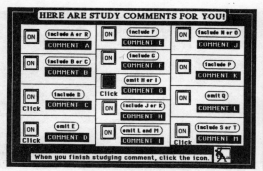

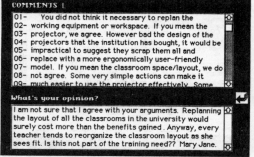

Figure 11. The Discussion Guide

Figure 12. One of the 13 Discussion Comments

3. Object Oriented Interface Design

An Object Oriented Approach to Hypermedia Authoring

Philip Barker

Interactive Systems Research Group, School of Computing and Mathematics, Teesside Polytechnic, Borough Road, Middlesbrough, Cleveland T2I 3BA, United Kingdom. Tel. 0642-342660. Fax. 0642-226822. Email. CLN5@UK.AC.DUR.MTS

Introduction

The electronic book metaphor is now widely employed for the design of multimedia instructional resources. It can be used in a variety of pedagogic design situations that require the creation of interactive, computer-based self-study materials. The utility and effectiveness of the metaphor can be significantly enhanced when it is augmented by means of the hypermedia paradigm. Using such an approach, this paper discusses an object oriented model for the design of reactive hypermedia page structures for electronic books. The implementation of the model using a conventional author language is described and the limitations of the operational system are then discussed. The design and fabrication of a courseware generator that totally automates the production of hypermedia pages is then described.

For some considerable time we have been involved in designing and fabricating a variety of different types of electronic book (Barker, 1990; 1991a; Barker and Manji, 1990). This work arose as a result of our realising some of the many limitations of conventional books as a means of supporting advanced interactive learning activity (Barker and Manji, 1988). Our earliest electronic books were based on the use of high capacity magnetic disk storage. We have also used video disk for the creation of high quality moving picture books (Manji, 1990). More recently, however, we have turned to the use of digital optical storage media for publishing much of our material (Barker and Giller, 1990). Digital optical media offers many attractive features in terms of storage capacity and robustness. Two types of digital optical storage are currently being employed for the production of our electronic books: compact disk read-only-memory (CDROM) and magneto-optical rewritable optical disks.

The basic conceptual model upon which our implementations of electronic books are based is illustrated schematically in figure 1. This depicts an electronic book as a collection of pages of electronic information. Each page in a book can serve two basic purposes. First, the display of information that may be of interest to some particular user. Second, the provision of a control interface. Through the control interface the user may: exit from the book; access other books; utilise the global book resources that are available; and gain access to local page resources.

Global book resources (such as a notepad facility, a bookmark or a glossary) are available from any other page within a book. They are sometimes referred to as 'reader services'. In contrast, as their name suggests, local page resources are primarily associated with the particular 'parent page' that hosts them - for example, a simulation, a picture, a sound narration and so on.

The basic model illustrated in figure 1 can be used as a basis for the creation of many other types of electronic book structure. The actual structure that is employed in any given situation will depend primarily upon the type of material that the book is to contain and the purpose for which the book is to be used. Most of the simple electronic book structures that we create consist of four basic types of page: a front cover; a contents page; a series of root pages; and a collection of target pages. The relationship between these is illustrated schematically in figure 2. Root pages are simply pages that can be reached directly form the contents page of any given book. Similarly, target pages are pages that are normally accessed from a parent root node although they could be accessed directly if their individual page numbers of their identities are known.

As can be seen form figure 1 each page of a book will have a set of control operations associated with it. The four most basic operations are used to support simple 'page turning' activity. That is, next page, previous page, go to page N and exit book. Because it is so easy to embed 'hot spots' or 'buttons' within pages, every page of any given book is capable of being made reactive. Control operations can therefore be represented by appropriately designed icons or they can be embedded within textual menu bars or pop-up/pull-down menus. In order to action a control operation a user would simply click on its reactive page area using a mouse device.

Electronic books can be classified according to the nature of the reader services that they provide and the types of information that they contain. Our taxonomy contains eight basic classes: text books; static picture books; moving picture books; multimedia books; hypermedia books; intelligent electronic books; telemedia books; and 'imaginary' books that are based upon environments that support artificial reality. This paper is primarily only concerned with multimedia and hypermedia books.

Multimedia and hypermedia electronic books have much in common but they differ considerably with respect to page reactivity and the way in which their page structure are inter-linked. Both types of book are based upon the use of pages that can embed text, static pictures, moving pictures and sound resources. However, as has just been mentioned, there is a major difference in the nature of the reactivity of their constituent pages. The reactivity of the pages of a multimedia book arises from three basic sources: page control mechanisms; the need to access local page resources; and the need to gain access to global book resources. In addition to these sources of reactivity, the pages of a hypermedia book will also embed hot spots that enable hypertext, hyperimage and hypersound links to be followed through to other related reactive pages of information. These additional hot spots embedded within the pages of a hypermedia book serve to identify the real (and major) difference between the two types of book. That is, multimedia books are essentially linear in their mode of presentation while hypermedia books use a non-linear approach.

Because of the importance of hypermedia books we have been investigating techniques for designing and authoring page structures for use within them. The basic models that we have been using are described in the remaining parts of this paper. Fundamental to this work is the creation of a hypermedia knowledge corpus and the use of object orientated techniques for both its design and its fabrication. Naturally, the provision of authoring tools is also of considerable interest to us. We therefore also describe some of the work that we have been undertaken with a view to offering authors of hypermedia books a set of automation tools to facilitate the creation of reactive pages of electronic information.

2. Hypermedia Books

Designing and fabricating electronic books is a difficult and time-consuming task. It is therefore important to ensure that well-founded models and guidelines are used as a basis for the design and fabrication processes that are involved. The basic design model that we use is illustrated schematically in figure 3. An extremely important aspect of the design model is the production of high quality end-user interfaces that will facilitate control and knowledge transfer. Some of the major interface design issues that are involved in electronic book production are discussed in more detail elsewhere (Barker and Giller, 1990). This paper therefore concentrates on the initial progress that is being made towards the realisation of design models for the creation of a hypermedia knowledge base.

The basic structure of a hypermedia page is illustrated schematically in the upper part of figure 4. A page is regarded as being composed of three elementary types of object: those which facilitate page control; context objects; and a spatial array of reactive references to other hypermedia page objects. Control objects correspond to the icons and menu items that facilitate page turning, global resource access, and so on. As their name suggests, context objects provide both the physical and the informatic background for the other two types of object that are embedded within a particular page.

All of the hypermedia page objects for any given book exist within a 'common pool'. This common pool is referred to as the knowledge corpus within figure 3. Each object in the pool is identified by means of a unique name. In figure 4 the page references to the supporting hypermedia page objects are denoted by small squares from which arrows emanate. The arrows point to the objects (within the common pool) which are activated when a user follows up the hypermedia references on any given page. These arrows therefore correspond to hypermedia links. Because objects are in a common pool (which is globally accessible by all pages of the book) there is no need for any duplication of hypermedia object as a result of different pages requiring to make reference to an identical item.

The structure of the hypermedia objects that are held within the knowledge corpus is illustrated schematically in figure 5. Essentially, all objects have the same binary structure which combines the material to be displayed with the mechanisms for handling end-user interaction and the object's own interaction with the other objects that are held within the knowledge corpus.

From root pages of the type depicted in figure 4 end-users of the hypermedia book can embark upon individualised explorations of the knowledge corpus. As they proceed the software management system that implements the hypermedia electronic book must keep a note of all the hypermedia objects that the user references - so that a back-track mechanism can be implemented. The system must also provide the end-user with a mechanism for 'marking' particular objects of interest so that they can be recalled and examined again later. A typical exploration path through a knowledge corpus is illustrated schematically in figure 6. In this illustration the knowledge corpus contains 20 nodes (labelled A through T) of which 10 have been visited. Some of the nodes in the graph structure are labelled with an ampersand (@) in order to indicate that these nodes have been 'marked' by the user so that they can be returned to at some later point during the exploration.

In order to enable users to navigate through the knowledge corpus associated with a hypermedia book it is important to provide an appropriate set of end-user commands. Obviously, the primary method of route selection through the corpus will be by means of the hot spots that define the reactive areas of book pages. However, in order to 'back-track' a special BACK-TRACK command will need to be provided. Similarly, a command will be needed to MARK a node. As is illustrated in figure 6, any implementation of a mark facility must allow any number of nodes to be marked. Such a facility is probably best provided by means of a list structure. As objects are selected and marked for subsequent re-visiting their names are added to the end of the list. In order to get back to a previously marked object a GOTO MARK command is needed. When this command is invoked it simply extracts and deletes the name of the object from the LIFO list and then passes control to the new object. In other words, the GOTO MARK operation returns the user to marked nodes in a 'most recently marked' order. The object marking process will also require a CLEAR command to be made available. When this command is invoked it would simply empty the mark list thereby enabling the user to start marking afresh with a new list. The semantics of the MARK and GOTO MARK commands need to be given much more thought if they are to be used to provide an optimally useful reader service. We shall return to a discussion of this point later. The back-track mechanism (activated using the BACK-TRACK command) works in an analogous fashion to the marking facility. Two other essential commands that must be provided are ROOT and EXIT. When it is selected the ROOT command immediately returns the user to the root page from which his/her exploration started. Similarly, when the EXIT command is selected it causes immediate termination of the book currently being studied.

3. The Implementation Environment

In order to implement the model described in the previous section we have been exploring a number of different implementation environments such as IBM's AVC, LinkWay, TenCORE, C, KnowledgePro, ToolBook and so on. The particular environment choosen for the work described in this section was PC/PILOT (Washington Computer Services, 1989). There were three primary reasons for choosing this environment. First, it is extensively used for CBT development within the author's organisation. Second, the author's institution has a site license for this system. Third, there are no built-in hypermedia facilities available within the PILOT system. This last reason is important since we wanted to see how difficult it would be to implement hypermedia using a conventional courseware development tool such as PILOT.

The PILOT language has its own run-time system which interprets source code files (PI.EXE) or encrypted versions of them (CPI.EXE). Each PILOT language statement has a standard format and can contain up to six basic parts: a label; an operation code (or 'opcode'); a modifier; a conditioner; a separator (:); and an operand (Barker, 1987). The label, modifier and conditioner are all optional items. The relationship between these items is illustrated in the command template shown below:

<label> <opcode> <modifier> <conditioner> : <operand>

From the point of view of applying an object orientated methodology, one of the most useful commands in the PILOT language is the 'link' command (L:). This command can take four basic forms:

[1] L: <module-name>
[2] L: <module-name>, <label>
[3] LX: <module>
[4] LX: <module>, <label>

Essentially, the simplest form of the command (format [1] above) causes termination of the module that issues it and then executes the module whose name is specified in the operand position. If the operand of the link command contains a label (as shown in format [2]) then execution of the new module commences at the label specified. When a link command is executed the state of the program variables is preserved, that is, the new module has access to all the variables (and their values) that were available in the calling module. If the link command is executed with an X modifier (formats [3] and [4] above) then all the variables in the calling module are erased before the new module is executed.

The way in which the link command is used to load in modules referenced in a hypertext page is illustrated in the root page object listed in figure 7. This shows the display part of the object (following the label *MAIN) in which hypertext terms such as 'telephone', 'gentlemen', 'beard' and so on are preceeded and anteceded by embedded commands for changing the colour in which the text will be displayed. In this case the commands used are # 14 (yellow) and #15 (white). That is, hypertext terms are shown in yellow and normal text is shown in white and both appear on a red background within their display window. Interaction with the text is via mouse pointing operations - the code following the label *LOOP assigns to the variables col and row the coordinates of the mouse cursor when the mouse button is clicked. Subsequent code analyses the coordinates of the cursor position to see if the user has selected a menu option or a hypertext term. If a hypertext term has been selected then the link commands are used to link to the appropriate module for handling the selected reference. Notice how each link command contains a conditioner that determines whether or not it should be executed.

The code at the beginning of the program (following the *INIT label) is used to set up the environment in which the hypermedia page (and the objects it references) will operate. Display text (and any embedded hypertext references that it contains) are presented to the user through a central CRT screen window that is generated by a viewport command (TS: V10, 60, 5, 20; E4). The last part of this command erases the window to colour red. The horizontal menu bar that is used to facilitate end-user interaction with the system is located in row 23 of the CRT screen. It presents the following command options to the user: ROOT, MARK, GOTO MARK, CLEAR, BACKTRACK and EXIT. Row 24 of the CRT screen is used as a transient message area where objects can display messages for the user to read. These are erased after a short time delay.

In order to implement the mark and back-track facilities a heap storage mechanism must be used. Three special commands are needed to achieve this:

```
FXH:        <size>
FOH:        <location>, <value>
FIH: <location>, <value>
```

The first of the above commands is used to allocate storage for the heap. The second command template is used when it is required to output a value to a particular location in the heap and the third is used to read a value from a specific location. PILOT allows only one heap to be created therefore the mark and back-track lists must share it. In the implementation shown in figure 7 a heap of 40, 000 bytes is created; the first 20, 000 are used for the mark list and the second 20, 000 are used for the back-track list. On the basis that the stored names of pool objects will each occupy 8 bytes, each list will be able to accommodate 2, 500 entries before overflow problems arise.

Another PILOT command that was found to be extremely useful in applying the object orientated methodology was the 'execute indirect' command (X:). This command takes as its operand a string constant, a variable or an expression (that evaluates to a string) and executes the PILOT command that is embedded within it. The way in which this command is used is illustrated in the listing of the back-track and mark list managers presented in figure 8. Within the mark list manager the system extracts the name of the required object from the heap. It then uses the concatenation operator (!!) in order to form a valid link statement which it then executes using the execute indirect command. A similar thing happens within the back-track manager (using the other half of the heap) except here the execute indirect has a condition attached to it.

Notice how the 'shallow' definition of the mark list manager leaves lots of scope for designing reader services to support the subsequent processing of the list of marked objects. Some of these possibilities are discussed later.

4. Automation Books

As can be seen form figure 7 the creation of hypermedia pages for electronic books can involve quite complex PILOT code. Ideally, authors of our hypermedia books should not need to know how to program. They should have available an appropriate 'toolset' that is capable of totally automating the production of all the objects needed to support the creation of the electronic books that they wish to produce. We assume therefore that the typical authors of our books will be quite proficient at using standard computer tools (such as word-processing systems or electronic paint packages) but will not be able (or wish) to program in PILOT or any other technical programming language.

In order to provide the toolset described above it is necessary to identify a basic template structure for each type of screen object used in a hypermedia book. Once appropriate templates have been identified it is possible to design and fabricate code generators that will produce the necessary code for each object completely automatically. We have been using the KnowledgePro system in order to develop code generators which totally automate code production for our hypermedia objects. KnowledgePro is a powerful knowledge engineering environment that contains a rich repertoire of list processing, string manipulation and file handling facilities (Barker, 1989). In the remainder of this section we outline how the automatic code generators work in the case of hypertext objects.

The creation of reactive hypertext pages requires the definition of two basic types of template: one to generate root pages and another to produce the reactive objects that are referenced through embedded hot spots. As has been mentioned previously, the only major difference between a root page and any other object is that the former contains extra code to set up the environment in which all other reactive objects must exist. In this section we shall therefore only consider the more general case of code production for reactive objects.

The overall task that the code generator must perform is to take an input text file (containing embedded hypertext references), analyse it and produce a PILOT code module that embeds the input text and supports end-user interaction with it. A typical input file is illustrated in figure 9. In the top line is a single word (in this case INDIA) which will be the name of the PILOT module that is generated. This word of phrase corresponds to the hot spot area used within some other 'host text' in order to reference it. Embedded within the text shown in figure 9 is a series of hypertext terms. These are delimited by % symbols. The program generator must analyse this file and produce a PILOT module called INDIA.PIL in which all leading % symbols are transformed into #14 and all trailing % symbols are translated into #15. The generator must then embed this text corpus within appropriate PILOT code which will (a) facilitate its display on the CRT screen and (b) handle end-user interaction with it. The generator also produces 'dummy stub' code modules for all the hypertext references it encounters in the body of the text that is displayed. The relationship between the input to and output from the code generator (for the data shown in figure 9) is illustrated schematically in figure 10.

The dummy stub code produced for each hypertext reference made in the text corpus is similar to that shown below:

```
TS:   M2?; V15, 55, 24, 24; E4
TH:   ORIENT.PIL has been referenced
W:        10
TS:   V15, 55, 24, 24; E1
L:        INDIA, LOOP
```

When such a stub is referenced it simply generates a message in the transient message area of the screen which informs the user that a reference has been made to it. The only action that the user now needs to take is to prepare an entry for the hypermedia knowledge corpus corresponding to this term. This must then be run through the code generator in order to produce the required definition which then automatically replaces the stub code which was generated earlier.

Code generators to support hypermedia authoring are an important design feature of our work since they enable 'non-technical' authors to create electronic books. Further details describing their specification and giving the actual definitions of our code generators are presented elsewhere (Barker, 1991b).

5. Discussion

The general requirements of a hypermedia authoring facility have been discussed in considerable detail by a number of authors (Barker and Proud, 1987; Barker, 1991c; Moore, 1990; Nielson, 1990; Gartshore, 1990). There are two basic requirements. First, an easy to use facility that will enable hypermedia nodes of any kind to be created and linked together in order to generate a hypermedia knowledge base. Second, the provision of a set of navigation tools that will allow users to access the stored material.

Ease of use with respect to hypermedia node production can be achieved through the use of automation techniques similar to those which were described in the previous section. However, having said this, the ability of authors to use the available automation tools will depend critically on how well their end-user interfaces have been designed. This aspect of hypermedia authoring is currently being investigated in some considerable detail (Lamont, 1991).

Ideally, the navigation tools that are provided must allow the user to access all the information that he/she needs in order to solve any particular problem. At all times, while a user is navigating a hypermedia network, it must be possible to backtrack to previously visited nodes, mark nodes of interest and have available orientation information. The orientation information is needed so that a user can always identify his/her current location within the knowledge corpus.

In the work described in this paper we have provided a back-track facility and a mark facility. We are also in the process of providing a 'map maker' tool that will provide the important orientation information that users may wish to make use of during their explorations of the knowledge corpus. The map maker simply looks at the list of visited nodes and draws a screen-based graph structure on the display monitor illustrating the context of these nodes with respect to the overall knowledge corpus.

In the work described in this paper we have provided a back-track facility and a mark facility. We are also in the process of providing a 'map maker' tool that will provide the important orientation information that users may wish to make use of during their explorations of the knowledge corpus. The map maker simply looks at the list of visited nodes and draws a screen-based graph structure on the display monitor illustrating the context of these nodes with respect to the overall knowledge corpus.

In the present implementation of the system described in this paper the mark list manager (figure 8) is very primitive in terms of the range of facilities it provides. Here, of course, there is much scope of improvement through the provision of a range of associated and relevant reader services. For example, instead of just providing a back-track capability, as it does at present, the mark list manager could generate a pop-out menu of marked nodes which would enable the user to select which one to see again. The mark list manager could also allow the saving of the underlying list structure as a 'stored profile' which the user could subsequently retrieve from store and use on some future occasion. Such stored profiles could form the basis of 'guided explorations' for other users. Obviously, much more development work needs to be undertaken in this area.

The major limitation of the work described in this paper lies in the fact that most of the development that has been undertaken to date has been based upon the use of hypermedia objects that are of a textual nature (see figure 9, for example). However, we are now actively extending the model to include other object types - static pictures, moving pictures and sound. Details of this work are presented elsewhere (Lamont, 1991; Richards, 1991).

One area that we are currently actively pursuing is the use of optical disk as a storage medium for our hypermedia knowledge corpus. At present we use a magneto-optical rewritable system in order to prototype our networks prior to creating them on CDROM. Because of their future importance with respect to portability issues we are now exploring the newly emerging optical disk standards - such as compact disk interactive (CD-I) and digital video interactive (DVI) - so that our work can exploit the technological facilities that these media offer.

All of the work described in this paper has been undertaken using the PC/PILOT author language. Of course, this involves quite complex programming activity. In order to reduce the amount of coding we need to undertake we are presently evaluating an automatic code generator called PROPI (Lamont, 1991). This system has a graphical user interface and produces PILOT code totally automatically. Our intent in using this system is to produce 'custom editors' that will automatically produce hypermedia objects and page structures for use with our electronic books. It is likely that these graphical tools will also provide the basis of the toolset that we provide for end-users of our system.

6. Conclusion

The electronic book metaphor described in this paper is a useful one for initiating knowledge transfer between different cognitive and perceptual domains. In view of its importance some considerable research effort has been devoted to its realisation in practical terms. One of the most useful approaches to the implementation of the electronic book metaphor that we have found (to date) is based upon the object orientated design paradigm. This involves describing page structures in terms of individual and autonomous hypermedia objects. These objects reside in a common pool which is referred to in this paper as the underlying knowledge corpus for the electronic book. This paper has described some aspects of the implementation of our electronic book model. It has also identified some of the current limitations in what we have achieved. Future work on this project will be directed at overcoming these limitations and increasing the generality of what has so far been accomplished.

Acknowledgements

The author wishes to acknowledge the intellectual contributions made to this work by Susan Giller, Charles Lamont, Karim Manji and Stephen Richards. The following organisations are gratefully thanked for the financial contributions they have made towards this research: The United Kingdom's Training Agency; the Science and Engineering Research Council;

A.P. Chesters and Associates; Dean and Whitlock Plc; and Teesside Polytechnic Higher Education Corporation.

References

1.   Barker, P.G.: Author languages for CAL. London: Macmillan 1987
2.   Barker, P.G.: KnowledgePro: A review and assessment, engineering applications of artificial intelligence, 2(4), pp. 325-338 (1989)
3.   Barker, P.G.: Electronic books. Learning Resources Journal, 6(3), pp. 62-68 (1990)
4.   Barker, P.G.: Interactive electronic books. Interactive Multimedia, 1(2). In press. 1991a
5.   Barker, P.G.: Automatic code generators for hypermedia authoring. Working paper. Interactive Systems Research Group. School of Computing and Mathematics. Teeside Polytechnic. Cleveland, UK 1991b
6.   Barker, P.G.: Tools for hypermedia authoring. In Aspects of educational and training technology, Vol. XXIV. Realising Human Potential. (R. Winterburn, ed.) London: Kogan Page 1991c
7.   Barker, P.G., and Giller, S.: An electronic book for early learners - a CDROM design exercise. The CTISS file, issue 10, pp.13-18 (1990)
8.   Barker, P.G., and Manji, K.A.: New books for old. Programmed Learning and Educational Technology, 25(4), pp. 310-313 (1988)
9.   Barker, P.G., and Manji, K.A.: Designing electronic books. Journal of Artificial Intelligence in Education, 1(2), pp. 31-42 (1990)
10. Barker, P.G., and Proud, A.: A practical introduction to authoring for computer-assisted instruction - part 10: Knowledge-based CAL. British Journal of Educational Technology, 18(2), pp. 140-160 (1987)
11. Gartshore, P.J.: A hypermedia tutoring system for design trainers. Hypermedia, 2(1), pp. 15-27 (1990)
12. Lamont, C.: Human-computer interfaces to reactive graphical interfaces. Outline PhD proposal. Interactive Systems Research Group. School of Computing and Mathematics. Teeside Polytechnic. Cleveland, UK 1991
13. Manji, K.A.: Pictorial communication with computers. PhD dissertation. Interactive Systems Research Group. Teeside Polytechnic. Cleveland, UK 1990
14. Moore, D.J.: Multimedia presentation using the audio visual connection. IBM Systems Journal, 29(4), pp. 494-508 (1990)
15. Nielson, J.: The art of navigating through hypertext. Communications of the ACM, 33(3), pp. 297-310 (1990)
16. Richards, S.: End user interfaces to electronic books. Outline PhD proposal. Interactive Systems Research Group. School of Computing and Mathematics. Teeside Polytechnic. Cleveland, UK 1990
17. Washington Computer Services. PC/PILOT language reference manual (version 4.4). Washington Computer Services. Bellingham, Washington, USA 1989

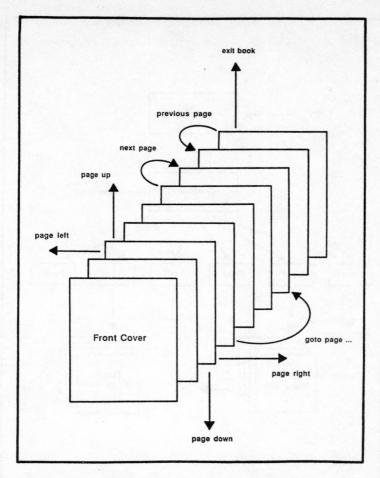

Figure 1. Conceptual model for an electronic book

144

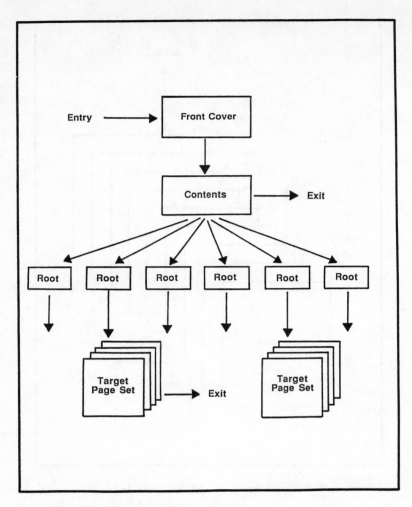

Figure 2. Structure of an electronic book

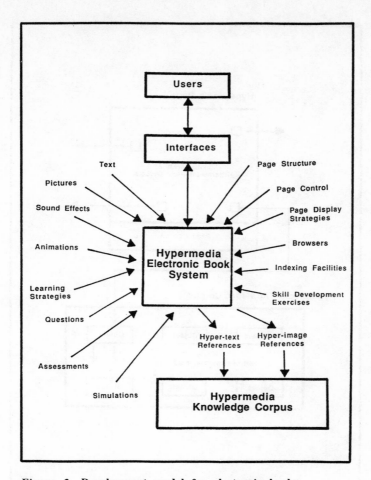

Figure 3. Development model for electronic books

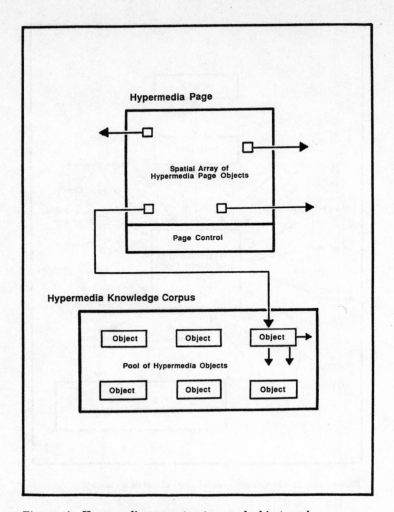

Figure 4. Hypermedia page structure and object pool

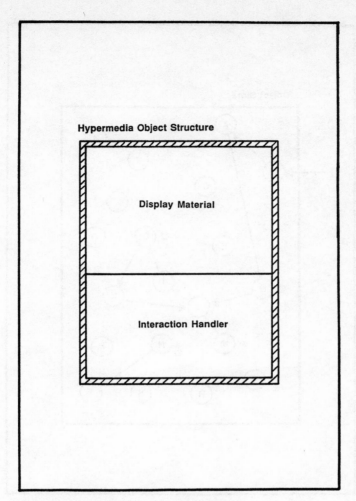

Figure 5. The binary structure of objects

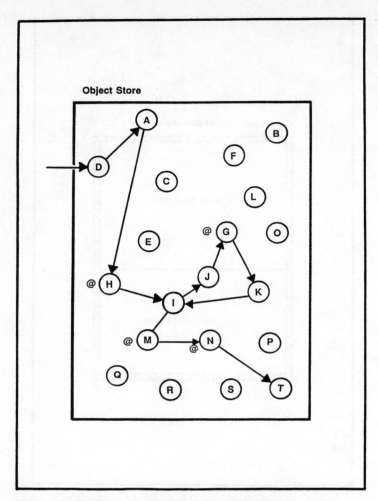

Figure 6. Explorations through a knowledge corpus

Listing of Hypertext ROOT node (ROOT.PIL)

```
*INIT
D:   M$(8),B$(8)
FXH:  4000
C:   M=0; B=20000

R:   Set up screen windows and menu bar
TS:  M2; B1; F15; E1
TS:  G08,23;CO
T:   #12ROOT#15
TS:  G16,23
T:   #12MARK#15
TS:  G25,23
T:   #12GOTO MARK#15
TS:  G38,23
T:   #12CLEAR#15
TS:  G60,23
T:   #12EXIT#15

R: Set up mouse
DX:  mouse$(150)
FX:  mouse.bin
FI:  0,mouse$

*MAIN
TS:  V10,60,5,20;e4
T: ROOT
:    The #14telephone#15 rang six times and it was then
:    answered by a tall #14gentleman#15 with a thick black
:    #14beard#15.  He asked me to whom I wished to speak
:    and what was my #14buisiness#15.  I informed him that
:    wished to speak to the #14master#15 of the #14house#15
:    and that I would not leave until I did so.
TH:

*start
R:  put node name on backtrack list
FOH: B,"ROOT    "
C:  B=B+8

*loop
V:  mouse$
C:  col=(asc(mouse$(7))-1)/2
C:  row=(asc(mouse$(8))-1)/8
```

Figure 7. Hypertext objects in PC/PILOT

```
R:   look for MENU OPTIONS
J (ROW<>23): KWORDS
J(col>8  & col<13) : ROOT
J(col>16 & col<21) : MARK
J(col>25 & col<35) : GOMARK
J(col>38 & col<44) : CLEAR
J(col>47 & col<57) : BACK
J(col>61 & col<66) : EXIT

R:   look for HIPERTEXT KEYWORDS
*KWORDS
L(row=6) : telephone
L(row=7) : gentleman
L(row=8) : beard
L(row=9) : business
L(row=10 & col<44) : master
L(row=10 & col<44) : house
j: loop

R: MENU OPTIONS
*ROOT
TS:  V9,40,24,24;E4
TH: You are already at the ROOT
W: 10
TS:  V9,40,24,24,E1
J:  LOOP

*MARK
TS:  V17,55,24,24;E4
TH: You cannot mark the ROOT object
W: 10
TS:  V17, 55,24,24;E1
J:LOOP

*GOMARK
L(M>0): GOMARK
TS:  V27,60,24,24;E4
C:  M=0
TH:  Mark list has been cleared.
W: 10
TS:  V39,70,24,24;E1
J:LOOP

*BACK
C:  B=B-8
L:  BACKTRAK

*EXIT
VX:  "mode co80"
E:
```

Figure 7. (Continued)

151

Listing of the Back-track Manager (BACKTRACK.PIL)

```
R:  Back-track manager - handles back-tracking
C:  B=B-8
J(B<20000):ERROR
FIH:  B,B$
X(B$<>"ROOT    "): "L:" !! B$
L:  ROOT,MAIN
*ERROR
TS:  V27,60,24,24;E4
TH:  Backtrack list is empty.
W:  10
C:  B=20000
TS:  V27,60,24,24;E1
L:  ROOT,MAIN
E:
```

Listing of the Mark List Manager (GOMARK.PIL)

```
R:  Mark List Manager
R:  Processes marked objects in the order
R:  most recent first etc.
R:
C:  M=M-8
FIH:  M,M$
X:  "L:" !! M$
E:
```

Figure 8. List managers in PC/PILOT

INDIA

The continent of India is situated in the %orient% and has much %mystique% associated with it. Many %novelists% have written adventurer stories about this country.

In the November of 1990 I was invited to visit India. My trip took me to three important cities: %Hyderabad%, %Madras% and %Bangalore%.

My trip was sponsored by the %British Council% and by the %State Bank of India%. My brief was to lecture on %Computer-Based Training%.

Figure 9. Input data for KnowledgePro code generator

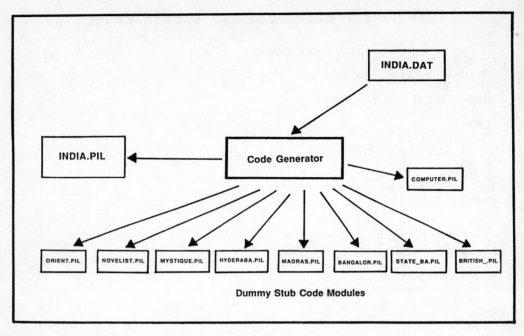

Figure 10. Code generator for hypermedia authoring

Manipulable Inter-Medium Encoding and Learning (An Extended Abstract)

Alan P. Parkes

Department of Computing, University of Lancaster, Lancaster LA1 4YR, United Kingdom. Phone: (0524) 65201 X3814. Fax: (+44) 524 381707. Email: app@uk.ac.lancs.comp

1. Introduction

I intend to focus on an analysis of user activities and the nature of learning in an emerging, and I believe, significant, subclass of multimedia computer systems. Systems in this subclass have two main characteristics. Firstly, the user is presented with an encoding formed in one medium (which I call the *external medium*) which refers to an encoding another medium (which I call the *base medium*). Secondly, the user is allowed to perform manipulative operations on the former encoding (the *external encoding*), these operations being *constrained* in such a way so as to ensure that the operations themselves, or the outcomes of those operations, represent operations or outcomes on the latter encoding (the *base encoding*). Such a set up I call a *Manipulable Inter-Medium Encoding* (MIME).

My presentation will proceed as follows. Using existing systems as examples, I will discuss the reasons for, and the power of, MIMEs. The systems emerge from different areas of computer science (information retrieval and intelligent tutoring systems research) and differ in the two media used in the MIMEs they embody. I will focus on some experiments which were carried out at Lancaster, based on a MIME-based learning environment in the domain of learning the proof of a theorem of Formal Language theory by manipulating a graphical representation of derivation trees. We will discover that the MIME-oriented view of user activities highlights problems overlooked by conventional (Human-Computer Interaction, Intelligent Tutoring System) methods of analysis, in terms of assessing the nature of the learning taking place, and the source, detection and remediation of learner misconceptions.

2. Manipulable Inter-Medium Encodings

I will briefly describe three MIME-based systems, and we will see how the MIME viewpoint allows us to see the common thread running through these disparate uses of MIMEs in the interface.

2.1 Examples of MIME-based interfaces

The three systems upon which I focus are Holland's (1989) Harmony Space system (base medium music, external medium: manipulable graphics); Pejtersen's (1989) BOOKHOUSE system (base medium: textual bibliographic data, external medium: pictorial representation of retrieval space) and Parkes"s (1991) CLANQUE system (base medium: video, external medium: natural language text). I will then discuss the reasons for, and factors addressed by, the particular MIMEs used. It should be noted that the intention is not to describe the technical details of the systems described: an overview is sufficient.

2.1.1 Harmony Space

Harmony Space was designed to present novices with little or no training in music to describe, analyse and experiment with harmonic progressions. The Harmony Space prototype consists of a computer linked to a synthesizer, the computer screen being occupied by a two dimensional array of note names arranged in such a way that (a) all of the notes of the diatonic scale appear in compact groups, (b) fundamental harmonic progressions of Western tonal music can be achieved by making straight line gestures with a pointing device (mouse). The chord sequences resulting from the gestures can be heard on the synthesizer. This allows novices to develop skills such as correctly accompanying sung performances of songs, given only simple instructions (and no training in playing a musical instrument).

2.1.2 BOOKHOUSE

The BookHouse system, represents an entire bibliographic database in pictorial form (using high resolution colour graphics). Areas of interest on the pictures can be selected by mouse. The entire system is represented as a library building in which one can "visit" different rooms in which there are pictorial representations of areas containing books on different subject matters. Two of the most interesting things about the system are the pictorial representation of (a) keywords (e.g. a paint palette to represent books on art, microscope and test tubes to represent science), this resulted in 108 icons for over 1000 keyterms, (b) the user's choice of the search strategy to be used (a picture representing four people using a library in different ways. Even features pertaining to books within a class are represented pictorially: for example, in the "working room" picture for fiction books, the geographical location of the book is symbolized by a globe.

2.1.3. CLANQUE

With the *CLORIS LAN*guage *QU*estion *E*ditor (CLANQUE) the user manipulates system-generated English statements describing photographic images in order to produce new statements which represent queries for new images to be displayed. The manipulation of the statements is achieved by performing activities familiar to users of "cut and paste" text editors i.e. the highlighting of phrases within the text. However, the system constrains the highlighting to be that of only "meaningful" phrases with the text.

2.2 What do MIMEs achieve?

All of the above systems use an encoding expressed in one medium to represent encodings expressed in another, and all provide facilities for manipulating the representative encoding in ways which are constrained to have meaning in terms of the other encoding. We will discuss the ramifications of this later, but first we shall consider what is achieved by the use of such inter-medium encodings.

A large number of tasks can be characterized as search in a space of encodings expressed in a particular medium. But the base medium representation of the search space may be too general to allow access to meaningful encodings to any but experts in that medium. Consider Harmony space for example. It achieves part of its success by a *reification* of the harmonic search space, which is hidden (to novices) amongst the huge potential search space of all possible combinations of notes, and sequences of these combinations suggested by conventional musical instruments (e.g. the keyboard). BookHouse captures a representation of the search space of a bibliographical database which overcomes several problems which would accrue to any attempts to use the database itself as its own search space.

The search space of some media is serialized: while one state is being visited, all others are hidden. Music has this feature, as does video. The overall structure of the bibliographic database is not apparent from the small part of it which can be viewed at any one time. Thus, the external encoding of the MIME can present us with a *wholistic* presentation of an otherwise *serialized* search space. The Harmony Space and Book House systems achieve this.

A further search space related consideration is that of the operators for effecting the transitions between states (i.e. encodings) of a medium. Often, we find that the existing operators require levels of skill only found in experts. Learning of skills in some aspects of a medium can often be fostered by capturing the salient conceptual content of that skill with respect to a certain task, or set of tasks, i.e. by isolating it in an alternative encoding in a medium which allows the difficult-to-acquire skills to be replaced by simple, manipulative operations (in harmony space, the chord sequences can be played by simply "dragging" the mouse through the graphical representation).

Then there is the nature of the base medium in terms of the information which it either does not directly express, or which it would be difficult for a user to indicate by operations performed directly on the base medium encodings. Consider the problem of expressing retrieval requests for related images by using the medium of video itself. Pointing at depicted objects on the screen is a useful way of specifying a request for further images featuring that object, but how can we indicate our interest in the *relationships between* the objects in a picture? To do this, we find we have to talk *about* the pictures by using an alternative medium. In the CLANQUE case, the alternative medium is language. To take this a stage further, how, while remaining in the medium of film, can we express constraints on the information which we wish the retrieved pictures to portray, particularly where these constraints may reflect abstract relationships which cannot be directly selected in pictures (e.g. "show me a picture of John's car" - the ownership relation will not be found in any picture, and nor is it to be present in the retrieved picture: we wish to see the car itself *but it must be the car which is owned by John*).

2.3 Problems with MIMEs (and other learning environments)

Thus, MIMEs can alleviate some of the problems associated with access to, or learning from or about, the encodings of a given medium. But there are problems associated with the use of MIMEs which relate to the subtleties inherent in the processes of user attribution of deeper meaning to simple manipulative operations performed on the external encoding. Theses problems have ramifications for the whole enterprise of design of, and assessing learning in, learning environments. This relates to the key question of learning with respect to a medium. To what extent can we take descriptions of constrained user activity in a representative encoding as a reflection of the learning that has taken place? To paraphrase this: can knowledge gained from a medium be demonstrated in encodings formed within that medium?

3. The HUGH studies

To investigate aspects of the nature of learning in MIME-based interfaces, I set up a series of studies centered around an experimental learning environment. The environment possesses several of the features outlined above, that is:

(a) it reifies the details (salient to a given task) of the search space of one medium in terms of another

(b) it represents a serialized search space wholistically

(c) what would be complex skills in the base medium are represented as simple manipulations (of a type with which the user is familiar) on the external encoding.

The system, and then the studies and the implications will now be discussed.

3.1 The Task

The chosen task was the discovery of a proof of the "uvwxy" theorem of context free languages (the appendix describes the theorem). The reasons for the choice of task were (a) it was unfamiliar to the available subjects (15 Department of Computing staff members); (b) it is sufficiently difficult to ensure that considerable mental effort has to be expended; (c) it has both a textual realization (as manipulations of productions etc.) and a graphical realization (as operations on derivation trees - often used in formal language text books, e.g. Rayward-Smith, 1983); (d) the operations on the graphics could be represented using operations familiar to the subjects (selecting, copying into a store, pasting etc.). The most useful feature of the task is that, while the interface could be made simple, and it would be easy for subjects to explain the effects of their actions on the graphical representation, to arrive at the proof of the theorem the subjects would have to derive an account of the semantics of the graphics (the external encoding) with respect to the textual, symbolic representations of grammars (the base encoding). It was the subjects' abilities to derive this account, the influences on those abilities, and the nature of the accounts themselves, which I intended to study.

3.2 The "HUGH" system

The HUGH system was implemented in HYPERCARD on a Macintosh SE. An observer (myself) provided assistance, when required, to the learner. In order to discover the nature of the users' accounts of the "inter-medium semantics", as described in the previous section, question buttons were placed at certain points in the system. On clicking a button, a question, and a window in which to type the answer appeared.

3.2.1. The background information

Interaction with HUGH begins with a sequence of five screens of information which are intended to remind users of the relationship between context free grammars (CFGs) and context free languages (CFLs), and the fact that any derivation of a sentence using the productions of a CFG can be represented as a derivation tree (DT). The task was described (exploring a graphical interface to intuitively prove a theorem about certain CFLs) and they were reminded of the defining characteristics of CFGs (single non terminal on left hand side of productions etc.). The learner was informed that in the system proper the lower case letters u, v, w, x and y are used to denote possible empty strings of terminal symbols. They were invited to attempt the questions (mentioned above) with as much detail as they wish, and told that they can attempt them again, if they come across the same question later on.

3.2.2. Overview of HUGH

Having read the introductory material, the user starts the session with HUGH, and is presented with the screen shown in Fig. 1. The scrollable window provides information about the initial formulation of the tree diagram on the right of the screen (see also Fig. 2).

As can be seen, the learner is informed that selecting a node may result in the subtree for which tat node is the root being selected. For the purposes of this extended abstract, we will concentrate on what happens when the upper A node (which, following Rayward-Smith, we will call "A major" is selected. This results in the display seen in Fig. 2, which shows the A major subtree as selected and a two option menu on the left hand side of the screen. Let us assume that the learner selects the "copy subtree" option. The display changes to that shown in Fig. 4. Assume that the learner selects the lower A node (we call it "A minor") in the right hand diagram (they all did, eventually). Fig. 5. shows the results.

Then, on selecting the "replace subtree" operation the display seen in Fig. 6 appears. Fig. 7. gives an overview of all the operations available.

The questions, which will be described at the workshop, were designed to elicit the users' accounts of"

(a) the meaning of the operations, either directly (Amin to Amaj; Amaj to Amin), or indirectly, when operations such as Amin to S and Amaj to S, which are not generally applicable, were performed - in these cases the questions was posed in such a way as to ask for a justification of the general legality of the operation,

(b) the scope of the diagrammatic representation (Root screen, end of session screen),

(c) the theorem itself.

4. Discussion points

This is a summary of some of the main points which have arisen (see Fig. 8). I believe them to be critical to all learning environments, including intelligent tutoring systems and computer-aided learning programs.   The detection and remediation of misconceptions is, of course of prime importance for both teaching and improving interface design. Particular points which arose form the HUGH studies are:

None of the subjects' misconceptions arose from "buggy" domain knowledge (as would be predicted by ITS methodology), or form a misunderstanding of the display-based results of the operations. In fact, the misconceptions arose from the users' accounts (or inability to form an account) of the inter-medium semantics. This suggests that, for learning environments, a richer methodology for detecting misconceptions is required than those currently available.

There were powerful *external-encoding-specific* influences on the attribution of meaning to the tree by the subjects. For example, the suggestion of the tree that the application of one *production* gets us from A *major* to A *minor* (several subjects thought this). This relates to the design of the tree itself. A learning environment has no ability to analyse the encoding specific influences of its own design, once that design is implemented.

There are also *external-medium-specific* influences on the attribution of meaning. There is the logical deficiency of the picture medium: the difficulty of representing disjunctions in the same picture without over-complicating the display. The HUGH initial tree represents a general situation, but only if inferences such as *for some grammars S and A could be the same, for some derivations the path to A may go down the leftmost (or rightmost) part of the tree,* etc. To make such inferences is made more difficult by the tendency of pictures to represent specific situations: the subject has to overcome the powerful suggestions made by the pictures. This extends to the operations on the external encoding. Users' prior experience with interfaces such as MacDraw, for example, did not encourage them to *reflect* upon the meaning of the operations. In this case, such reflection was a critical component of the learning process. In view of ITS researchers' claims about graphical representations encouraging reflection, this is an important point.

Finally, there are the *inter-medium-semantics* influences. Most of the users' misconceptions only came to light when the users attempted to translate between the two encodings. Since an explanation of the display-based effects of the operations was readily available to the subjects, this meant that the users' difficulties in arriving at the inter-medium-semantics only manifested themselves when they tried to express those semantics in a medium which could refer to both encodings (the answers to the questions which they gave).

Appendix. The uvwxy theorem

The "uvwxy" theorem, in an agreeably intuitive form (see Beckman, 1980), can be expressed as:

Any sufficiently long sentence of an infinite context free language L, can be written as $s = uvwxy$, *where* v *and* x *cannot both be empty, so that all strings* uv^iwx^iy, $i \geq 0$, *are also in* L.

Note that u, v, w, x and y are used to denote possibly empty strings of terminal symbols, and that the superscript "i" represents i copies of the preceding string (empty if i = 0).

To "prove" the theorem, consider the tree in Fig. 1. If a sentence is of sufficient length then the same non terminal (A) must appear twice on a path. Since the grammar is context free, the derivation from the top A can be repeated any number of times from the bottom A, each time yielding a sentence of the language.

HUGH is short for "HUGHvwxy".

References

1. Beckman, F. S.: Mathematical Foundations of Programming. Reading. MA: Addison-Wesley 1980
2. Holland, S.: Interface design for empowerment: A case study from music. To appear in A.D.N. Edwards and S. Holland, (eds.). Multimedia Interface Design in Education. NATO ASI Series F, Vol. 84. Berlin: Springer-Verlag 1992
3. Parkes A.P.: Manipulable inter-medium encodings and information retrieval. To appear in RIAO '91 conference Intelligent Text and Image Handling. Barcelona, Spain. April 2-5 1991
4. Pejtersen A.M.: A library system for information retrieval based on a cognitive task analysis and supported by an icon-based interface. In Proceeding of the 12th Annual International ACMSIGIR Conference on Research and Development in Information Retrieval. Cambridge, MA. pp. 40-47. June 1989
5. Rayward-Smith V.J.: A first course in formal language theory. Oxford, UK: Blackwell 1983

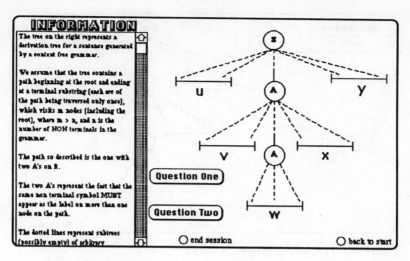

Figure 1. The Root Screen of HUGH

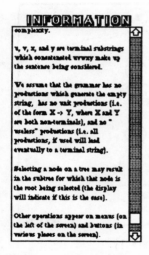

Figure 2. Continuation of the Information Window

162

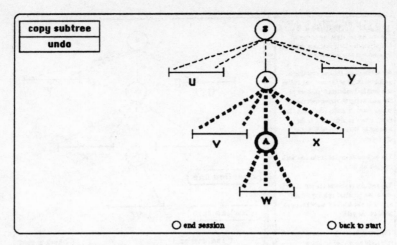

Figure 3. The Display Shows A major Selected

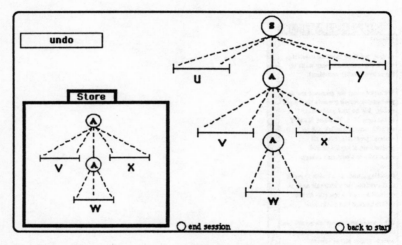

Figure 4. The result of "copy subtree" at Figure 3

163

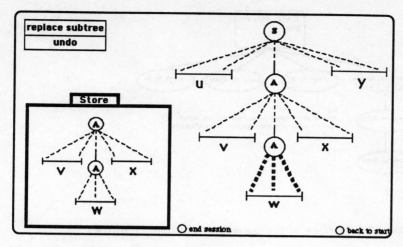

Figure 5. A minor selected at Figure 4

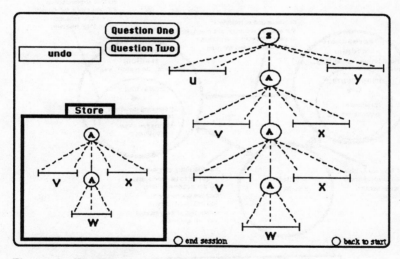

Figure 6. The Effects of "replace subtree" at Figure 5

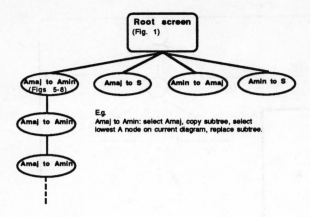

Figure 7. Overview of the Operational Structure of HUGH

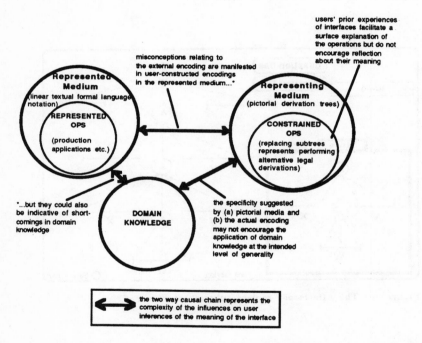

Figure 8. Sketch of the Base Medium, External Medium, Domain Knowledge Relationship

Interactive Instruction: Evolution, Convolution, Revolution

David M. Tuttle

Corporate Training, 5225 Wiley Post Way, Salt Lake City, Utah UT 84116, USA. Tel. (801) 537-7800. Fax. (801) 537-7805

Introduction

The creation of interactive multimedia learning environments presents some unique challenges to the instructional designer. With hypertext and hypermedia technologies, we have the opportunity to create learning environments never before possible. And the revolution in hardware will make this technology available to an increasing number of learners. This presentation will review the "evolution" that is occurring in the design of interactive learning environments, the "convolution" we are experiencing with the rapidity of change taking place in the field, and the "revolution" that continues to drive the development of better, faster, cheaper delivery systems.

We have learned over the course of a decade of developing interactive courseware training interventions that there are certain questions that are critical to the success of any project. One of the first things we learn is that the first definition of a problem -usually the one the client comes to us with- is generally not the best definition of the problem.

So very quickly, we must move from a micro to a macro view of the problem in order to see it in a total learning context. It is important to understand the political, cultural, personal and psychological constructs of the environment so that issues can be addressed intelligently in the design of the instructional intervention. Unless we are able to effectively touch the emotions, and address the "burning issues," we will fail to make lasting changes in attitude or performance. It has been our experience that performance improvement follows attitude adjustment.

Knowledge Assessment Tool (KAT)

One tool that is continuing to evolve is what we are calling a Knowledge Assessment Tool or Technique and it involves a methodology for capturing critical subject matter, assess a person's understanding of that material, and sequence a learning path through the content, effectively distinguishing between experts and novices.

With the U.S. Air Force maintenance technician training project, we are using the concept of Knowledge Assessment Tool (KAT) to develop the cognitive strategies for teaching better, faster and cheaper troubleshooting skills on the flightline. This process, which requires excellent subject matter experts to provide the content, usually independent from material in the technical manuals, reliably differentiates novices from experts in terms of system knowledge and ability to effectively troubleshoot a problem. Further, the KAT approach enables us as developers to learn much about the nature of the audience and of the learning environment. The process stimulates experts and novices alike to learn more about a given system, participants report they find it relevant, interesting and even exciting...

Specifically, KAT help us during the pre-assessment phase to:

- identify critical subject matter
- assess Individualization's knowledge level on a given system or topic both before and after the instructional intervention
- define a body of knowledge in terms of sequence of learning, associative clusters of information, and student "pathing" through a course
- determine course prerequisites (If individual already knows, why teach it?)

Unlike some pretests in more traditional courseware, the KAT is used to both evaluate and to guide learning. That is, once learners have established their performance level for any section of the KAT, they will be encouraged to continue to another section of the KAT if they meet the "pass" criterion. If they do not meet or exceed this standard, the KAT will provide "prescriptive advice" about where they are weak and how to "fill in the gaps." They are then directed into courseware related to that section of the KAT. Likewise, following instruction, another version of the KAT -post KAT- will be used to very mastery of knowledge and troubleshooting ability.

So once we have the skills and knowledge identified through the KAT process, multimedia gives us the possibilities we have never enjoyed with other delivery systems. In fact, a training intervention developed with this technique doesn't look like a normal training intervention, because it's audience-centered, rather than technical manual-based.

What are some key differences in the look and feel of "audience-centered" instruction?

1. Attitudinal and affective elements for dealing with first impressions and mind set.
2. Multimedia applications that place learner in conflict situations and require proactive decisions to resolve or respond to them.
3. Emotional segments that appeal to basic loves, fears and frustrations...
4. An essentially "messy" look that does not necessarily divide up the world in neat little packages with convenient solutions.
5. An iterative quality that encourages repetition and reviews, with the idea of improving or perfecting responses each time through a problem situation.

On the Air Force Maintenance Training project, development of KAT includes the following steps:

1. Identify the most significant [maintenance] problems from existing data.
2. Identify master troubleshooters from the [flightline] to use as SMEs.
3. Review existing documentation to prepare for KAT interviews.
4. Conduct KAT development interviews, including basic knowledge survey and PARI (problem, action, result, interpretation) trace.
5. Develop KAT items.
6. Conduct KAT item review by SME panel.
7. Prepare final item revisions and prepare for KAT validation.

Because we began with a clean slate, the Air Force couldn't understand what we were doing. The usual assumption that content is in the technical manuals has been superseded by the new assumption which says that while some of the "whats" may be found in technical orders, virtually none of the "hows, whens or whys" are... We believe that the content and how to interact with it effectively is found in "Jonesy's head," or in other words only in the mind of the master troubleshooters. So the major function of the KAT approach captures what's in his or her head in a way that can be shared with novice troubleshooters.

The more we work with the KAT structure, the more we realize the revolutionary instructional potential of this methodology. This advancement in the analysis and structuring of knowledge compliments the parallel advances being made in the design of multimedia and hypermedia learning environments.

Audience and Outcomes

Even the title of the conference suggests that by creating the right kind of environment, learning will take place -almost in spite of our interventions! With that orientation, may I begin with the proposition that we want to teach *something to someone* and that correctly identifying these two factors of the equation makes all the difference. And that when the context for that learning is accounted for, then a real difference takes place.

Once we have determined more or less exactly what will make a difference in a training intervention, the task is only half done. The Master Teacher knew what He wanted to teach and knew it was important for His audience. So how did He do it? Certainly one approach was to let the learners know when they had done something worthwhile. Another was acknowledging where they were in terms of understanding or experience. And another was recognizing that each individual can make a difference. Somehow HE touched the heart or the emotions, the mind or the intellect, and the ear or action -the doing of the word, not the hearing only.

Metaphorically speaking, our interventions must touch the HEART -we must pluck the positive and negative *emotions* in a way that then opens the MIND or intellect to a *desire* to grasp and understand, so that finally the EARS can hear and *process* the needed information. So, in order to have engaged learners -involved, interacting, assessed participants- we need to call upon all the senses, focusing the learning through the various media at our disposal.

Union Pacific Railroad

What does it require to open the heart, mind and ears to understanding? Does appealing to the heart really open the mind and allow the ears to hear and eyes to process information? Our experience with another client has shown again the importance of creating an emotional link in the learning environment. With Union Pacific Railroad employees, the tradition of railroading runs deep in families. And appealing to that love -to those traditions- touches heart strings and emotions and feelings and attitudes.

But sometimes traditions pull us into a routine -even a rut and it takes some mind-expanding experience to jolt us out of the familiar, the ordinary, the "way it's always been done." So we confront the learner with reality therapy- a dose of frustrations and fears so they realize we know where they're coming from and what they're feeling right now. And once the heart is right and the mind is open, then we can begin to hear what we need to be hearing: CHANGE, progress, technical, interpersonal, network responsibilities, etc. And change is really what education is all about- to quit doing the things that don't work and begin doing the things that do! And multimedia has the potential to make those kinds of changes, individual by individual.

A special music video production was created to help UPRR employees make this move from where they were to where they needed to be. Visually, trainees were exposed to both the cherished traditions of the railroad as well as its frustrations. Further, our analysis showed that it was critical to show system users that even though they might have problems with the way things were being done, that the railroad was aware of their feelings and open to the kinds of change required to solve the problems.

How often do we fail to even acknowledge the underlying causes of performance failure? With UPRR, for example, the problem was not so much one of incompetence as of inattention. It was not so much that conductors couldn't report their work -car setouts and pickups- as not realizing how critical their report was to the effective functioning of the entire information network!

And the problem was not simply at the conductor level. We had middle managers and even upper management who refused to acknowledge a problem even existed and whose efforts actually tended to cover up the non-performance of their subordinates, attempting to cast blame on some other group within the organization...

And remember, when UPRR came to us, they said "we need training in how to use the on-board terminal -the OBT." Well, yes, they did need training in how to use a computer terminal to do reporting that had been done previously through paper and pencil and phone calls and fax machines, but that wasn't all they needed. So Wood's Law of Problem Definition was proved again: The first definition of a problem is never the best... But even though the first description is rarely the best definition of the problem, it's a good, pleasant starting point. But from there we need to see how high the ceiling is and how low the floor is. It just so happened that the ceiling for UPRR was the entire company culture and a need for a shift in orientation -about a 12 foot ceiling! And the floor for was where the characters in fields fit on screens -about elevation 0-foot!

And what they had told us they wanted was "training on the OBT -the on-board terminal." But in order to create training that would make a difference, we had to know WHO we were teaching, WHAT they needed to learn and HOW best to cause change to occur.

In summary of this point, we have learned that unless and until we deal with culture, any changes will be temporary at best. And unless we have an accurate idea of what really needs to be taught, a lot of time and effort will be wasted. We spend a great deal of effort to analyze our audience - to get a feel for their point of view, their frustrations, their expectations, hopes and fears, so that these issues are addressed in the design of the course.

Affect and Instruction

How do we approach an instructional problem that goes beyond the simple place tab A in slot B type instruction? But, is even Tab A, Slot B instruction that simple? What if the person has a bias against placing tab A in slot B? Suppose there are management/labor relations conflicts that affect when tab A will be inserted into slot B? What if the inserters are angry with the supervisors? What if the inserters think the slot and tab builders are jerks?

What role does AFFECT play in a purely "training" problem? Is there such a thing as a pure training problem? To what extent do outside factors impinge on the training presentation? We could add other questions, but the lesson we have learned in our experience is that the larger learning environment always affects the instruction or training, whether it has been formally acknowledged or not.

The Multimedia Dilemma

Right now, the creation of multimedia learning environments is a convoluted, complex and expensive process. Today, multimedia is available only to the elite with lots of money! At $13,000 per workstation, this technology is not available to the masses! And until a revolution occurs in the delivery system technology, it will not reach the masses...

Authoring systems are complex and not easily mastered and they represent only the tip of the multimedia iceberg. By comparison, the creation of an award-winning film or movie is easy! It is essentially mono-media and requires only that the audience sit passively in front of the screen -after paying their entry fee! Participants do not interact with the movie, they do not determine pace or direction, and they do not experience a personalized path through the presentation. By contrast, multimedia requires advance organizers, menu structures, feedback mechanisms, remedial loops, answer-processing routines, score-keeping algorithms, and performance reporting systems. In short, multimedia may be, as the warning labels we see elsewhere, hazardous to your emotional and mental health and economic well-being!

Creating an authoring environment for multimedia development today is a complex and sometimes formidable undertaking. After reading the hyperbolic claims of a leading authoring system which claimed, among other things, that it "creates lessons that are impossible to sleep through," and "can help your students learn faster, retain, and perform better," one developer [Robert S. Becker, *Instruction Delivery Systems*, p.6 March April 1991] put it bluntly: "What rubbish! The installation of an authoring system is only one of several events leading to the creation of courseware." He then goes on to show four major areas of development activity, including 1) instructional design and development, 2) graphic design and production, 3) film and video production, and 4) engineering and programming. I show these merely to illustrate how convoluted the multimedia process is today. Now, to provide some perspective and lead into a prediction, let's review some recent convolutions in the area of instructional design.

Five-Level Instructional Design Strategy

Level 1

This is the overall strategy where values are taught, where the Big Picture motivation is provided and where desire-building begins. This is like the BIG WHY for the course or courses. This is the soul of the course, the underlying message and medium of the enterprise. In this level of design we are interested in the unifying symbols that provide continuity and transitions between the elements of instruction. This level is almost slogan-like in focus and simplicity of purpose.

The headline is the hook. Oglevie and Mather required 55 good headline ideas from which they selected the top three, leaving the final decision to the design team. This is where the theme or mission statement is established: "I am the lifeblood of the system." "My job is critical -I run the RR," for example.

Level 2

In this level we reinforce the Performance Macros -how do I perform, how do I get the job done. This is the 5 (plus or minus 2) steps taught in all exercises. This level is characterized by the "message" you can put in your back pocket to refer to in the process of completing the rest of the course. This is, for instance, where the technician for the F-15 and F-16 aircraft learns the troubleshooting steps for any problem:

1. Verify indication -Gather additional information
2. Duplicate problem
3. Check simplest fix first -gauges, plugs, pressure, wiggling wires
4. Start with most obvious component first -most likely failure (shoot back in geographical regions, then back up one step)
5. Space splitting -based on most probable to least probable fault (try to eliminate as many non-possibilities as possible in each move)

It's also the level of design where the Characteristics of Effective Troubleshooters are incorporated into the overall fabric of instruction:

Creative - vision of possible approaches and solutions is not limited by artificial internal mental walls; open-minded and teachable, curious, energetic; like challenges (believes all problems have a solution).

Self-motivated - takes pride in work, perfectionist, high standards of work quality, committed, dedicated, positive attitude, confident.

Patient - persistent, good at focusing and concentrating on a task; willing to sort through tedious details to track down the problem; observant, perceptive, noticing details most others overlook; has endurance.

Big Picture - understands own role and why it is important and is dedicated to learning everything about a given system; asks why; is analytical, a problem solver.

Dependable - willing to take responsibility; has integrity; does not accept a superficial solution.

Level 3

At this level of design, the Course Level, we are interested in the knowledge of intra and inter-system components and diagnostics for assessing knowledge. Questions, games, progress checks, context-sensitive problems, guided and unguided simulations and other strategies are addressed.

Level 4

In this level of design, we are concerned about how to share knowledge of Components, Connections, Interactions, Block Diagrams, etc. On the Air Force project, for example, for each of these content areas users get the following instructional options:
* Block Diagrams - where relationships are practiced
* Components - where they can query an "expert" for additional information
* Connections/Interactions - where there are options to be tutored on a particular area
* One-Step Troubleshooting - where symptom and cause are taught

Level 5

In this level we design the detailed activities for each Knowledge Areas. As one of our colleagues said: "The theme of level 1 had better come across in the frames of level 5, or we have missed the point of it all... The challenge is to put the fingerprints of levels 1 and 2 into frames at level 5."

The Hardware Revolution

In the early 70's, interactive developers were using the $3,000,000 PLATO mainframes, where line costs alone cost $2,500 per month. When the Apple II was introduced, one of these developers bought this computer with his own money, hired a graduate student from Egypt to convert his entire math curriculum to this $1,700 machine, and said goodbye to the mainframe.

Many revolutions are spawned by economic breakthroughs. In the mid-70's the $300,000 mini-computer moved the decimal point one place to the left and created another revolution. An in the early 80's, the decimal was moved again so we can now have computers for $3,000 that do more than the mainframes did a decade earlier. Revolutions seem to occur in powers of 10. I predict that by 1993, the multimedia revolution will enable the UPRR to move the decimal on their $13,000 workstations one place to the left and actually get more for less. They will have more storage and memory, video on chips - digital video, digital audio - and less: no videodisc players, expensive graphics overlay boards, etc. Now when this happens, we will be seeing the day multimedia will truly be available to the masses. But then the challenge will be to increase our productivity in the creation and authoring of the courseware and training that will be delivered on these new platforms.

Another component in this revolution is the societal demand and expectation for dramatically improved training systems. "I want my MTV" will be heard and technology will follow with better, faster and cheaper delivery systems.

Nevertheless, progress rarely takes hostages. My colleague Dr. Norm Wood used to give a lecture entitled: "Killing Sacred Cows to Beef Up Learning." This attitude holds particular relevance for today's turbulent development world. In the arena of productivity we are seeing more and more technical tools for problem definition, data gathering, needs analysis, content dumps. KATs or Knowledge Assessment Tools have provided the beginnings for systematically structuring knowledge for delivery via hypertext environments. Another area of significant progress is in the determination of "ceiling heights" and "floor depths" - scoping a project for budget and timeline allocations. And finally, there is a mini-revolution in the design of overview courses, course maps, macro menus and instructional shells.

4. Multimedia Learning Projects: Applications

Interactive Learning Using a Videodisc Connected to a Computer Review of Seven Prototypes

Philippe Marton

Groupe de Recherche sur l'Apprentissage Interactif (G.R.A.IN), Département de technologie de l'enseignement, Faculté des sciences de l'éducation, 1466, Chemin De Koninck, Université Laval, Quebec, 10, Canada G1K 7P4. Tel. (418) 656-2770/3769. Fax. (418) 656-7347

Introduction

This article reviews research in the field of interactive learning using a videodisc connected to a computer conducted by the G.R.A.IN group between 1983 and 1989.

During this time, the G.R.A.IN groupe was made up of: Professor Philippe Duchastel, Maurice Fleury, Jacques Rhéaume, and Philippe Marton; master's students Jean-Claude Duguay, Denis Drouin, Claire Mainguy, Marie-Pierre Lévesque, Louis Houle, Guy Trépanier, Brigitte Maillard, and Lunda-Mukuna; and doctoral students Max Giardina, of the Département de technologie de l'enseignement, Faculté des sciences de l'éducation, Université Laval; and Denis Rhéaume, guest lecturer, INRS du Québec.

1. Objectives of the G.R.A.IN Group

- To systematically develop varied interactive multimedia learning prototypes;
- To experiment with different interactive learning technological environments;
- To develop methodological principles underlying design and development;
- To pinpoint and explain fairly complex interactive learning design models;
- To assess the effectiveness of learning in these new situations;
- To assess the impact on learners of these new technological environments;
- To develop evaluation instruments and procedures related to these new learning situations;
- To propose educational applications for these new technologies.

By pursuing the foregoing objectives, we developed the seven prototypes discussed in this report. However, the driving force behind our research was the striking development of information and communications technologies, with a view to seeking valid, efficient educational applications.

Without a doubt, these technologies offer new ways of developing even greater interactivity, through new images and new messages integrated into new, more impressive and "intelligent" technological environments, thus making it possible to build innovative, worthwhile, efficient learning environments, and devise novel educational situations. An entire, important new sector has sprung up, one which is suited to research in educational technology.

2. Development and Evaluation of the Seven Prototypes

Between 1983 and 1989, the G.R.A.IN group developed seven interactive learning prototypes using videodisc and computers at the undergraduate level at Université Laval.

We decided to develop applications in physical education (two prototypes) and theology (two prototypes), because the professor responsible for the course content in both fields were the first to accept. The field of educational technology (three prototypes) reflected my interests and needs as the instructor responsible for the course devoted to educational visualization, to which videodisc technology seemed well suited. Above all, it offered considerable audio-text visual input in the classroom.

To facilitate the presentation and understanding of the prototypes, we felt it would be advisable to introduce each one according to the degree of complexity (A to G) and not in the approximate chronological order in which they were developed, indicated by the project number (1 to 7)

A. Educational Visualization Prototype

(i) *Development*

This project was undertaken in conjunction with the Université Laval educational innovation program and was designed to satisfy the particular needs of the educational visualization course, which was already organized in the form of mixed learning modules, i.e. modules centred on learning situations involving 25 to 30 students, and individualized learning situations.

Above all, the project was carried out to satisfy the instructor's needs for group learning situations in the classroom.

Mention should be made of existing audio-text visual resources, i.e. 350 transparencies, 600 slides, 20 films and a number of videos.

The project entailed preparing existing materials for the master video copy. The bulk of the work was carried out on a computer; each of the transparencies contained lettering and visual elements, bearing in mind the location of the flaps. This lengthy (550 hours), delicate operation was effected by Jean-Claude Duguay, who spontaneously volunteered in class to perform it.

(ii) *Evaluation*

A systematic evaluation was conducted when the prototype was first used in the classroom in the fall of 1984:

- We decided that a student who had taken the old course would make an excellent observer-commentator.
- For 15 weeks, all of the observer-commentator's observations on the students and the instructor were recorded in a logbook. After each course, the observer-commentator also recorded the instructor's observations and reactions noted or felt in the classroom, and the instructor's responses to questions put to him during a brief interview.
- Three questionnaires requiring closed or open answers were distributed to students at the end of the third, ninth and fourteenth weeks, and at the end of the course.

B. Educational Visualization Diagnostics Prototype

(i) *Development*

The idea for this prototype came to mind while we were using prototype A described earlier. We thought it would be useful for students to have access, in an organized manner, to all of the audio-text-visual resources used by the instructor in the classroom. To this end, we did not want to use an overly complex computer system. We designed the project, and as soon as the Macintosh HyperCard system was available, we were able to carry it out. The environment cost roughly C$7 000.

Aside from the period of initiation to HyperCard software, the remainder of the work was fairly straightforward. Our objective was to use questions of various types to enable students to be individually diagnosed with regard to course content, based on the audio-text-visual resources on videodisc and, when their answers were inaccurate, to obtain complete answers drawn from the same sources. At the end of the module, a result sheet and individual prescription are printed out; the students place the reports in their ongoing evaluation file.

C. Videoscope Language Prototype

(i) *Development*

This prototype was developed to satisfy students' needs for individual initiation to the videoscope language devised by Jacques Sainte-Marie, in order to program interactive situations using an IBM PC connected to a videodisc, the Visage interface, a single touch-sensitive screen and a key-board.

Jean-Claude Duguay developed the prototype, under the supervision of Professor Jacques Saint-Marie. The prototype makes it possible to pinpoint and demonstrate the potential of videoscope and to propose exercises for its realization. A guide provides advice and enables students to preserve the main information. The environment cost roughly C$8 000.

D. Biblical Geography Prototype

(i) *Development*

Using the videodisc produced in conjunction with project 2, Denis Drouin, a master's student, developed the prototype under the direction of Professor Jacques Rhéaume.

This is the first application by the G.R.A.IN group of the HyperCard software in a specific learning situation, involving a fairly unsophisticated technological environment using two screens: a Macintosh SE computer connected to a Pioneer videodisc using the Voyager interface and a video monitor. The environment cost roughly C$6 000.

The objectives pursued, i.e. locate, identify, name, are those found in the portion of the course given by Professor Jean-Claude Filteau, who acted as an advisor during the development of both biblical geography prototypes.

E. Fertile Crescent in Biblical Geography Prototype

(i) *Development*

This prototype and the one that follows (F) are the G.R.A.IN group's first two projects. From the outset, the group wished to developed prototypes involving extensive interactivity and using a single screen.

Initially, our aim was to set up two development teams which would, for the first time, solve the same type of technological and educational problems by meeting regularly to discuss the difficulties encountered and the solutions contemplated or found, while working together in constant interactivity. For reasons which are too complex to outline here, the experiment, although worthwhile, unfortunately lasted for only a few months during the initial project. Subsequently, both teams held what were, at best, sporadic discussions. Nonetheless, two worthwhile prototypes were developed, markedly different in terms of their design and level of interactivity, i.e. project E, involving only a keyboard, and project F, using a touch-sensitive screen.

The prototype was evaluated in the G.R.A.IN group's initial technological environment, centred on an IBM PC, a Sony LDP-1000.A videodisc, a monitor with touch-sensitive screen, and the Visage-1550 interface, which made it possible to overlay computer and video visuals. Space does not permit us to describe all of the steps needed to achieve this configuration.

Suffice it to say that, for want of driving software to operate these technological units, we were able to produce the first two prototypes thanks to Professor Jacques Sainte-Marie, who adapted the Videoscope system of the Microscope language that he devised.

Professor Jacques Rhéaume supervised the team throughout the project.

F. Human Body Movement Prototype

(i) *Development*

As we noted earlier, this prototype was developed at the same time as prototype E and involved the same technological environment, although it uses only the touch-sensitive screen, which we feel is more user-friendly.

The content of the prototype is part of the curse given by Professor Benoît Roy, who acted as an advisor throughout the development phase and was consulted frequently. Professor Roy, who is responsible for the course, reached all educational decisions.

I supervised the work team; Max Giardina, a doctoral student, produced the prototype.

The objectives pursued were those pursued in the course, i.e. describe, locate, define, demonstrate and enumerate the axes, planes or movements of the human body.

One striking facet of the design is that it uses a summary page, a dispatcher through which the student has access to resources and to which he can return when he wishes.

The summary page also breaks down various parts and, in addition to actual learning fields, provides exercise fields, access to a supplementary image bank, a glossary, a summary block, and a self-evaluation test.

During each learning sequence, the student can control videodisc functions, i.e. freeze-frame, slow motion, return to the beginning, and continue. Moreover, in several places the user can review, go into greater detail or return to the summary. The environment cost roughly C$12 000.

(ii) *Evaluation*

The G.R.A.IN group conducted three trials involving 50 students. To this end, we had to develop evaluation instruments tailored to this new situation. Several trials were attempted and we decided on the situational, and semi-structured interview, with spontaneous answers recorded on audio tape. A cognitive level test was carried out on a 1/2 inch VHS videocassette, focusing on questions posed on a written document.

G. BIOMEC Prototype, Designed to Solve Problems in Physical Education

(i) *Development*

This prototype was developed in conjunction with Max Giardina's doctoral research; his thesis, defended in September 1989, explains in detail the bases and development methodology elaborated, the findings of the trial conducted among students, and the observations of Quebec educational technology experts.

At present, this prototype is the most effective, sophisticated interactive program available. Mr Giardina sought to evaluate the concept in all its complexity, with particular emphasis on its cognitive facet, not just its mechanical and technological aspects.

The environment consists of the IBM-INFO-WINDOW interactive system, using a touch-sensitive screen and a keyboard, an IBM AT computer, and a Pioneer LDV-6010 videodisc.

The IM-SATT computer system drives and manages the configuration; it includes an expert system shell and noteworthy potential in the field of artificial intelligence. The environment cost roughly C$20 000.

One noteworthy feature of the design is the separation of knowledge and the decision-making process; thematic knowledge, which shapes conceptual interrelationships; pedagogical knowledge, which shapes tutorial processes; and the learner's knowledge, which shapes the developing cognitive effect.

The system developed is fluid, flexible and dynamic because of the types of interactivity made possible, and constant adaptation to changing conditions. It might be said that the inferences and relationships established by the system make the prototype somewhat "intelligent".

3. General Observations and Reflections on the Experiments

Our first observation is that these new information and communications technologies are indeed outstanding.

In the wake of the development and evaluation of the seven prototypes, we have noted the extent to which they have generated interest in educational methods, and, in particular, teaching and learning. There is no doubt that the prototypes have considerable educational potential. Our work in this respect merely suggest possible future applications.

A coherent, structured educational approach must be adopted in conjunction with these new technologies; they cannot be approached intuitively or with limited knowledge. They demand a systematic, rigorous approach, the adaptation of new work methods and, above all, a multidisciplinary approach, whose main advantage is to draw together individuals with varied backgrounds engaged in a broad range of disciplines.

These experiments clearly revealed the varied capacities, effectiveness, power and importance of interactivity, a complex concept which depends on the degree of control exercised over the dialogue, reasoning, diagnostics, prognostication and so on that the system is able to carry out and that is made available through the learner.

Moreover, these experiments clearly stress the importance and relevance of the audio-text-visual messages in these new technological systems. As we have stated on a number of occasions, audiovisual documents, which were thought to be outmoded, are coming back into their own and occupying their rightful place.

From another standpoint, the new technologies enable us to experiment with varied, specific technological learning environments, configured in a broad range of manners, from the simple to the complex. Moreover, their vital presence bolsters the importance of the formative evaluation throughout the development process.

The new technologies constantly question systems designers about learning, teaching and educational methods by demanding answers, all of which have not yet, unfortunately, been clearly formulated.

Without a doubt, new technologies lead to *new learning situations*, which school systems and training programs will have to face in the near future and which teacher training systems and programs must consider immediately, failing which they risk being left behind.

The key factor is the importance and urgency of research in this sector. How can we have fallen so far behind? How can we have forgotten, in the realm of education, to invest in research? Why are we once again investing in a disorganized fashion in excessive quantities of this new equipment? One would think that the salespeople are more powerful than the teachers.

Research must be conducted before widespread use of this equipment. Above all, we must rely on human beings before relying on machines, regardless of how remarkable the latter are. A machine will never be able to decipher a desire in human eyes.

Research devoted to the educational applications of these new technologies is much more important than other forms of economic or military research, as it is intended to study, analyse, evaluate and develop new systems centred on training human beings, to be operated by human beings, with a view to ensuring their full development.

We must promptly establish through applied research how to design, develop, evaluate and operate these new technological systems, and how human beings react, behave, appreciate and learn using such systems.

4. The Focus of Future Research

Regardless of the country, priority must be given to research focusing on the educational applications of new information and communications technologies.

This priority must be reflected in a specific plan which clarifies who is to do what, where, when, why, how and with what.

To avoid costly duplications and the wasteful dispersal of energy, initiatives must obviously be carefully planned.

The importance of training researchers in faculties of education must also be acknowledged and, more particularly, in educational technology departments or sections. Such departments are responsible for the quality and relevance of training for researchers. Research and development groups must be established and provided with the means of properly training masters' and doctoral students through *applied* research, and systematic academic training based on the educational applications of new training technologies, as they should be called.

In this way, it will be possible to systematically develop and evaluate, in collaboration with the research community, prototypes for education and training which use the new technologies.

It should subsequently be possible to use these prototypes in industry to produce educational materials, as it is not the role of the university to produce them. This could facilitate more extensive collaboration between the universities, industry and the research community.

It should be noted that, in April 1989, representatives of over 130 countries attending the UNESCO-sponsored Congrès de l'Informatique et l'Éducation in Paris acknowledged that it was necessary to invest further in the search for educational applications, develop more educational and training prototypes, and properly train educators and trainers in the development and use of new information and communications technologies.

This conclusion is in keeping with observations recorded by the OECD in its 1986 and 1988 reports devoted to the same topic.

D.M. Gayeski proposes a thorough review of research on new technologies and notes that educational methods must guide research, that we must find new design strategies, seek and broaden learner participation, and develop and evaluate interactive learning and training systems.

In his view, the challenge is to standardize equipment, channel research initiatives, disseminate educational innovations and develop effective, efficient products. We fully concur with all of the foregoing observations and proposals.

In the realm of educational technology in Quebec, it is essential to group researchers, adopt ambitious objectives leading to excellence and provide financial support for research now under way. If we so desire, Quebec or the Saint Lawrence valley could become a centre of excellence with regard to the educational applications of new training technologies.

References

1. Anderson, J.R.: Cognitive Psychology and Its Implications. 2nd ed. New York: W.H. Freeman 1985
1. Allard, Kim E.: The Videodisc and Implications for Interactivity. Paper presented at the annual meeting of the American Educational Research Association, New York. 11pp. 1982
2. Andrews, K.F.: A Study of Effectiveness of Instructional Feedback Provided by Interactive Videodisc Instruction. Ph.D. thesis, University of Texas, Austin, p. 30004 in Vol. 46/10 (Dissertation Abstracts International). 1985
3. Andriessen, J.J., and Kroon, D.J.: Individualized learning by videodisc. Educational Technology, Vol. 20, No. 3, pp. 21-25 (1980)
4. Bork, A.: Personal Computers for Education. New York: Harper and Row, 1985
5. Brockenbroughs, A., and Merril D.: System-assigned strategies and CBI. Journal of Educational Computing Research. Vol 1, No. 1, pp. 3-21 (1985)
6. Bunderson, C. Victor, et al.: Instructional systems development model for interactive videodisc training delivery systems. Vol.1: Hardware, Software and Procedures. Orem, Utah: Wicat Inc., 108 pp. (1980)
7. Cohen.: Interactive features in the design of videodisc material. Educational Technology. 1984
8. Currier, R. L.: Interactive videodisc learning systems: A new tool for [educational create visual lesson]. High Technology, Vol. 3, No. 11, pp. 51-59 (1983)
9. Dalton, D.W.: How effective is interactive video in improving performance and attitude? Educational Technology. 1986
10. Davidove, Eric A.: Design and production of interactive videodisc programming. Educational Technology. 1986
11. Daynes, Rod.: Experimenting with videodisc. Instructional Innovator. Vol. 27, No. 2. pp. 24-25 (1982)
12. Debloois, Michael L.: Videodisc/Micro-computer Courseware Design. Englewoods Cliffs, N.J.: Educational Technology Publications. 1982
13. Dubreuil, Bernard and Beaufils, Allen.: Vie de châteaux, une application de vidéo interactive. Paris: INRP. 1987
14. Eastwood, Lester F., Jr.: Motivations and Deterrents to Educational Use of "Intelligent Videodisc" Systems. St Louis: Washington University Center for Development Technology. 57 pp. 1978
15. Garrigues, Mylène. "Peau d'Ane", vidéodisque interactif de français langue étrangère. Paris: CNDP. 1986
16. Gayeski, D.M.: Interactive video: Integrating design 'levels' and hardware 'levels". Journal of Educational Technology Systems. Vol. 13, No. 3. pp. 145-151 (1985)
17. Giardina, Max.: Interactivité, vidéodisque et intelligence artificielle. VIe Colloque du CIPTE, Orford, Québec. 1987
18. Giardina, Max and Maillard, B.: Conception et développement de modules d'apprentissage interactif à partir d'un magnétoscope couplé au micro-ordinateur. Proceedings of the 5e Colloque du CIPTE. TELUQ, Montreal. 1986
19. Guilliams, Isabelle.: Allao, un système d'apprentissage et d'évaluation de la lecture labiale à partir d'un vidéodisque interactif. CNET, Bulletin d'audiophonologie, annales scientifiques de l'Université de franche-comté.
20. Hon, D.: The promise of interactive video. Performance and Instruction Journal, Vol. 22, No. 9. pp. 21-23 (1983)
21. Jonassen, D.H.: Interactive lesson designs: A taxonomy. Educational Technology, Vol. 25, No. 6. pp. 7-17 (1985)
22. Kearsley, G.P., and Frost, J.: Design factors for successful videodisc-based instruction. Educational Technology, Vol. 25, No. 3. pp. 7-13 (1985)

23. Keating, Carol Ann and Marton, Ph.: Recherche bibliographique sur le vidéodisque et l'apprentissage interactif. Université Laval: Département de Technologie de l'enseignement, No. 110. 127 pp. 1984
24. Laurillard, D.: Interactive video and the control of learning. Educational Technology. 1984
25. Levin, W.: Interactive video: The state of the art teaching machine. The Computing Teacher. pp. 11-17 (1983)
26. Lipson, Joseph.: Design and development of programs for the videodisc. Journal of Educational Technology Systems, Vol. 9, No. 3. pp. 227-285 (1980)
27. Marton, Ph.: La programmation télévisuelle : une première évaluation des applications dans l'enseignement. Revue DIDASCO, Vol. 1, No. 1. 1983
28. Marton, Ph.: Aspects pédagogiques d'un système d'apprentissage interactif par vidéodisque couplé à l'ordinateur. Proceedings of the VIe Conférence internationale sur la télévision éducative. Montréal. June, 1986
29. Marton, Ph.: Interactivité et apprentissage. 10e Colloque de l'ADATE. Château du Mont Sainte-Anne. October 31 1986
30. Marton, Ph., Duchastel, P., and Giardina, M.: Vidéodisque et EIAO : Une technologie en émergence. Symposium international Cognitiva 87. Paris. May 1987
31. Marton, Ph., and Rhéaume, J.: Conception et développement de deux modules d'apprentissage interactif sur vidéodisque couplé à l'ordinateur. Proceedings of the 5e Colloque du CIPTE, TELUQ. Montreal 1986
32. Marton, Ph., Sainte-Marie, J., and Giardina, M.: Apprentissage interactif par vidéodisque couplé à l'ordinateur. Colloque du Groupe québecois de télématique et médiatique (GCTM). Montreal. April 8-9, 1987
33. Molnar, Andrew R.: Microcomputers and videodiscs. innovations of the second kind. Technological Horizons in Education, Vol. 7, No. 6. pp. 58-62 (1980)
34. Pollarx, Stillwell P.: Interactive video directory. Performance Instruction Journal, Vol. 22, No. 9. pp. 36-51 (1983)
35. Reigeluth, Ch. M., and Garfield, J.M.: Using videodiscs in instruction: Realizing their potential through instructional design. Videodisc and Optical Disc, Vol. 4, No. 3. pp. 199-215 (1984)
36. Rhéaume, J.: Le design interactif. Proceedings of the 5e Colloque du CIPTE, TELUQ. Montreal. 1986
37. Sainte-Marie, Jacques.: Microscope Plus. Québec: Presses de l'Université Laval. 1987
38. Schramm, W.: What [does] the research say? in Quality in Instructional Television. Honolulu: The University Press of Hawaii. pp. 44-79 (1972)
39. Schroeder, J.E.: A pedagogical model of instruction for interactive videodisc. Journal of Educational Technology Systems, Vol. 12, No. 4. pp. 311-317 (1984)
40. Sinnet, D., and Edwards, S.: Authoring systems: The key to wide spread of interactive videodisc technology. Library Hitech, Vol. 2, No. 4. pp. 39-50. pp. 39-50 (1984)
41. Sturm, Rebbeca.: High technology breakthrough: Interactive videodisc. Wilson Library Bulletin, Vol. 59, No. 9. pp. 10-13 (1981)
42. Sustik, Joan M.: An interactive videodisc project in art history. Performance and Instruction, Vol. 20, No. 9. pp. 10-13 (1981)
43. Tuscher, L.J., and Harvey, F.A.: Developing authoring tools and demonstration courseware for intelligent interactive videodisc systems. Technological Horizons in Education, Vol. 13, No. 3. pp. 85-88 (1985)
44. Williams, D.: An interactive video module. Videodisc News. pp. 12-13 (1981)
45. Willis, B.D.: Formats for the videodisc: What are the options? Educational and Industrial Television. pp. 36-38 (1979)
46. Wooley, R.D.: A videodisc/portable computer system for information storage. Educational and Instructional Television. pp. 38-40 (1979)

Discussions on Two Multimedia R & D Projects: The Palenque Project and the Interactive Video Project of the Museum Education Consortium

Kathleen S. Wilson

Bank Street College of Education, 610 West 112th Street, New York, NY, USA Tel. (212) 932 1494

Introduction

This paper briefly describes two multimedia research and development projects with which I've been involved over the past six years: Bank Street College's Palenque Project and Museum Education Consortium's Interactive Video Project. These projects will be considered together in this paper, because the interactive multimedia prototypes developed for each share a pedagogical bias toward discovery-based learning, as well as a variety of other design characteristics, despite the fact that they were designed with different hardware systems, content areas, target audiences, and learning contexts in mind.

Since there are many ways of defining interactive media, or multimedia, my use of it here will refer to computer-based learning environments that allow for the electronically integrated display and user control of a variety of media formats and information types, including motion video and film, still photographs, text, graphics, animation, sound, numbers and data. The resulting interactive experience for the user is a multidimensional, multisensory interweave of self-directed reading, viewing, listening, and interacting, through activities such as exploring, searching, manipulating, writing, linking, creating, juxtaposing, and editing. The hardware systems involved typically include a computer with extended memory, a storage device (such as a videodisc, CD-ROM, or large internal hard disc), an input device (such a joystick, mouse, touch screen, or keyboard), a board inserted into the computer (for image compression/decompression of for image capture, display and graphic overlays), and a color, stereo monitor, or two, for the integrated display of images and the presentation of sounds.

The Palenque Project

Palenque is a Digital Video Interactive (DVI) multimedia prototype that was developed at Bank Street College in New York City as a collaborative research and development project with

RCA/GE's David Sarnoff Research Center from 1985-1987. (DVI technology was originally developed by RCA and GE, but is currently owned by Intel.) Three versions of Palenque have been made to date: (1) the original Palenque "silver", which has been used by GE, and later Intel, since 1987 for marketing and trade shows, and (3) a Palenque museum product, based largely on the original prototype for children, which has been under development at Bank Street since 1990 with funding from Wings for Learning. From 1987 to 1988 in-depth observational research was conducted with children using the original Palenque prototype at Bank Street College to see their strategies for using it, what they learned from using it, and how they understood its structure and complex connectivity.

Palenque is based on themes, locations, and characters from the *Second Voyage of the Mimi* television show, which is produced at Bank Street College as part of a project in science and math education. The *Mimi* project includes a television show, computer software, and print materials and introduces science concepts to children in a motivating and "real world" way. The "science" of the *Mimi* is archeology, and the location is the Yucatan peninsula in Mexico. In the television show, a cast of scientists and children explore the Yucatan's ancient Maya ruins and learn about the ways that archeologists attempt to reconstruct and better understand an ancient culture like that of the Maya.

The Palenque interactive multimedia prototype has incorporated this theme to the extent that the user's experience is based on a user-directed surrogate travel exploration of one of the ancient Maya sites, Palenque, and on the perusal of an multimedia database, called the Palenque Museum, related to various things that are found in the course of the exploration. Users control a joystick to take self-directed "walks" around the Palenque site, visit temples of interest, wander through the rainforest surrounding the site, see 360 degree panoramic views, or zoom in for close-up details of glyphs and stone carvings. Several characters from the *Mimi* television show can be selected at certain spots to find out more information about the various things discovered while exploring the Palenque site. In addition, a genuine archeologist is available to give the user expert information about Palenque and about the ancient Maya if desired. A camera can be selected at any time to "take pictures" of things of interest. The pictures are automatically stored in a photograph album for later viewing.

The Design Research Goals for the Palenque prototype originally included:

1.   Developing an engaging discovery-based experience for 8 to 14 year old children and their families to use at home that piques their curiosity about a new content area and encourages them to explore an information space according to their own interests, in any sequence, and to any level of detail;

2.   A second design goal for Palenque was ease of use via a highly visual user interface, and

3.   A third design goal for Palenque was to incorporate six integrated, interwoven components around a central theme (the ancient Maya) and place (Palenque). The six components of Palenque are:

(1) Video overviews to set the context and to introduce features, video characters, and content.

(2) An Explore Mode, organized spatially, with surrogate travel experiences around the site at Palenque and access to related information.

(3) A Museum Mode, organized thematically and hierarchically, with a multimedia database of four theme rooms: a Maya glyphs room, a Palenque history room, a Palenque map room, and a rainforest room.

(4) Tools, such as a camera and album, dynamic "you-are-here map of the Palenque site, and 360 degree pan feature.

(5) Games and activities, such as a treasure hunt game, glyph game, and rainforest symphony game that allow for image and sound manipulation.

(6) Characters, including a boy, an archeologist, and a museum guide, that represent different points of view, and serve as guides and information providers.

The Palenque prototype, in many ways, instantiates the Bank Street School for Children's pedagogical bias toward the creation of discovery-based multimedia learning environments. This approach is evidenced throughout Bank Street College, in both its non-electronic and electronic learning environments. The basic characteristics of this approach, which has many of the attributes of research-oriented adult learning environments, include:

1. *Child Centered Learning* -- starting where the children are in terms of capabilities and interests and building from there and encouraging self-directed exploration and inquiry based on each child's curiosity. This self-motivated learning is not "free form" but guided by the implicit structure of the classroom, materials, activities, and/or teacher.

2. *Direct Experience and "Real World" Connections* -- children are encouraged to see the connections between what and how they are learning in the classroom and the larger world around them and to begin to extrapolate from the particular to the general.

3. *Interaction* -- learning is characterized by interaction on many levels, child with child, child with teacher, child with materials, child with world outside the classroom.

4. *Analysis and Action* -- children are encouraged to learn through doing: asking questions, constructing, exploring, researching, and manipulating objects and processes. Learning is active, experiential, analytical, expressive, and collaborative. Children become observers, investigators, researchers, producers. They are encouraged to question things and people around them, and to be constructively critical.

5. *Engagement* -- active and deep engagement with learning tasks is encouraged. This involves time and resources intensive activities that allow children to pursue individual interests deeply.

6. *Collaboration* -- children are encouraged to work with others to solve problems and accomplish tasks.

7. *Interdisciplinary Learning* -- various traditional curriculum areas are integrated through theme-based activities. Learning to see and make relationships are emphasized.

In 1987 we showed the Palenque prototype to several focus groups, including Museum Educators, Exhibit Designers, and Curators. Among their comments about Palenque were the following. They felt that the "intellectual space" and the way it is probed via open investigation meshed extremely well with the exhibit designer's goal of encouraging open-ended exploration in a typical museum exhibit. Also, they commented on the importance in Palenque of different options for different users and uses, and a variety of difficulty and interest levels. Many members of the Museum Education Consortium were involved in our Palenque focus group testing and decided, after seeing Palenque, that they would like to develop a prototype for museum visitors with the educational philosophy inherent in the Palenque design.

The Interactive Video Project of the Museum Education Consortium

The Museum Education Consortium, which is coordinated through the Museum of Modern Art in New York, was started in 1987 by the directors of Education Departments of 7 Art Museums:

1. The Art Institute of Chicago
2. The Boston Museum of Fine Arts
3. The Brooklyn Museum
4. The Metropolitan Museum of Art
5. The Museum of Modern Art
6. The National Gallery
7. The Philadelphia Museum of Art

Among other things, these museums came together to discuss issues of concern to museum educators. In particular, they were interested in exploring the potential roles, if any, that technology might play in museum and art education in the future. Toward this end, they started the Interactive Video R & D Project, with funding from the Pew Charitable Trust, The Getty Trust, and the Andy Warhol Foundation, to develop interactive multimedia prototypes. This work has focused on several key question, including:

1. How do you collect and store the appropriate images, sounds, text, and graphics for educational interactive applications?
2. What interactive video programs will be most useful for two audiences: museum visitors and art teachers?
3. How do you determine the content and design of these programs?

To start to answer these questions the Project focused on several research and development activities from 1988 through 1991: (1) extensive content, image, and film research, as this was a content-driven project; (2) experimentation with high resolution imaging, including HDTV filming and digital scanning for high quality display of images of paintings; and (3) the development and formative testing with users of two interactive prototypes for demonstration purposes: one is a prototype for Museum Visitors, which I will focus on here, and the other is prototype for teachers.

At the core of both prototypes is a common multimedia database, stored partly on a videodisc in analog form and partly on the computer's hard disc in digital form consisting of approximately 1000 images of paintings, drawings, preliminary sketches and sculpture, with selected details, pans, and zooms; documentary photographs, films, motion video clips, historically appropriate music; and explanatory and bibliographic text information. These assorted pieces of multimedia information complement major works by 4 artists from the Impressionist and Post-Impressionist periods: Cassatt, Cezanne, Monet and Seurat.

The goals of the Museum Visitors Prototype share much in common with the goals of the Palenque Project, despite the fact that Palenque was designed for children to use at home and the Museum Visitors program is being designed for adults to use in museum settings. These goals include:

1. Piquing curiosity and fostering self-directed exploration in an engaging way so that the experience of using the program is enjoyable as well as informative and is based on each user's individual interests and evolving knowledge base.

2. Offering easy access through a highly visual interface to a rich, multimedia information base so that users will come away with an increased understanding of different ways to look at and think about paintings, through an exploration of selected works of art from the Impressionist and Post-Impressionist periods.

3. Introducing users to new ways of learning to look at and reflect on original works of art in the museum galleries.

Like the Palenque prototype, the Museum Visitor's Prototype has several interwoven components. These include:

(1) A video overview with a video guide to introduce the content, characters, and features used in the prototype and to demonstrate briefly how to use it.

(2) A "Paintings" framework for looking more closely at selected paintings and exploring a variety of formal features and considerations: zooming to close-up details, hearing audio commentary about the paintings, seeing comparisons to other works, etc.

(3) An "Artists" framework for visiting the artists' studios, learning more about their life, their technique, their thoughts, seeing collections of their paintings, etc.

(4) A "Context" framework for learning something about the times and places in which the artists worked, seeing documentary photographs and film clips about them, etc.

(5) An introductory level dictionary of related terms.

(6) A visual timeline with a number of cross-referenced categories: politics, art, culture, science, leisure.

(7) Four characters with commentary from different points of view: a museum educator, an historian, a museum visitor, and a young art student.

(8) Tools, such as a video controller to control motion video clips and to step through sequences of still images.

(9) An "attract loop" of images from the prototype cycling on the monitor, with accompanying music, when it is not in use to attract visitors over to the program.

When the museum visitor first sits down to interact with the Museum Visitor Prototype, he can make a variety of choices about what he wants to see, hear, learn, and do. Perhaps he'd like to start with an explanatory introductory overview, which is a brief video clip with a narrator explaining and demonstrating the interactive program. If he wants to look at a particular painting more closely, he can choose the Paintings option from the menubar at the top of the screen. This option will access a screen that looks like a gallery wall of photographically realistic, high resolution images of paintings. He can then choose a painting from this wall, for example, Monet's *Waterlilies*. Once a painting is chosen, he sees it enlarge to fill the center of the screen. Icons appear at the bottom of the screen which represent a variety of options for finding out more about the chosen painting: label information, audio commentary form each of the four characters, a brief biography of the artist, zooms to close-up details, direct looking and ideas to ponder, and comparisons to other paintings.

If he decides he wants to know more about the artist who painted *Waterlilies*, he can chose the Artists option on the menubar at the top of the screen at any time. This will take him to Claude Monet's studio, which is depicted with a colorful graphic image, based on a photograph of Monet's studio in Giverny, France. Icons at the bottom of the screen represent options to see an original photograph of Monet's studio, or to step through all the paintings by Monet that are stored in the database. Objects in the graphical studio menu, such as a silhouette of Monet, canvasses, and a stack of letters, are pointers to things like a more detailed biography of Monet, a look at his series paintings, a chronology of his paintings, letters he wrote, and a photograph album of his friends, family, and benefactors. In the studio, he can use a video controller to compare paintings with film clips of the objects painted. For example, how can access a screen that displays one of Monet's Parliament paintings juxtaposed with a filmed pan across the facade of the Parliament building in London.

If he decides he wants to know more about the times and places in which the artist worked, he can chose the Context option on the menubar at the top of the screen. This will take him to Monet's garden at Giverny, where he painted his many *Waterlilies* paintings. Like Monet's studio, this menu screen is depicted with a colorful graphic image, in this case based on the aerial view of the garden. Icons at the bottom of the screen represent options to see photographs of the garden as it looks today, film clips of things like the surface of the waterlily pond, the variety of paintings that Monet painted at Giverny, and a film clip showing a walk around the garden before it was reconstructed. Highlighted locations on the graphical Giverny menu are pointers to documentary photographs of Monet in the garden in the late 19th and early 20th centuries.

With this variety of options available to the visitor at all times, the Museum Visitor's program is designed to be a discovery-based educational experience. The expected interaction time is 5 to 15 minutes. The target audience is broadly defined as adult museum visitors who are not experts in art or art history but rather "intelligent novices."

Some key issues in the design of the Museum Education Consortium's Interactive Video R & D Project have been:

1. What is the most appropriate *pedagogical approach*?
   In Phase I of the project the design of the interactive learning was based on a recurring stylistic question (Is this by?). In Phase II a discovery-based approach was the basis for the design.

2. What is the *best use of interactive video* technology for museum educators? What difference will it make?
   Some preliminary answers include: (1) storage in one place of works of art now distributed around the country and world plus contextual, complementary information to help illuminate these works, (2) the ability to investigate works of art at close range via panning and zooming for close-up details, (3) the ability to compare and contrast works of art side by side for research purposes, as well as for the creation of personalized presentations and lectures, (4) to provide the ability for users to see and hear multiple points of view regarding selected works of art.

3. What is the *target audience*? (How do you define museum visitors?) What is the *target context*? Where will interactive multimedia programs be used? (in the museum lobby? in the library? near the galleries? in the education center?)

4. What is the expected *interaction time*/ (5 to 15 minutes for museum visitors? 30 or more minutes for teachers?)

5. What kind of *content research* should be done for the multimedia database? How much? By whom? (Should you rely on art historians? cultural historians? museum educators? generic researchers? a combination?) What is the best way to obtain the images/films/sounds for the multimedia database? (Do you use image/film/sound research and *acquisitions* experts?) What are the issues involved in rights clearances?

6. How do you *evaluate the effectiveness* of these interactive multimedia prototypes to meet your goals with your target audience?

7. If you are developing a *research prototype* (as we were in Phase II) how do you determine what that is? When is it "complete" as a prototype? (Is it a design document?

8. What is the most *appropriate hardware and software* to use? Since things change so fast, how do you determine this? (The final development system for the Phase II prototype include a Mac II computer, with a Pioneer 4200 video disc player, an Electrohome color monitor, and Truevision's Nuvista image capture board. A custom C program was written. The graphics package was Pixel Paint.)

9. Can we develop an interactive video prototype that will *encourage seeing the "real" works of art* in the galleries?

10. Is the *image quality* of existing systems good enough to display works of art? (This led to research into scanning and digitizing images at high resolution as well as HDTV filming with Rebo studios in New York.

Features Common to These Two Discovery-Based Designs

Palenque and the Museum Visitor's Prototype share several design features that seem to foster the discovery-based approach. One is the creation of exploratory experiences in multidimensional, simulated world. Another is the accompanying user interface. These two components are completely interwoven in these designs, but have been separated here for the sake of this discussion.

Simulated discovery environments are often designed to be experienced as small, controllable worlds to be explored, transformed, and enjoyed. The two described here have bounds on them in terms of content, for example, the use of one ancient Maya site rather than an encyclopedic Mexican database, which helps to give them a sense of coherence and an implicit structure for novice users. The use of intriguing topics and aesthetically appealing images and sounds adds to the inherent motivation to explore these bounded environments. Attention and curiosity are also enhanced by a certain amount of ambiguity which exists due to the fact that so much is purposely distributed or "hidden" in the environment in order to be investigated, manipulated, and "found" by the user in his own way.

Ideally, in a discovery-based experience, users know intuitively how to navigate within the environment, and have a sense of the kinds of things they'll find there, but not necessarily the specifics of what they'll find along the way. Some characteristics these discovery-based experiences hare are:

(1) *narrative elements as organizers* (such as the use of video characters, and specific themes and places);

(2) *movement* (a sense of control over fluid movement through and being in the environment; visual as well as intellectual movement through information);

(3) *access to multiple perspectives and points of view*, as well as multiple media formats,

(4) *discovery* (surprise, diversity, multiple levels of penetration through information);

(5) *activities* (manipulation of information, images, sounds; puzzles, games, questions);

(6) *appeal* (multisensory, emotional, and intellectual appeal all lead to a sense of pleasure, fun, enjoyment, and accomplishment; high realism via high resolution images, sounds, graphics);

(7) *personalization* (the ability to reflect on, or to transform information, to reconstruct it and make it meaningful in one's own way).

In both prototypes, various interface conventions have been used to promote information access and manipulation. Both were designed to be as intituitively easy to use as possible. The hope is that eventually the interface will become transparent to users, allowing them to focus on their investigations of the content. Functional and organizational metaphors, such as allusions to taking a trip in Palenque, were used from time to time to facilitate navigation. Interface conventions that are consistent in availability and function, such as the use of menubars and icon panels, have been used to help users establish a sense of knowing what to do, how to do it, and where they are, while exploring these novel environments. Some of these interface features include:

(1) *contextualizing* (through the use of video overviews and audio commentary);

(2) *multiple options* (through a variety of menubar and icon panel selections available on the screen at all times);

(3) *visual, spatial access* to and organization of information (through the use of pictures as menus, places as organizational structures, pictographic icons as buttons and landmarks, maps, timelines);

(4) *locational information* (through highlights, arrows, maps, signs, labels, "your location" windows);

(5) *reversibility* (the ability to "go back" at any point, to do something then undo it, to interrupt things, to get to the main menu directly, to exit quickly);

(6) *direct, quick feedback* (quick system reactions, system acknowledgment that a user input has been made).

Next Steps

In the course of its development from 1985 - 1987, the design of the Palenque prototype benefited greatly from an iterative process of formative research with child users. This process involved testing successive versions of the evolving prototype with children from our target audience of eight to fourteen year olds. During these ongoing testing sessions, we observed children using the Palenque prototype and attempted to assess issues to appeal, comprehension, and interface usability. Changes were made in the design based on these observations, as well as on interviews with children after each use. We are now in the process of assessing the effectiveness of the Museum Visitor's Prototype with visitors to two of the seven museums in the Museum Education Consortium. The results of this formative testing will be fed back into the evolving design of our prototype and will point to potential future directions for the Consortium to take with interactive multimedia in the museum context,as well as in other learning environments, such as classrooms and homes.

References

1. Ambron, S., and Hooper, K. (eds.).: Learning with interactive multimedia: Developing and using multimedia tools in education. Redmond, WA: Microsoft Press 1990
2. Ambron, S., and Hooper, K. (eds.).: Interactive multimedia. Redmond, WA: Microsoft Press 1988
3. Bolt, R.A.: The human interface: Where people and computers meet. Belmont, CA: Lifetime Learning Publications 1984
4. Brown, J.S.: Learning-by-doing revisited for electronic learning environments. In White, M.A. (ed.). The Future of Electronic Learning. Hillsdale, HJ: Lawrence Erlbaum Associates 1983
5. Brown, L.K.: Taking advantage of media: A manual for parents and teachers. Boston, MA: Routledge & Kegan Paul 1986
6. Bruner, J.S.: Acts of meaning. Cambridge, MA: Harvard University Press 1990
7. Bruner, J.S.: After John Dewey, what? New York, NY: Bank Street College of Education Publications, #54 (1961)
8. Bruner, J.S.: Models of the learner. Educational Researcher, pp. 5-8, June/July 1985
9. Bruner, J.S.: The process of education. Cambridge, MA: Harvard University Press 1977
10. Bruner, J.S.: Toward a theory of instruction. Cambridge, MA: The Belknap Press of Harvard University Press 1982
11. Dewey, J.: Experience and education. New York, NY: Collier Books 1938
12. Dewey, J.: The child and the curriculum, the school and the society. Chicago: Chicago University Press (1965)
13. Gibbon, S.: The electronic learning environment of the future. In White, M.A. (ed.). The Future of Electronic Learning. Hillsdale, NJ: Lawrence Erlbaum Associates, Publishers 1983
14. Laurel, B. (ed.).: The art of human-computer interface design. Reading, MA: Addison-Wesley Publishing Company 1990
15. Luther, A.C.: Digital video in the PC environment. New York, NY: Intertext Publications 1989
16. Mitchell, L.S.: Our children and our schools. NY: Charles Scribner's Sons 1950
17. Mitchell, L.S.: Young geographers: How they explore the world and how they map the world. New York, NY: Bank Street College of Education 1934
18. Nickerson, R.s.: Using computers: Human factors in information systems. Cambridge, MA: The MIT Press 1986
19. Norman, D.A., and Draper, S.W.: User center system design: New perspectives on human-computer interaction. Hillsdale, NJ: Lawrence Erlbaum Associates, Publishers 1986
20. Shapiro, E., and Biber, B.: The education of young children: A developmental-interaction approach. Teacher's College Record, 74, 1 (1972)

21. Shulman, L.S., and Keilsar, E.R. (eds.).: Learning by discovery: A critical appraisal. Chicago: Rand McNally & Company 1966
22. Tally, W., and Char, C.: Children's use of the unique features of interactive videodiscs. New York, NY: Bank Street College of Education, Center for Children and Technology 1987
23. Wilson, K.: Palenque: An interactive multimedia digital video interactive prototype for children. In Conference Proceedings. Conference on Human Factors in Computing Systems, ACM/SIGCHI and ACM/SIGGRAPH, Washington, D.C. 1988
24. Wilson, K.: The interactive video research and development project of the Museum Education Consortium. Visual Resources, Vol. II, pp. 395-400 (1991)
25. Wilson, K.: The Palenque design: Children's discovery learning experiences in an interactive multimedia environment. Doctoral dissertation, Harvard University, Graduate School of Education, Department of Human Development and Psychology 1988
26. Wilson, K.: The "Voyage of the Mimi" prototype videodisc. Bulletin of Science, Technology and Society, Vol 6, No. 3 &3, pp. 321-323. University Park, PA: STS Press 1985
27. Wilson, K.S., Brunner, C., Hawkins, J., and Webster, K.: A design scrapbook of discovery experiences in multidimensional worlds. Hypercard Project for Apple Computer, Inc. 1987
28. Wilson, K.S., and Hawkins, J.: Designing for inquiry: Exploring roles for technology. Paper presented at the American Educational Research Association Annual Meeting, Washington, D.C., April 1987
29. Wilson, K., and Tally, W.: Classroom integration of interactive multimedia: A case study. NY: Bank Street College Center for Technology of Education 1991
30. Wilson, K., and Tally, W.: Looking at multimedia: Design issues in several discovery-oriented programs. NY: Bank Street College Center for Technology of Education 1990
31. Wilson, K., and Tally, W.: The Palenque project: Formative evaluation in the design and development of an optical disc prototype. In Flagg, B. (ed.). Formative Evaluation for Educational Technologies, pp. 83-98. Hillsdale, NJ: Lawrence Erlbaum Associates, Publishers 1990

Some Techno-Human Factors in Interactive Video Based Language Learning

François Marchessou

Université de Poitiers, OAVUP, 95 Avenue du Recteur Pineau, 86022 Poitiers, France.
Tel. 49 45 32 26, Fax. 49 45 32 30

Introduction

Interactive video and multimedia learning environments should not remain laboratory-centered *techniques* serving only as a basis for a number of limited demonstrations and experiments. Our assumption has been that design and experiments should be both a continuous ongoing process spreading over a number of years and an attempt to address some of the learning issues university students have to face in a context of mass education.

1. The Framework

Since the early 1980s, there has been an advanced "English as a foreign language" course at the Université de Poitiers involving first 70 and later up to 90 students divided into two sub-groups. University regulations stipulated that each of those sub-groups would attend one 90-minute class per week, devoted to the study of "oral English". This was the institution's "allotment", the students' schedule comprising a number of other classes devoted to translation activities, the study of another foreign language, courses in management studies, etc.

As the command of an oral language involves a definite amount of exposure to unsegmented quantities of spoken material for aural comprehension skills as well as the opportunity to (actually) speak, one could no longer assume that the limited amount of time available for contact hours could be supplemented by individual study as would have been the case for a regular lecture course in literature, history, etc. There is little opportunity for exposure to spoken English in a French university and one of our original aims was to *recreate a simulated environment* primarily through the use of "authentic" video material.

We were aware that, video as Gabriel Salomon has pointed out, is linked in students' minds with television and is thus considered as an "easy" entertaining medium not as a learning tool likely to demand much involvement and effort on the learner's part.

This has led to the designing of an activation software which would transform the video material into a programmable linguistic package aimed at specific content objectives. On the *metacognitive* side, we have thus been attempting to develop student and small group activities aimed at fostering a spontaneous, ongoing, peer learning process. Our specific *cognitive* language goals were focussed on the devolment of listening comprehension skills, on the acquisition of vocabulary in context through enriched connotative associations and on the discovery of the diversified layers of culture which underlie the English language in the countries where it is spoken.

The semi autonomous multimedia seld study sessions were to be organized alongside the regular contact classes without replacing them. Students were free to organize themselves in groups and choose their own schedules, knowing that the interactive video modulesat their disposal were not an optional adjunct to the main (i.e. classroom) course but a major component which was to be fully assessed through the regular exam process.

The tools at our disposal (i.e. both the hardware and the software) are in fact closely linked with the objectives outlined above. *Video is the original starting point*, the source of unsegmented linguistic material. As we wish to reinforce the "current" aspect, the stress on the contemporary language and cultural issues, non copyrighted "off satellite" sequences are recorded, reedited and subsequently activated with the help of the S-VAO authoring software. Ech work station consists of a PC-AT computer with VGA graphics which operates a standard 3.head VHS video player. Video tape is the chosen medium in spite of its obvious mechanical limitations because it makes it possible to record and activate "off air", regular, "authentic" broadcasts, in a matter of hours, a process which is not yet accessible through videodisk technology. The choice, however, is not a final one and the software can essily be adapted to activate other video or sound media of an analog or digital nature.

Each work station can accomodate a maximum of four students, the stress on peer learning being an essential factor in the multimedia environment. The software consists primarily of an authoring system which enables instructors to produce lessons geared to the specific learning needs of a specific group of students. No prior knowledge of informatics is required of the teacher and the system operates on a simple, user-friendly set of instructions, in plain (i.e. French or English) language. Multiple choice questions, keyword or sorting out exercices can be selected and the system makes a provision for open-ended questions in which the students' answers are not analyzed but simply recorded by the computer. The system enables the designer to provide responses adapted to the students' answers whethner they are 100% correct, part correct, part wrong or 100% wrong.

Although constrained by the mechanical limitations of video tape, the software does nevertheless enable the students to perform a certain amount of navigation from one sequence to the previous one with great accuracy, each frame ono the cassette being time-coded prior to being activated.

The commentaries, questions, etc... will remain displayed on the computer screen as long as the students wish to keep them, since control of the learning pace by the person and the group is *considered as an essential part* in the flexible learning process. Within the multimedia learning environment the computer is *the activator* of the video-based system which could be categorized as a *partner* not as a full expert tutor, if we accept Monique Linard's categories. [4]

The system does not at this stage of its development provide voice recognition capability and oral expression exercices based on the production of small video programs by the students are organized on a regular basis, alongside the "contact" classes and indepedent interactive video sessions.

2. Towards an Assessment

After 5 years of on-site experimentation, it has been possible to assess some of the *metacognitive developments which are activated through the interactive video process and to identify the actual cognitive gains*.

2.1 Entering a multimedia learning environment on a regular basis in any school or university even in the hi-tech 902s, does represent a break away from what is rightly or wrongly considered as the routine succession of lectures and lab workshops. The novelty of the process carries a positive connotation for the students and this has to be taken into account when trying to identify the *actual metacognitive gains*. A careful presentation of the system, software and objectives of the modules by the instructors is a prerequisite for a successful appropriation of an interactive course. Students generally come with positive representations of video which is considered as a "realistic" entertainment, bringing actual "slices" of foreign language expression not as a difficult educational medium calling for a great deal of mental effort. Their representations of computers, on the other hand, are often tinged whith fears of an arcane, complex machinery that will make impossible intellectual demands and faithfully record their linguistic failings and lack of technical expertise. This survey of learner's preconceptions has been extensively analysed at various stages in the history of educational media by G. Salomon and more recently in a series of articles published in *Educational Technology Research and Development* . [1]

Once presentation has allayed the initial fears and changed some of the representations, the student will become fully involved in the interactive video process and actually enjoy the flexibility it affords.

The teachers' view of the metacognitive gains and the students' own impressions at the end of the year may in fact differ slightly as was shown in a survey which was carried out at the very end of a 6-month term. The instructors had noted an overall departure from the individualism and passivity which are frequently to be found in a large university setting where students hardly know each other. The positive, metacognitive acquisitions which have been noted in a distance teaching context were also to be found in an interactive video enrironment: [3] the small group's self-regulation and work organizing habits came out very forcefully in our general appreciation of the students' performance. The cohesion of the small study groups which had been attending the multimedia sessions was further evidenced by the fact that the same members of a group remained together for video expression activities which were another element of the course but had no direct link with the multimedia process.

The students' *own ratings of the metacognitive elements* as reflected in their answers to the questionnaire, were in fact quite different. They were asked two sets of questions about their "a posteriori" impression both of the multimedia experience and the learning process in general and of the self-instructional and small group "human" side. In the majority of the answers the multimedia experience was rated above human interaction. The highnest score was in fact awarded to the question about the gain in "awareness of communication technologies in an international, multicultural context" with 83% of the students considering their progress in the field as having been "very important" while 10% considered it as "not so important". Interactive video thus seems to appear as a powerful motivation factor making language students aware of and eager to know the "global electronic village" beyond the school's borders.

The second highest rating was to be found in the answers to the question about "the ability to operate, to activate new technologies". 73% of the students did in fact consider that this was a "very important" asset in the course. Third came the "consolation of acquisitions", the fact that 60% of them believed that the various media involved (i.e. video, sound, written elements, peer stimulation, etc...) had actually helped reinforce their acquisition of the foreign language.

The purely "human" factors which had seemed so important to outside observers although not considered unfavourably, did not benefit from the same enthusiastic endorsement: a general question on the "convivial set-up of small groups for self study" was considered as very important by 53% of the students polled while 30% felt it was only "quite important" and 10% considered it "unimportant".

An end of year survey of that kind has to be replaced in the light of the "novelty" factor we have mentioned above but it does nevertheless reflect among those 3rd year university students *an awarenes of the close interrelation between multimedia technology and the learning process.*

2.2 The cognitive gains were easily measured by the existing university evaluation process based on regular vocabulary and comprehension tests. An overall comparaison with the previous course setup which did not include the interactive video sessions, has shown that, after several weeks, retention of vocabulary, the *ability* to recall words in their original (i.e. video) context ant to re-use them spontaneously in another situation constitute definite gains. It is interesting to note at this stage that *memorizing* and subsequent *recall* and *contextualizing* are *in fact based on the word as it was heard and shown in the video material*, not on the sentences and exercices using the same word and displayed on the computer screens. In one particular example in which a BBC newcast served as the basis for an interactive module, the announcer sait "inflation falls below 10% but an early cut in interest rates is *ruled out'* and the picture showed a supermarket check-out counter with the figure 9.4% superimposed on the merchandise being purchased. At that stage the computer "froze" the picture and asked the student to provide synonyms for "ruled-out". This was followed by response and by reinforcement pages offering various relevant uses of "rule out" and followed by the admonition "Do not rule out the possibility of finding a job abroad!" In nearly all the "recall" answers, "rule out" was linked with "an early cut in interest rates". This and many other similar examples tend *to reinforce our impression that video alone, is a passive medium but that once it has been actived by the computer, it will be the predominant source of actual learning material*, the computer being only the indispensable, "friendly" activator.

The same testing process has also revealed a *greater ability to analyse and infer* from various sources in the target language. It had previously been noted that French students of English event at that advanced stage, found it quite difficult to identify the common points and the differences in two magazine articles on the same subject. In the present case, they were tested about four weeks after having worked on an interactive video module focussing on the burning oil wells in Kuwait, in the aftermath of the Gulf War. They were presented with an article from *The Economist*, dealing with the same subject. They had little difficulty in pinpointing the differences (i.e. the varying degrees of assessment of the ecological disaster) between the two views of the situation, even though the video module was only present in their memories and, unlike the written text, not readily available. In the students' written reports, the argumentation presented was based actually on the very words and expressions that had been activated and assimiled ("damaged beyond repair" etc.).

Inference may *lead* to *linguistic agglutination* although further evidence in this respect will have to be systematically collected. It has been repeatedly noted that students' written productions, notably in the written tests, will include words or expressions borrowed from several interactive modules. It remains however to be determined whether this agglutination is the result of a strong deliberate urge to please the instructor in charge of testing or the spontaneous manifestation of a well-assimilated acquisition process. G. Solomon' assumption that video is perceived as "easy" and unlikely to elicit much mental effort, will appear in a different light once students are fully involved in an "interactive video" learning environment. In that case, video is appreciated as the "reality" element, the source of authentic linguistic material and the computer-induced process there, is not only seen as a mechanical tool, but as a comfort provider which *reassures* the learners by offering them an element *of control and the awareness that they are actually learning from the video.*

3. Rising Expectations

If an ongoing flexible learning process based on multimedia activation is to be organized and maintained, a number of *human and technical factors* have to be taken into consideration: first and foremost is the need to organize a resource unit to support the production of multimedia packages and the maintenance of the learning stations and to "tailor" the video and computer material to the specific needs of new groups of learners. It is also essential to modify and reproduce the modules according to the elements of feedback recorded throughout the course.

An efficiently designed self-instructional system should be presented as an added dimension in the learning environment not as a cheap mechanical substitute for "contact" classes involving a person-to-person relationship. Within the university framework, the course involves both the traditional classroom activities and the small group autonomous interactive video sessions. In a distance learning context, the multimedia process will stimulate the students and raise questions which cannot all be answered by computer. The need for human communication has to be addressed and if face-to-face student-teacher gatherings cannot be organized, modern telecommunications, from the telephone to videoconferencing will help bridge the social and geographic gaps as is already the case within such extended organizations as The Knowledge Network in British Columbia and TI-IN in the United States.

As we have seen in our evaluation of student responses (see 2-1 above) multimedia instruction will foster a great awareness of the close interrelation of the potentialities of the new media and of the excitement that goes with the consciousness that one is actually acquiring knowledge. Our experience is that students will spontaneously wish to appropriate new media once they have become fully involved in one type of multimedia. With the Poitiers classes, after having activated their command of the language through interactive video, the students were eager to go beyond the "procedural", computer activated, step-by-step modules and to express themselves freely by really using the newly acquired words and phrases, through ... a new medium ... the videoconderencing facilities provided by the satellite-based EUROSTEP [2] TV channel which features live panel discussions broadcast from London which can easily be accessed by telephone!

The same intellectual curiosity applies to the software: at one stage the learners will wish to discover the software which operates the multimedia, from the instructor's side, to see for themselves how the authoring system works, why they have failed or succeeded in a given exercices. If we go back to foreign languages, with the specific difficulties of multilingual communication in European meetings, multimedia are also perceived as tools enabling people to develop the ability to "jump" from one foreign language to the next, from English on the video screen to Spanish on the computer without going thtough their native French, a simulation-cum acquisition process which may open vast new prospects.

The "snowballing effect", the ad-hoc addition of other media is now on its way. Can the educators, designers of packages and teachers keep up with the student-induced pace? In spite of many promises, the question is still unanswered.

References

1. Cennamo, S.K., Savenye, C.W., and Smith, P. Mental effort and video-based learning: the relationship of preconceptions and the effects of interactive and covert practice. Educational Technology Research and Development, vol. 39, No. 1 (1991)
2. EUROSTEP, the educational channel for Europe, Rapenburg 63, 2311 GJ. Leiden, The Netherlands.
3. Lebel and Michaud. Canadian Journal of Educational Technology, Vol. 19, No. 2.
4. Linard Monique. Des Machines et des Hommes. Editions Universitaires, (1990)

Audiovisual, Spoken and Written Languages: An Interacting Trilogy for the Teaching of Foreign Languages in an Interactive Multimedia System

Martine Vidal

Université de Poitiers, CFIAP. Faculté des Sciences, 40, avenue du Recteur Pineau, 86000 Poitiers, France. Tel. 49 45 37 61

The multimedia environment has been considered from many angles, characterized in diverse ways, and put to multifaceted uses in the past few years.

Often typified by the nature and number of technical devices and appliances set together, usually interfaced to work simultaneously or alternatively with the help of a computer or computer-like apparatus, the multimedia environment surprises one by its polymorphous aspect and compass, both in reality and in the user's mind.

It may range from a mere television screen, more or less mysteriously linked to the rest of the world, to an elaborate local workstation, revealing or concealing (according to the pride and purpose of its creators) multifarious tape recorders, videodiscs, CDs with or without ROM and/or video, sound digitizing electronic cards ... all struggling together – and even working together, to end up on a screen or through a loudspeaker, wherever they come from, according to the "interactive" order in which they are called up to play their score.

Well knowing – having worked doing so with and at that kind of array and still – that what sometimes looks like a wild-wired monster sprawling on my desk will eventually become tame, manageable and even powerfully useful, in perhaps a miniaturized form too, I chose today to focus on only one aspect of the multimedia environment, i.e., what it feeds on:

– the fact that it is the meeting place of *multiple languages: image, sound, written and spoken words*, which interact into a new one, made of all the others.

And, because it is the easiest and most "transferable" of interactive systems including textual and audiovisual information, technically speaking, I will refer to a workstation made of a *computer connected to a videodisc player*.

Two reasons for thus concentrating our talk on the manipulation of different types of languages involved in a multimedia environment:

1. Being responsible for the organisation of quite diversified trainings in the field of "new" technologies, we are struck by the fact that trainees are often bewildered by the constant "zapping" from one form of language to another (image to text, to sound, to

graphics, ... and vice versa) or by the fact that they are generally expected to efficiently master the "zapping" themselves afterwards.

Working on the adjustments between languages, and on the peculiar interactive syntax produced by multimedia interactive systems, has thus appeared a necessity, for which we have produced technical and pedagogic tools.[1]

2. From one language form to another: the teaching of foreign languages is a domain where the use and study of interacting images, sound, written and spoken words is manifest. Therefore, although this interplay between different forms of languages is useful and relevant in many other fields, it is quite convenient to exemplify it today as a tool for the teaching of foreign languages.

1. Processing Among the Languages Involved in an Interactive Multimedia System

One has to bear in mind that an interactive system is a space where the creators of the system and its contents, are communicating with the users of the system, with the help (or in spite of!) a screen, and that the users will travel in that space *only* where they are allowed to by the creators, except if they escape the whole thing by switching it off.

A maze is built, accesses are devised according to specified purposes, clues are provided; and although it all seems a question of pressing keys on a keyboard, or setting switches on and off various machines, progressing through that maze is not so much a "man to machine" dialogue as a remote "man to man" dialogue, fixed by necessity, limited to the area granted by the creators of the system and its contents. And with as much spontaneity in the exchanges as what one gets on a telephone connected to an answering machine, as compared to a direct telephone conversation.

Yet, however fixed, the exchanges, or travels, from one written or spoken information to another in the same written or spoken form, are not too difficult to organise of follow.

One is usually able to anticipate the information that could follow, or apprehend a new information that actually follows, or extend an information, or expatiate on it, as long as it is in the same written or spoken form. Because one has usually been educated and trained in that form ever since childhood.

For example, if, in France, on my MINITEL (Service télématique) keyboard and screen, I write *SNCF*, and press the *ENTER* key, I am not surprised, and even able to understand the

---

1   Among which the software VideoLog, an authoring system allowing one to combine text, video, and digital images in an interactive way, driving videodiscs, CDV, CD or videotape. This software is distributed in every school or teacher training centre using interactive equipment in France: several hundreds are now part of the Ministry of Education's network of "Ateliers Images Interactives".

ensuing page on the screen, offering time tables, information etc. about trains in France. Although this supposes that I know what *SNCF* means, I can always look it up in some book, and have explanations in a written form somewhere.

But what happens when a piece of information starts encoded in a written form, for example, and ends up delivered in an audiovisual form? When and how is the transition between word and image done? And how to put that transition to best advantage and efficiency, so that the various pieces of information will not appear as a mere chancy juxtaposition but as a meaningful whole, as a completed jigsaw puzzle, where the different forms of languages are justified and used in an effective way according to purpose.

One has to be wary of sheer technological prowesses and accumulation, of the allurement of a "collage", more artistic than pertinent, pleasant to consider but of an unfortunately extravagant pedagogic economy (if one has pedagogy in mind...).

1-a) A Question of Access, Organisation and "Immediateness"

When everything is encoded in the same written or spoken language, going from one piece of information to another asks for no other adaptation, on the part of the user, than what is asked of him while following or taking part in a conversation. If some of the information is in an audiovisual form, the transition with that part of the information will be more natural if it is as "immediate" and "conversational" as the rest, if it is inserted in the general flow of the conversation.

So far the only audiovisual tools with which we have been able to work on this aspect are videodiscs (and other "optical memories" such as CDVs).

Indeed no other tool for storing audiovisual information allows one to easily manipulate, i.e.: access, isolate and organise the audiovisual elements so as to create endless meanings, with an accuracy similar to that of a spoken language.

1-b) Reminder from Silent Movies

However, working on the transition between text and images is not new: in many silent movies, we find that the text often played other roles than supplying the missing sound track.[2]

- In Chaplin's *THE KID*, for example, the first few texts have nothing to do with a spoken dialogue. They introduce each character *before* we see him or her: and not only do they typify the character (*"The woman whose sin was motherhood"*) but some texts are

---

[2] A more extensive study of the links between image and text in silent movies: Martien Vidal: Le Dicible Exédé, in "MIRES", Office Audiovisuel de l'Université de Poitiers, No. 2, automne 85

related to each other across the pictures (another character is simply introduced by "*The man*", an apparently useless subtitle - everybody can see it is a man - when not linked with the text introducing the female character) as if the written story was mingled with the visual narrative. But the link between text and image can be more than a "well-informed" denotation on the part of the text: the character of *the tramp*, played by Chaplin, is first seen having a walk in back alleys, where garbage and rubbish keep falling from the windows, generally onto his head, so that when he finds an abandoned baby (*the kid*) lying on the ground, he remarks to a passing lady with a pram (already garnished): "*you dropped this*". The idea of *dropping* being in bud-shape in the image, it blooms in the text.

Text and image can thus be of use to each other, to create of modify a meaning. According to the aim, many links can be designed between them, creating a kind of narrative where the syntactic elements are either text or image.

Yet, what seems relatively simple in the case of silent movies, picture books, comic strips, etc...gets more complicated in an interactive multimedia system.

1-c)   When "Syntagm" and "Paradigm" Exchange Positions

Whereas a linear narrative, whether including diverse forms of languages or not, usually has a set syntax, and is deciphered form the beginning to the end with rarely a second thought, an interactive system may offer a web to travel on, with decisions to take at every crossroad.[3] So that the next syntactic element in the narrative (let us still call it a narrative) is one among several propositions, each proposition being in a paradigmatic position. The chosen one will get inserted, as a syntagm, in the narrative the user unrolls as he travels on. And those several syntactic elements can be any of the languages conveyed by a multimedia system.

---

[3]   Analysing interactive progress: Martine Vidal: <u>Lorsque l'erreur est séduisante,</u> in APTE, No. 4 "Les Ecrans Interactifs", 1988.

2. A Few Simple Examples in Foreign Language Teaching, Among Those Shown Today[4]

2-a)

A video sequence is shown to the trainee. It represents the first stage in a succession of actions. The trainee has to choose a sentence, on a list, describing the action represented, or announcing the next stage in the succession of actions.

If he can't choose correctly, this first stage, or action, will be repeated and never progress.

If he chooses correctly the sequence goes on, showing the next stage: either announced by the trainee when he chose the sentence for it, or offering a visual action, and aid, for the trainee to describe afterward. In both cases, announcing or describing, the trainee creates a narrative, drawing upon visual or written elements that he links together.

In this example, right and wrong possibilities quite limit the conceivable potential narration.

2-b)

A more open linking of image and words.

A poem is written on the computer screen" by a very simple action, one can add as many as one likes of any of the 54 000 stills of a videodisc, to each verse of the poem.

The poem can then be "read" starting from the stills or from the words, each form of language influencing our perception and understanding of the other.

2-c)

The audiovisual language is usually made of image, sound, and spoken language.

One notices that by temporarily removing one of those three channels of information, one can draw attention to it, i.e.: the withdrawn information or language.

With a videodisc, this can be done very minutely, word by word, producing, for example, a commentary where some objects or actions, exist only by their visual representation, and not by being named or described verbally. The trainee will have to supply the missing verbal

---

[4] For a more extensive description of the uses os interactive video in language teaching: Martine Vidal: Interactions de langages, in "Une Approche Multimedia des Pratiques Pédagogiques", Ministère de l'Éducation Nationale, Direction des Lycées et Collèges, Département de l'Innovation Pédagogique, March 1991. et Martine Vidal: Audiovisuel Interactif et Enseignement des Langues Vivantes, in "Stratégies pédagogiques et outils pour l'enseignment des langues vivantes", Centre National de Documentation Pédagogique, November 1990.

information to fill the gaps, thus producing, acting, and not merely passively watching or listening. On the reverse this can be done with gaps in the visual information, the trainee having then to match bits of soundless video to the spoken words he heard cut off from their visual accompaniment.

3. Benefiting From Counterpoint

As we cannot lengthily describe here all the processes by which image, sound and words, can be interactively combined so as to lead the trainee to *build* his/her knowledge rather than submit to information, let's just compare the multi-languages interactive system to a contrapuntal musical composition.

The trainee will not get the full score, unless he is able to rebuild it, or play his/her own voice in the melody, and still make musical sense.

As in a musical fugue, the trainee's part gets support from all the instruments (image, sound, words), sometimes simultaneously, sometimes separately, but ever mindful of each other, following "imitative:, "answering", "free", etc... patterns.

Where harmony lies between all the voices, doubtless every voice is mastered: and each voice is mastered with the help of, and in conjunction with the others. (See **2- c**, above).

Assisting the trainee to build his/her voice is the role of the multi-languages interactive system.

To Conclude

The whole pedagogic problem lies then not so much on the information the user obtains or is lead to, but on how he reacts to it and *what he does with it: how he inserts it in his personal "syntax", and builds a knowledge and know-how out of "bridging", i.e.: structuring the different forms of languages involved in the multimedia systems.*

The user has to make his way, and structure his information, among sound, image and word.

The few examples shown today deal with foreign language teaching, and mostly autonomous uses of interactive multimedia systems. Many other uses exist of course, and in many different fields, but we find that the most appropriate and fruitful are those where the system goes beyond the handling of the audiovisual language as a mere illustrative device, and integrates it as part of the language manipulated by the system, along with the spoken or written word, building the three into one multimedia language.

And let us note, with poems, since we are here, on paper, dealing with the written and visual forms only, how the visual form and the written text can complement each other.

One poem, Lewis Carroll's figured verse, in *Alice in Wonderland*, relates in form to the narrator, the Mouse, and more precisely, its tail; the other poem, dating back to the 18th century, uses a technique frequently employed today in the lettering of advertisements, book jackets, TV titles, and so on, takes the visual shape of its objects. And all for our better understanding.

```
        Fury said to
        a mouse, That
            he met
             in the
                 house,
             'Let us
             both go
             to law:
        I will
        prosecute
        you. -
            Come, I'll
                take no
                    denial;
                    We must
                         have a
                              trial:
                                   For
                                 really
                              this
                                  morning
                                      I've
                                   nothing
                                    to do.'
                    Said the
                    mouse to
                  the cur,
                   'Such a
                       trial,
                     dear sir,
               With no
              jury or
             judge,
             would be
                 wasting
                 our breath.'
                     'I'll be
                     judge
                  I'll be
                  jury,'
                 Said
                     cunning
                     old Fury;
                         'I'll try
                           the whole
                                 cause,
                                 and
                            condemn
                         you
                              to
                              death
```

Charles-François PANARD (1674-1765)

```
                    Que   mon
                    Fl ac on
                Me semble bon !
                  Sans lui
                    L' ennui
                  Me nuit;
                  Me suit,
                  Je  sens
                  Mes sens
                  Mourants
                  Pesants.
              Quand je le tiens
            Dieux ! Que je suis bien !
          Que son   aspect  est  agréable !
        Que je  fais cas de ses  divins présents !
      C'est  de son sein fécond, c'est de ses heureux flancs
      Que   coule  ce  nectar  si   doux,  si  délectable
      Qui  rend tous les esprits, tous  les coeurs satisfaits.
      Cher objet de mes voeux, tu fais  toute ma gloire;
      Tant que mon  coeur vivra, de tes  charmants bienfaits
      Il    saura    conserver    la   fidèle   mémoire.
      Ma  muse, à te louer  se consacre  à  jamais.
      Tantôt dans un caveau,  tantôt sous une  treille,
        Ma  lyre, de ma  voix  accompagnant le  son,
      Répétera cent fois cette aimable chanson :
        Règne sans fin, ma  charmante bouteille;
        Règne sans cesse, mon  cher  flacon.
```

Interactive Language Learning:
A Multimedia Approach in Chile

Max S. Echeverría

Departamento de Español, Casilla 82-C, Universidad de Concepción, Chile. Fax. 56 412 43379

1. A "Bit" of History

It was about three years ago at our University of Concepción, Chile, that we decided to renew our Language Lab. At the time of analyzing the different purchasing alternatives, however, we realized that a fundamental discussion was going on: there was no agreement as to the convenience of insisting on traditional language laboratories for the language teaching task. Several issues were raised relative to the communicative, functional and interactive approaches to language teaching and the need to focus on learning rather than on teaching. The occasion seemed appropriate for a change: we needed a media room with richer and more diversified means; the audio from a tape recorder sounded extremely poor indeed.

We then thought it indispensable that the computer should be the central unit. We kept the audio recorders and added some videotape recorders with TV sets. The Language Learning Resource Center had come into being.

The next step was acquiring the basic software. From Wida Software in England we purchased several authoring packages especially designed for CALL activities (Computer Assisted Language Learning). Word processors, databases and graphics packages in addition to a couple of high level programming languages completed the picture. Thus far we had the instruments: it was now necessary to make the orchestra play ...

For the last two years we have being trying to make this orchestra play at least some simple pieces; it has not been easy. Lack of technical support and qualified staff is just one of the natural handicaps in our Third World countries, especially when sophisticated technologies like computers and video are involved. Compatibility, communication and interfaces are the usual kind of problems we have to face. Solutions are often costly and sometimes inexistant. We have overcome these limitations, though, with imagination and effort. In this presentation I will give you an overview of the interactive programs we presently have in Concepción for our first and second language students.

2. Nature and Type of Programs

2.1. Interactivity

We have a variety of programs, traditional and innovative; they all share, however, one fundamental feature: the fact of being interactive. The reason is obvious: we believe language learning is better accomplished if the learner is driven to participate actively in the process.

2.2. Individualization

Although the programs have been adjusted to the needs of our college students, every user has the possibility of setting his own working pace according to his own interest and capacity. In this sense we can say that the learning process becomes individualized.

2.3. Student-Instructor Interaction

Normally the students work in pairs at each workstation. Due to this and according to the nature of the task, the problems posed by computer are discussed between the subjects before they react to input an answer. Consequently a linguistic interchange takes place which often leads to an information exchange involving the instructor who has been called on to clear things up. Notice that the motivation of the student at this time makes this opportunity unique for knowledge acquisition: he needs information to go on working out solutions.

2.4. Program Types

2.4.1. Quizzes and Drills

Most of the self-access activities available at the resource center have been developed by using authoring packages which, as you may well know, are a kind of software shell where the instructor fill in the linguistic material; from then on the software itself takes charge. Typical programs are:

a) *Gapmaster*. The learner explores the contents of gaps in the text: e.g. words, parts of words, short phrases, etc.

b) *Storyboard*. A text reconstruction task in which learners try to rebuild a text by guessing the word deleted.

c) *Matchmaster*. An authoring package for matching activities: pairs of words, sentence-halves, questions and replies.

d) *Vocab*. A vocabulary building program; it provides a range of games and activities based on common lists of words and context sentences entered by the teacher.

Several other drills have been developed in Pilot language.

2.4.2. Simulations and Adventures

Text adventures and simulations carry a great value for language study, namely because they put the learner in a communicative situation, which is essential to modern language teaching methodology. "London Adventure" is an excellent example of this kind of software. It simulates a trip to London. We will describe it later on.

2.4.3. Generative Programs

A generative program is one that creates or "generates" new situations or elements by integrating the answers previously given by the user. By this recourse the more you use the program the more "intelligent" it becomes.

2.4.4. Hypertext

Hypertext is a kind of software that is producing a sort of revolution in knowledge transfer on the basis of text. Hidden information is linked to actual strings present on the screen. The user can select a word or phrase and immediately a window is opened at that point to let related information come forward. Explanations or comments are thus linked to a surface node. Likewise, the new screen may have more links to new paths which you may choose to explore or not. This structure allows the user to read the text in different ways, thus establishing different relationships. Fig. 1 illustrates how hypertext works.

One of the major advances hypertext has over regular printed text is the fact that the reader decides what to read: he is not committed to a single linear direction. According to his particular interests he can choose to explore a specific term, concept or subject available as a link: multiple readings are possible. The hypertext software we have been using has been Text-Pro from Knowledge Garden, Inc.

2.4.5.   Hypergraphics

Extending the idea of hypertext, Knowledge-Pro applications allow the user to have links or "hot-spots" on a graphics screen. In this manner we can associate text to graphics and graphics to other graphics. By means of a hypergraphic link you can zoom-in on a specific point of a picture, give details of a section and then explain through text. Fig. 2 illustrates this approach.

2.4.6.   Audio Integration

Sound is fundamental for language teaching. Linguistic signs are primarily phonic. For this reason handling an audio source through the computer is an ideal arrangement. So far we have not been able to have available an appropriate interface to a tape-recorder. We are investigating the use of digitalized voice.

2.4.7.   Interactive Video

Using the video in combination with computer programs capable of handling the presentation and selection of video fragments is a much powerful tool with a high motivational plus. Not having the adequate interface, we intend to use 2 monitors: one for the video and another for the program output. If the video units are kept short then it is possible to establish the interaction with the user through the computer program.

3.   Degree of Program Development

It should be noted that the programs we have made reference to and which will be described below are at a different level of development. Some of them are in full use, others are in an experimental stage, and several ones are just a project.

4.   Topics and Areas Covered

There are six areas that we have covered with our programs so far:
   a)   English as foreign language
   b)   French as foreign language
   c)   Spanish as native language

d) Latin
e) Linguistics
f) Translation

5. Program Description

In this section we will describe the most representative programs for each area, it will be stated in every case the objectives, the type of program, stage of development and characteristics of the software.

5.1. English as a Foreign Language

5.1.1. London Adventure

A trip to London is simulated in which the student plays the role of a visitor who has to purchase several goods in different places and then reach the airport in time for this flight back home. Produced by the British Council, this program is ideal for functional language learning in context.

5.1.2. Text Reconstruction Programs

Storyboard and *Gapmaster* offer typical text rebuilding tasks. They are of a special importance for the language learner because of the psycholinguistic abilities which are called for in order to accomplish the job. *Fun With Texts* and *Double-Up* are authoring programs allowing text reconstruction and other game-like activities with the same texts the teacher has entered only once.

5.1.3. Reading Comprehension

A hypertext software called *Black Magic* has been used to write texts devoted to enhance reading comprehension in English. The links incorporate lexical, grammatical and cultural information, according to the students' requirements. About a dozen of texts are currently in use with undergraduates.

Sequitur, which is Latin for "what follows", is the name of a clever piece of software by John Higgins where you have to decide what is the right continuation line for giving coherence to a text you have been reconstructing line by line.

5.2. French as a Foreign Language

5.2.1. Vicat

It is a program written at Brigham Young University intended to give the user structural information, practice and testing in French irregular verbs. From menus on the screen the student can select verbs and tenses and then choose practicing or testing with the selected subset. In full use with 1st and 2nd year students of French.

5.2.2. Creative Textual-Oriented Text Rebuilding

Traditional text reconstruction is little more than the Cloze method of gap-filling. A creative teacher of French at our University has developed a series of exercises where clues are provided which narrow and specify the range of the task. In one of them a student is given an abstract of the subject the text is about; thus providing the learner with a background knowledge that guides his decisions when reconstructing the text. In another case the student must rebuild a dialogue, but he is previously given precise information about the characters, their status and personal characteristics, and their goals in communicating with each other. In this form the reconstruction task requires from the student an integration of linguistic, sociolinguistic, pragmatic and world knowledge. We call this a *textual orientation* because of the application here of fundamental notions provided by Text and Discourse Linguistics.

5.2.3. "Avec plaisir" Video

Undergraduates study French with the well-known "Avec plaisir" video course. Although still a project, the possibility of adding an interactive computational complement to be available at the resource center is under consideration.

5.3. Spanish as a Native Language

5.3.1. Ortografía

The user's Spanish spelling competence is assessed by means of a series of drills. Software under development. Full version will include tutorials on the subject.

5.3.2 Sintaxis

A series of drills devoted to syntactic analysis of Spanish. (Software under development.)

5.3.3. Argumentación

This is an interactive video project intended to teach Spanish speaking college students how to argue in Spanish. On the basis of actual situations the video will analize the structure of argumentation in action and the software will permit the user to interact to see the consequences of his decisions. This is an ambitious project in association with Dr. Max Giardina currently at Université Laval, and waiting for funding from a Canadian agency.

5.4. Latin

5.4.1. Latin Grammar

Several Pilot programs are available to train students in the use of Latin declensions and verb conjugations. More than 20 programs have been prepared by one of our Latin instructors.

5.4.2. "Pro Multis"

"Pro Multis" is a Latin expression meaning "in favor of many". It is a project of an interactive video program devoted to the teaching of Latin language and culture. Short video recordings will show monuments, inscriptions and documents related to the Roman Empire. The computer will then reproduce some of the scenes shown and, through hypergraphics and hypertext, will review and extend the information presented in the video.

5.5. Linguistics

The software in this section is intended to help students introduce into the scientific study of language.

5.5.1. Linguistic Concepts

This is a generative program based on the structure of the well-known computer game "Animals". The user thinks of a linguistic concept or discipline, then by means of a series of yes/no questions the program tries to guess which concept it is. If it cannot then it asks the user to formulate a yes/no question to distinguish between the concepts it "knows" and the new one. Next time the run will be more "intelligent", the knowledge base being larger now. Written in Quick Basic.

5.5.2. Fundamental Linguistic Concepts in Hypertext

A hypertext tutorial on the nature of language. So far the only working module is the one on the definition of language. It is being implemented in Knowledge-Pro.

5.5.3. Articulatory Phonetics

The study of the speech apparatus and all the diagrams characterizing specific sound articulations is made possible through the use of hypertext nodes linked to "hot-spots" in graphics screens. The PCX-graphics have been created with a scanner. Program under development.

5.5.4. Doctor

The famous AI program by Joseph Weizenbaum simulates a conversation between a doctor and his patient. We use it with Linguistics students to discuss the nature of conversation, natural language computer simulation challenges, linguistic transformations and production rules, etc. A Spanish version will be used to implement new "scenarios" for linguistic transactions.

5.6. Translation

A translation tool our students are beginning to use is the text-manager **Mercury-Termex** that allows users immediate access to an on-line dictionary from which they can input information to be "pasted" onto the text on the screen. Termex also allows the user to create and keep a personal glossary to supplement the regular dictionary.

6. By Way of Conclusion

Hypermedia has been defined as "the ability to build connections or links between two or more pieces of information" (PC AI 5, 2, 1991, p.46). Among the types of information that can be linked together are text, graphics, audio, and video. Linguistic communication being an essentially multimedia transaction considers a hypermedia approach to language learning as its natural habitat. Looking for a better way to teach languages we have quickly realized how well the new technologies will help us develop more sound and efficient language learning tools.

221

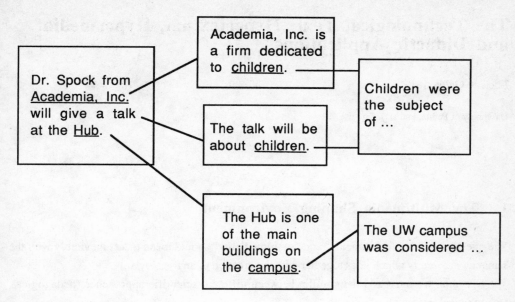

Figure 1.

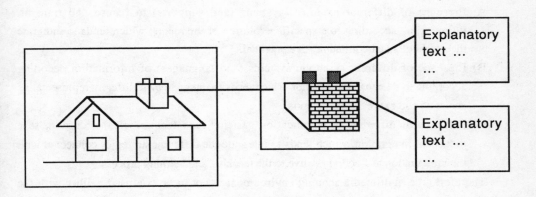

Figure 2.

The Technological Text: Hypertextual, Hypermedial and Didactic Applications

Luciano Galliani

University of Padua, Padua, Italy

1. The Multimedia Shaping Environment

The question of what "multimedia" and "multimediality" should mean meets inevitably with the semantic ambiguity which goes together with the creation of any neologism.

To this, we must add the conflict between different scientific approaches (pedagogical, technological, informatical).

We can call multimediality "a shaping environment which is determined by the integrated use of information and communication technologies".

This implies a three fold articulation of the

A) Presence of different technical systems (and supports) to record and transmit information, according to a specific evolution of the media, which tends to integrate their technological-communicative potential.

B) Presence of different symbolic systems (and languages) of information decoding according to a textual combination which tends to integrate their different representative semantic and expressional potential.

C) Presence of different communication systems (and technologies) according to a didactical integration, which tends to integrate the different strategies connected with the presentation and action relative to the teaching and learning processes.

Therefore, the multimedia shaping environment is not to be confused neither with the media sequence, nor with the hypertexts or hypermedia.

The media sequence is referred to the complex of the educational technologies connected with communication and information, processing and products.

The hypertext is referred to a specific generation of software featuring the possibility to deal with informative texts, not in the linear-sequential form, but according to knowledge paths that are open and multi-branched. With the hypermedia we are in an evolutional hypertextual software phase, that is, the possibility in the knowledge path to associate with or relate to not only language texts, but also to texts that are fixed and animated icons, and musical or sound ones.

A more subtle ambiguity comes from the fact that often a learning environment is technologically led by a computer, or better, by a hypermedia software: it appears that every synergy of communication and knowledge which is present in putting together the information handling and research (hypertext) with the analogical and/or digital storage of date (optic memory).

In reality, to lead a learning technological environment is determined by the pedagogical design of the authors and is entrusted to the relational strategies of users, teachers, and scholars.

It is the users who move and act in the multi-media environment.

The taxonomical model of the multi-media environment is a tridimensional space defined by the axes of representation of media, languages and methods.

Multimediality and interactivity can thus be defined as two "functions" (in the *algebric* sense) of the learning technological environment, as they establish a constant relationship between the variables (technical-communicative, linguistical-cognitive, methodological-didactical) relative to the whole of the media, languages and strategies.

Multimediality therefore is not to be identified with the mere availability of several media, as it usually is, but with their integration, led by a taxonomy which interrelates the features of the different media with the didactical functions of educational communication. The production of materials structured for teaching, the so-called "multimedia packages" cannot limit itself to have various media overlap (videotape + book or booklet + CAI or CBT software), thus ignoring that to each technological-linguistic system are to be given the task of different communicative aims.

The integration between material and print, videotapes, series of slides and/or transparencies, evaluation texts, informatic software and all what is available as far as the technology of informatics and communication, must have as a clear stand the specific didactical functions derived from the teaching-learning processes (motivation, phenomena description, analysis, abstraction, communicative performance, evaluations, etc.).

The complexity of a multimedia teaching environment goes therefore far beyond simplifying the software or products, although valuable, available in the *educational* market.

The point is, in fact, the complexity of the formation process, finalized to the creative reorganization of one own's mental field (knowledge) and behavior (psychomotorial, affective and relational abilities).

If it is true that the competences in the formative contexts are built in a privileged way by acting directly on the *events* (natural, social or artificial) seen as "communication worlds", then a multimedia and interactive technological system becomes the environment with the highest degree of learning.

2. Research as Applied to the Technological Text

In order to deepen this context we have undertaken an inter-university research project (University of Padua, Messina, Bari, Florence) lasting 2 years, financed by the Ministry of University and the Scientific and Technological Research, with the aim of studying the communicative texts of technological nature geared to formation and their didactical application by means of multi-media methods of integration together with hypermedial and hypertextual interaction.

The research - which starts with the pedagogical stand of educational communication meant as speech and interpersonal relation teacher-student - develops the analysis and texts around four problematical cores:

A) The perceptive-cognitive, technical-linguistic, content-structural and pragmatic-relational components of texts (writings, graphics, iconics, sound and audiovisual ones) finalized to didactical and educational communication;

B) The means of multi-media integration between the different textual components of the creation of a taxonomy geared to didactical communication strategies;

C) The cognitive and didactical potentials of an interactive handling and a non-linear access to information;

D) The possibility to improve (efficacy-efficiency) the learning processes through the automatized and interactive mastering of a plurality of media and/or communicative supports.

In general, the research is geared to showing that innovation in the didactical environments and of informatical systems does not depend much on the introduction of new technologies (audiovisual, informatical, telematic) but more on testing and evaluating the efficacity-efficiency of texts and single and integrated media, and of interactive strategies of hypertextual and hypermedial nature.

Specifically, the research is aimed to prove the "superior functionality" of the technological text, handled with hypertextual and hypermedial systems, in respect to the development of cognitive and relational processes, which are essential to learning and that are: plurilinguistical representation of information, modular organization of knowledge, network-type handling of information, interdisciplinar study of problems, autonomous construction of knowledge paths, associative research and selection of information, direct action on representative models of reality, intrinsic motivation, multifunctionality and multiusers context.

The research is developed by validating the didactical functionality of the technological text, through the elaboration and application of taxonomic grinds, the prototype design of hypertextual and multimedia software (1 year) and their production and testing-evaluation in different formative situations (2 years).

The Group of the *University of Padua* is conducting an in-depth analysis of the different communication dimensions of the technological text by exploring the interactivity of multi-media didactical environment, by means of the application of taxonomic grids and the production of hypermedial software, where it will be verifies the formative context together with its cognitive and relational functionality.

The Group of the *University of Messina* is conducting a study on the mediatization of the teacher-student educational relation in the technological formative systems, characterized by the use of audiovisual and informatical media, with special reference to the acquisition of specific cognitive abilities in exploring and solving problems, using also purposely-made software.

The Group of the *University of Bari* is conducting a research applied on the evaluation and testing (in a formative situation) of hypertextual and hypermedial software with didactical functions, produced in Italy and abroad, to verify their interactive strategies and linguistic functionality of the text (graphics, iconics, sound).

The Group of the *University of Florence* is conducting a specific hypertextual book versus the printed book, with and operative application on medioeval history, by creating in a Macintosh environment with Hypercard a Hypermedial Data Base with didactical paths for elementary and primary school.

In respect to the research development, the Group of Padua, in charge also of the general coordination between the four Universities - has elaborated three operative proposals which foresee the design - production - testing - evaluation of:

1) *a hypertextual model* of modular courseware on communication, centered around the relational interdisciplinar approach and geared to educators for the creation of differentiated teaching actions and to students for self-learning connected paths;

2) *a hypermedial model* on the study of artwork on Vincent Van Gogh, centered around a contextual access (hystorical-geographical-biographical) and an interdisciplinar one (artistic-iconological-psychoanalytical) and geared to high-school students;

3) *a multimedial model* to have access to the cultural works of the "Fondazione Collodi" (librarian mediatecharian laboratory, architectural-museographical) centered around the pluritextual relation (the numerous translations and abridgements: written, visual, audiovisual, theatrical and musical regarding Pinocchio) beginning from a hypermedial approach to exploring the Park visited every year by 200 000 children and adults.

The first two proposals are supported by Apple multimedia and Apple University, the third is conducted in collaboration with editel.

For models 1 and 2 the final standards will bring to the CD+ROM synergy and interactive videodisk, whereas model 3 will foresee the CD-TV Commodore.

The Training of Primary and Secondary School Teachers in Hypertext: Analysis of an Experience

Altamiro B. Machado and Paulo Dias

Project Minerva, Universidade do Minho, 4719 Braga, Codex, Portugal. Tel. (351) 67 64 94

Introduction

The experience in the training of primary and secondary school teachers hypertext to use under the framework of Project Minerva is focused. Some comments on the nature of hypertext technology and in its application to the development of instructional courseware are made. The results obtained by teachers without any programming experience are described. Having in consideration the problems detected, an alternative course structure is proposed.

1. The Role of Project Minerva in the Introduction of New Information Technologies in Education in Portugal

The introduction of New Information Technologies (NIT) in primary and secondary schools in Portugal has had a substantial development since the setting up in 1985 by the Minister of Education of an official programme - Project Minerva. This programme presents several innovative characteristics and has been pointed out as a model for the introduction of NIT by international organizations such as OCDE, the European Community and UNESCO.

One of the most praised innovations of this programme has been the fact that universities and colleges of education were commissioned to implement it. Several consequences resulted from this decision, the most dramatic being the nature of the efforts made in Portugal in teachers training in NIT.

In several centres and colleges of education in Portugal this training has emphasized the educational uses of commonly available software such as wordprocessors, databases, spreadsheets, desktop publishing programmes, etc. This approach, although recently validated by the fact of being also adopted as the main strategy in the use of NIT in the new curricula resulting from the 1988 Education Reform in the United Kingdom, has deep educational foundations in the need to introduce innovation in schools in all sorts of ways.

However, the need for more educational specific tools has been present for a number of years. A variety of so-called second generation tools with a large potential use in education, such as hypertext, simulation tools, symbolic computational tools, syntactic analyzers and translators have been tested.

2. Instructional Design and Hypertext Technology

One of the most popular of the second generation tools has been hypertext. Hypertext supports an educational environment radically different from traditional CAL. With an hypertext educational environment the user can explore and interact with knowledge in a non-linear and interactive way using several representational systems such as text, graphics, video, sound, voice and animation.

Knowledge is not just a collection of facts. Hypertext excellence in multi-representational data processing plus the autonomy that it gives the learner to grasp and restructure its contents makes hypertext an excellent instructional tool oriented to the active learning process whereby the learner discovers and restructures the information links in an interactive way.

Hypertext educational environments have already proved being excellent tools to promote meaningful learning. With hypertext the learner tends to interiorise information by means of a complex cognitive activity of interconnecting knowledge and ideas, building new links in the pre-existing information network and restructuring it.

However, the large freedom hypertext allows in the structuring and use of information is sometimes perceived as a source of difficulties in the design of hypertext products by school teachers used to a linear school curriculum design.

3. The Initial Courses in Hypertext

An extensive programme of training courses in hypertext has been offered to teachers in the framework of Project Minerva using both HyperCard for Macintosh computers and Guide for IBM compatibles.

The aim of these courses is to introduce teachers to the design of interactive instructional educational strategies using hypertext technology and to the development of courseware applications. The programme was developed for teachers with no computing programming expertise and its contents were:

    i)   the fundamentals of hypertext technology;

    ii)   contents organization in HyperCard;

    iii)   Interfacing techniques in HyperCard;

    iv)   stack design; and

    v)   HyperTalk commands.

This expertise has however shown two classes of problems. One relates to the quality of the products - HyperCard Stacks - developed by teachers in the three month period following the course.

The other problem relates to the enormous difficulties that teachers without previous programming experience face when dealing with a programming language such as HyperTalk.

A more thorough analysis of these problems reveals that an average school teacher after following these courses:

- had an extreme difficulty to organize information in a hypertext educational environment,
- had no full understanding of the need of a carefully planned specification phase in the development of life cycle of hypertext products,
- found great problems in handling, at an application level, a programming language such as HyperTalk.

Taking into accounting these considerations, alternative approaches to the teaching of hypertext to school teachers have been formulated.

4. An Alternative Approach

Different alternative approaches have been considered to restructure this training course. An active approach has been selected to encourage initially an intuitive discovery learning process.

The training course comprises two parts. The first one is a three days long and is intended to give an overall view of hypertext technology supported by HyperCard.

The second one is taught after several weeks of interval and has a normal duration of five days.

In the first part of the course a presentation of HyperCard is made by the lecturer. Then, students are encouraged to explore in an unstructured way and as extensively as possible several stacks, finding linear and non-linear access to the information and modeling the intuitive meaning of the contents links.

Finally, an analysis of the stacks guided by the lecturer is made.

The approach used in this part is based in the same educational principles of the teaching of reading skills using a global strategy.

No mention of the nature and syntax of the instructions of HyperTalk is made in this first part of the course.

In the second period of the course a different approach is used. In this part an emphasis is made to the introduction of concepts that teachers must manipulate when specifying and developing an hypertext product.

The structure of the second part of the course comprises:

a) a theoretical phase with:
-   an introduction to the specification of information systems using concepts from the theory of relational data bases such as data normalization and entity-relationships diagrams;
-   an introduction to software development methodologies using concepts such as software life cycle and documentation using several types of graphics, etc...;
-   an introduction to the basic concepts used in object oriented programming languages;
b) a description of HyperTalk in a formal way;
c) the development of a project from scratch using the concepts introduced in the previous phases.

5. Conclusions

The analysis of the products developed by teachers in the three months period following the completion of the course has shown a dramatic improvement when compared with the previous course structure.

Changing the instructional paradigm from a formal one in the first course to the global one in the second course has provided a more effective awareness of hypertext technology and significant improvement in the design of instructional HyperCard stacks. We have, however, arrived to this conclusion in an informal way.

Next July a MSc. student will begin looking at this problem in a more rigorous way. Special care will be put in the specification of several different course structures.

Training Drivers to Detect Visual Indicators or The Trials and Tribulations of the Uninitiated in Interactive Video

Maurice Fleury and Jacques Rhéaume

Groupe de Recherche sur l'Apprentissage Interactif (G.R.A.IN), Département de technologie de l'enseignement, Faculté des sciences de l'éducation, 1466, Chemin De Koninck, Université Laval, Quebec, 10, Canada G1K 7P4. Tel. (418) 656-2770/3769. Fax. (418) 656-7347

Introduction

Over time, all drivers develop visual strategies, depending on the type of vehicle driven and the conditions encountered. According to Têtard (1985), a strategy comprises three basic components:

(1) the perception of relevant indicators;

(2) the processing or interpretation of these indicators;

(3) decision-making or the manoeuvre executed.

Simply stated, driving a vehicle consists of knowing what can happen (anticipation, prediction) in order to know where to look and what to look at (selective search for information). If "knowing how to look" is the key, consideration should perhaps be given to training drivers to quickly detect significant indicators in particular situations.

Until last January, driver training in Quebec driving schools lasted 40 hours, including two hours devoted to the detection of indicators, and 10 hours of driving.

Since then, a new regulation has called for 12 hours of driving and a theoretical course tailored to the student driver, depending on the results of a pre-test.

In both instances, we feel it is germane to question current driver training and to propose special measures to enhance such training, bearing in mind that:

(a) 85 percent of road accidents are due to human error;

(b) 90 percent of driving skills rely on vision;

(c) current driver training programs are inadequate because they are overly condensed.

To overcome these shortcomings, we deem it appropriate to propose that student drivers engage in a series of training activities centred on information in order to offset their lack of driving experience.

Purpose of the Research

The main purpose of this study was to design and validate a series of driver training learning activities centred on gathering visual information in a wide array of significant situations.

The activities, which were both theoretical and practical, were based on the following working hypotheses:

H1: skill in detecting visual indicators is acquired with experience;

H2: repeated exercises develop sound habits;

H3: a novice driver can accelerate the development of his reflexes in simulated situations.

Problems Encountered

Under the circumstances, the problem we were facing was multi-faceted, although it focused primarily on the following questions:

(1) Among beginners, is it possible to significantly increase the rate of detection in simulated situations of indicators relevant to driving?

(2) Is the integration of such teaching material into the training program likely to enhance the situation?

Experimental Material

After meeting a number of intervening parties, attending information sessions, and viewing 30 or so films and videos used in training, we concluded that we must propose activities which were as realistic as possible and give each participant the opportunity to react to realistic situations.

Without overlooking practical considerations under actual driving conditions, we agreed that interactive video would be the most suitable choice. Indeed, it satisfied all of our requirements in that it offered:

(a) a replication of driving conditions;

(b) the desired array of situations;

(c) a quick succession of exercises;

(d) a record of student performance;

(e) a record of reaction time;

(f) graphics and animation.

We acquired IBM equipment, including a PS2/50 computer with 6 MB of RAM and 65-MB hard disk, connected to an Infowindow workstation and a Pioneer 1000-A videodisc. We used Professional Pilot software.

This is the point at which our trials and tribulations as researchers began.

Creating Modules

It should first be pointed out that three of the six modules planned to cover our objectives were informative and that no practice was proposed. The three modules involve 102 minutes of viewing and were produced on videocassettes. The titles and playing times are as follows:

Module 1	*La vue : c'est la vie*	72 min
Module 4	*Marge de sécurité*	15 min
Module 5	*Être vu*	15 min

Each of the other three modules includes a theoretical section lasting between 10 and 15 minutes, and a practical section, lasting between 15 and 20 minutes. We will now focus on the latter section. The titles and playing times are as follows:

Module 2	*Voir haut, loin et large*	27 min
Module 3	*Interroger l'environnement*	27 min
Module 6	*Repérer les problèmes*	27 min

Production Problems

The design and planning stages were fairly straightforward as they entailed establishing the broad outlines of the content of the theoretical section of each module, based on the three themes selected. I estimate that between four and six weeks were devoted to this task.

Filming was much more difficult. Over two consecutive summers, we devoted at least 10 to 12 weeks to daily filming sessions. The diversity of sites, the variety of situations and the quality of the video picture were constant concerns.

All told, we had nine hours of video which had to be edited down to 45 minutes. Bearing in mind that the practical section of each of the three modules lasts roughly 15 minutes and that each illustrated sequence runs on average to 10 seconds, that meant 90 different sequences per module, for an overall total of 270 sequences in the three modules.

It is easy to imagine how confusing it was to put the videos in order.

Were we to repeat the experience, we could enhance picture quality by using time-code KSP cassettes instead of KCA cassettes. Because we had to copy the selected sequences, we ended up with fourth of fifth generation pictures, which are far from perfect.

Programming was organized in blocks of 150 hours per module, which strikes us as satisfactory.

A Word on the Final Product

Although the finished product is flawed, we are satisfied with it and are confident about a future project.

Initial experience is always the most instructive; it is what we remember the most vividly. I learned that the experience is an exciting one, that the challenge is worthy of any true artist, and that the desired learning among students drivers can only be enriching and significant as it is tailor made. Future experience will confirm this observation.

In the near future, I hope to quickly finalize, in collaboration with a graduate student, a teacher training project already under way, to convince any remaining skeptics that we are offering a remarkable general training and educational tool.

Learner Control Versus Computer Control in a Professional Training Context

Christian Depover and Jean-Jacques Quintin

Unité de Technologie de l'Education, Université de Mons-Hainaut, Belgium

Introduction

Following an analysis on the inherent advantages and disadvantages of learner control on learning contents and strategies in a multimedia environment, the authors emphasize the difficulty in reconciling the freedom offered to the learner concerning the choice of contents and the requirements of professional training.

Based on a multimedia system devoted to metal protection through the use of zinc, the authors propose a number of arrangements to be made in a learning environment to be used in a professional training context. These arrangements contribute in defining a "focused exploration" strategy that consists in orienting learner attention by using focusing elements such as questions adjusted for learner progress and prior structuring elements. This strategy also integrates assistance in the establishment of a conceptual network in learning with the use of an individual "conceptual map" that can be presented to the learner, at his request, at any time.

The exploitation of the possibilities offered by an interactive video, in particular when it is based on a media giving immediate access to every part of the visual support, generally gives the learner free access to information. Without the usual limitations of the linear sequence imposed by the traditionnal visual supports, the conceptor must exploit the possibilities offered, keeping to a minimum the limitations imposed to the learner. Unfortunately, this learner freedom is not always compatible with the knowledge acquisition that should be mastered following a training program. This difficulty is particularly real in a context of immediate professional training. In this context, the long term advantages we expect from the learning process capacities of self regulation do not always compensate for the possible weaknesses of certain goals which would not be well mastered after training.

1. Origin of control in a learning situation

Learner control in a learning situation must not be considered as a dichotomous variable expressed in terms of all or nothing but rather as a continuum, from a point of no control, where all decisions would be placed under the responsibility of an external design, to an approach where all decisions would rest in the learner hands.

In order to establish this continuum we must consider the nature of the elements on which control will be based. More specifically, the learning contents on one hand, and the strategies on which the instructional process will be based on the other hand (Figure 1).

Within each of these dimensions, more specific factors can also be established depending whether content control is based on the choice of the goals that must be mastered, the level at which these goals will be mastered, the sequence chosen to study these goals... In addition, control on the instructional strategy will be more or less important depending if it is based on the choice of the strategy itself (expositive instead of rediscovery) or certain components of this strategy: number and level of difficulty of the problems, response delay, access to specific help, choice of examples...

Although this analysis of the instructional-learning process in relation to the level of control can be applied to any pedagogical situation (external control can be exercised by a teacher or by an automated instructional system), we will limit its use, for the purpose of this paper, to the characterization of computer assisted multimedia instructional systems.

As for the continuum from which we have just described a few essential articulations, the instructional systems based on the exploitation of hypertexts take an extreme position in terms of the freedom left to the learner, whereas the classic computer assisted instructional systems characterized by a learner evolution strictly pre-determined would be located at the other extreme of this continuum.

Applications which use the exploitation of resources from interactive audiovisual supports in order to propose learning environments simulating reality often favor learner control. To justify this choice, the notion of facilitating the transfer to real situations is usually stated. However, under this openly stated justification, there are other motives that are less often mentioned like, for example, the difficulty to perform a detailed pedagogical analysis from which a valid choice of didactic strategies controlled by an external design would be made. As PLOWMAN (1988) deplored it, we rarely find designers with a special interest in the analysis of pedagogical variables conditioning the efficiency of a multimedia instructional system. They usually are too preoccupied with the problems inherent in the technical implementation of a technology which they do not always perfectly control.

2 . Advantages and limitations of learner control

Next to the subjective elements we have just described in trying to explain the designers' interest in applications which point out learner initiative, we find a certain number of objective elements which justify this approach in the available literature.

Thus, MERRIL, starting from a learning structure based on a strategy of isolation later formally stated in an instructional theory (Component Display Theory, MERRIL, 1983), clearly demonstrated the interest existing in a regulation, by the learner, of his own learning process. A number of other authors like TENNYSON (1980), CAMPANIZZE (1978), SEIDEL et al (1978), have also demonstrated an interest not only in the advantages but also in the limitations of learner control.

In addition to these experimental results, the choice which consists in favoring learner control is also frequently based on arguments which, although less clearly established, seem to rely on plausible hypotheses. In particular, the notion that control by the student (in part or completely) would lead to induced benefits such as the development of certain metacognitive skills is now commonly accepted. These benefits would, among other things, concern the development, by the learner, of skills in the management and planning of his own learning. However, the way to favor the emergence of these metacognitive skills through a confrontation with an environment favoring learner iniative does not seem to be clear. Can we consider, as some authors seem to imply, that all that is needed is to let the learner control his own learning in order for him to develop a skill in this field or, on the contrary, must we prepare specific interventions to help him reflect on his own learning strategies? As we will explain in this text, based on the presentation of a multimedia system concentrating on the use of zinc in anticorrosion, we believe that the development of a real metacognitive skill is rarely spontaneous and that, on the contrary, it requires the establishment of a number of structures capable of inducing the learner to reflect on his own learning strategies.

Another factor which we believe has played an important role in the development of this interest in learner control is the realization by the researchers in artificial intelligence of the failure to give intelligent tutoring systems a student model on which instructional strategies adapted to the learner individual characteristics would be based (SELF, 1988). This inability to discern learner characteristics, in addition to the difficulty in arriving to a format of the field being taught that is sufficiently flexible to permit a real adaptive tutorial (CLANCEY, 1987) have lead certain authors to propose intelligent instructional models where the control is distributed between the system and the learner (DEPOVER, 1988). CUMMING and SELF (1989), use the term "collaborative instruction" to characterize this allocation of responsabilities in learning management.

The development of cognitive psychology also had an effect on the conception of multimedia systems. In particular, the "schema" concept already proposed by BARTLETT in the thirties (BARTLETT, 1932), and later formally stated by researchers in artificial intelligence (MINSKY, 1975, SCHANK and ABELSON, 1977) largely contributed to the recognition of the importance of the "waiting system" (prerequisites, prepresentations...) with which a student faces learning. Considering the difficulty in recognizing this waiting system which is specific to each individual, it is not surprising that learning controlled by the learner has appeared, in the eyes of a number of designers, as an easy way to favor the integration of new knowledge to the cognitive structure characterizing each learner.

However, learner control does not solve all the problems of the multimedia systems designer wishing to respond to the students' needs and expectations. In particular, research seems to demonstrate that the effectiveness with which a student is capable of controlling his learning is extremely variable.

Thus, authors like DEPOVER (1987), ROSS and MORRISSON (1989) have presented a number of parameters susceptible to affect control effectiveness:
- learner's age;
- learner's level of knowledge in the field;
- progress during the course;
- complexity level of the material
- familiarity with the content.

Based on this data, particularly data concerning the characteristics of the learner , it is difficult to continue to accept the idea that learner control, whatever the circumstances, is a solution to the difficulties encountered in the recognition of individual particularities in a multimedia instructional system.

The problems encountered in the initial use of hypertexts in an educational context only reinforce this idea. Thus, most authors mention the students' weaknesses observed when they must "navigate" efficiently in an hypertext environment. Furthermore, JONASSEN (1988) adds that the integration of knowledge presented through an hypertext in a learner cognitive structure is rarely satisfactory, in particular when the document is not well structured.

In order to favor the setting of new knowledge in the learner cognitive structure, we propose to construct, as the student progresses in the course, a "conceptual map" reflecting the relationships network that is established progressively between the different notions studied.

3. Learner control management in a context of professional instruction

Despite the attractive aspects of the possibility to give the learner control of his own learning, it is difficult to accept the disadvantages, especially in a context of professional training.

As a number of reports on the pedagogical use of hypertexts and the pedagogical exploitation of microworlds like the turtle environment (LOGO) have demonstrated, it is difficult, even impossible, to expect which skills will be mastered by the learners when free to set their own learning process.

In order to take into account the requirements that are specific to professional training, and at the same time exploit high interaction level video to its fullest, we propose to adopt a pedagogical approach we will designate as "*focused exploration*".

This approach consists in directing the learner's attention by using focal and structural elements susceptible to let the student master a number of specific skills, and at the same time giving the learner a number of possibilities to control his own learning.

Looking at the focal elements used, the questions proposed to the students play a particularly important role in the multimedia instructional system ("zinc in anticorrosion") we will use as reference to illustrate a pedagogical approach based on focused exploration.

A number of reports have clearly recognized (DALTON and HANNAFIN, 1987) the benefits associated with the use of questions in the interactive exploitation of videos. HANNAFIN and PHILLIPS (1987) have demonstrated that the integration questions, i.e. those that require from the learner a relatively elaborate level of data processing (gathering data from different places, making a critical synthesis of a number of data...) play a particularly beneficial role in learning as opposed to factual questions (on isolated facts) that might, even if they favor too much the retention of data isolated from their context, negatively affect the memorization of certain elements for which questions are not directly asked.

Other reports, while confirming interest in the questions, point out the necessity to use them judiciously especially when video support authorizes a major interaction (SCHAFFER and HANNAFIN, 1986). In particular, in setting an instructional process using focused exploration, we must give special attention to provoking, with specific questions, an active research of information and also to have the learners integrate this information in more and more elaborate structures in order to give rise to a progressive organization of the conceptual network associated with the skill to be attained.

4. Components of a strategy using focused exploration

The strategy which uses focused exploration established in the multimedia course "zinc in anticorrosion" consists in part in proposing to the learner more and more explicit approaches of the same industrial process.

The level of cognitive requirements associated with each approach of the process will be defined through three parameters:

- nature of the proposed questions;
- presence of focusing structuring elements;
- level of detail of the comments proposed during the visit.

Therefore, for each industrial process that the learner will have the opportunity to discover (figure 2), a free exploration will first be proposed through which he will be able to follow the progress of a piece through the processing operations that it will undergo in order to obtain an optimal protection against the risks of corrosion (level 1).

The second level of the industrial process approach consists in proposing a visit, during which the attention of the learner will be directed, using focusing structuring elements, towards a number of characteristics (place of application, preparation of the surfaces, coating application method, notice of the process). These characteristics will define the axes uniting the conceptual network links we want the learner to be able to control after having completed this part of the course.

Under this part of the process study, the learner is lead, in order to satisfy the requirements of the questionnaire that will be proposed to him, towards only process video sequences which illustrate the different phases of the establishment of a protection technique.

The third level of this strategy using focused exploration consists in directing the attention of the learner not only to the exploration of the video images but also to the analysis of the textual comments accompanying these video sequences. Based on the information he will gather from the video sequences and their accompanying comments, the learner will be able to answer the questions that will be proposed to him following the completion of this third level of exploration.

As mentioned previously, learner evolution through different industrial processes allowing the protection of metals through the use of zinc is directed by focusing structuring elements chosen in order to let the student rediscover the particularities associated with each process. Based on these structuring elements, but mostly on the progress of the requirement level, a more operational knowledge of the diffenrent process characteristics will be elaborated and will permit the learner, during the next phase of his learning, to develop a real skill in dealing with specific problems linked to the protection of metals.

In order to ensure a progressive exploration of the different processes while at the same time protecting the self regulating possitilities of the strategy offered to the learner, the questions' level of difficulty will be adjusted by taking into account not only the level at which the study of a particular process is realized, but also the order in which these processes are approached by each learner.

Learning the connections that exist between each process and its characteristics will mostly call upon mental images, the elaboration of which is suggested by the very realistic applications allowed by a multimedia environment. It is symptomatic to realize that when we ask learners on which basis they recall a particular connection between a process and one of its characteristics, they most often state audiovisual elements particularly outstanding: "A metallic beam comes down in a bath in an incredible crash".

In order to help the learner build up a global structure which associates the specificities of each process with the distinctive features of different situations where zinc protection is justified, the system is managing, as the learner progresses, a "conceptual map"* adapted to each individual learning evolution. This conceptual map progressively relates each studied process to its application conditions through a series of characteristics but also, under the learning phase dedicated to a choice of processes, with each situation describing a specific corrosion problem.

Figure 4 presents the state of the conceptual network associated with the electrozincing process in addition to the links that can be established between application conditions of this process and two corrosion problems that were submitted to the learner.

The analysis of the relationships network established on one hand between each process and its characteristics, and on the other hand between each corrosion problem and its requirements allows to emphasize privileged circuits underwhich all the requirements of a particular problem meet the process characteristics (this is the case, as far as electrozincing is concerned, with problem 2).

These circuits define the superior level relationships directly associating certain situations with certain processes using a progressive generalization technique that should allow to avoid passing through intermediate relationships such as those that link processes' characteristics to the requirements of the situations or the deviation through secondary relationships such as the coating adherence level which allows to associate the electrozincing application modality with the adherence requirements that characterize a particular corrosion problem.

Using this generalization technique, we could, as SCHANK (1980) suggests, prepare a memory storage based on more general structures built on a generalization of different relationships networks, but also, by creating automatisms of a superior level, give learners a skill close to professional expertise where intuition and reasoning by analogy play a determining role.

---

* This conceptual map is in fact the materialization of the conceptual network associating the different processes with their application conditions.

5. Hypermedia type environment

Besides the two components we have just described (gradual cognitive requirements and conceptual map), a strategy using focused exploration is perfectly compatible with most of the possibilities usually offered to the learner in an hypermedia type environment.

Thus, in the course "zinc in anticorrosion", the learner will have at his disposal different navigational assistance systems such as an "instruments panel" (figure 5) that will help him visualize his position in the course or, he will be able at all times to visualize the level of operation where he is located (figure 6) by pressing a specific function key.

Most of the possibilities of action on the unfolding of his learning will be presented to the learner in an initiative cartridge presented at the bottom of the screen. This cartridge will be more or less complete depending on the initiatives available at a specific time. Chart 1 describes different initiative formats available to the learner through the initiative cartridge.

As part of the progressive discovery of the different industrial processes, the learner will be able to control permanently the video sequences proposed to him.

At first, he will have the opportunity to select, based on a schematic representation of an industrial process evolution (figure 7), the video sequences that correspond to the stages he wishes to analyze.

In the course of presentation, he will be able to stop the image in order to study certain details, review certain sequences or return to the process general schema in order to select another stage to be studied.

At all times, the learner will have the possibility to be given a general view of the process where textual structuring elements will be proposed in order to ease the links with the theoretical aspects studied in the first part of the course, or recalled by the learner as part of the technical records.

6. Road to the future?

The possibility of proposing learning environments that respect the particularities of every learner has always been an essential preoccupation in educational technology research. Taking this interest into account, it is not surprising that the development of systems based on hypertexts has raised an important interest, even a certain fascination. However, after the initial enthusiasm, a number of difficulties did appear, in particular concerning the capacity of the learners to manage their own learning in an independent way, in an often complex environment.

In particular, in a professional training context, the difficulty inherent to an "hyper" type environment to control what the student is really learning is often inconsistent with the necessity to give the learner specific skills following an often time limited training.

In order to take into account these constraints, we propose to integrate, in a multimedia environment offering numerous possibilities of learner control, a certain number of tools capable of helping the learner manage his own learning.

It concerns elements susceptible, on one hand, to focus learner attention, in particular a questionning procedure the level of requirement of which will be adjusted in order to take into account the progress chosen by the learner and, on the other hand, to materialize, through the presentation of an individual "conceptual map", the progressive establishment of the conceptual network by each learner. This should give the learner a mirror of the evolution of his own learning process, which he will be able to consult at any time.

In a version of the training system being currently developed, the learner would be able to obtain certain explanations regarding certain links from which he would not (or not anymore) perceive the significance by being placed back into the situation where these links were put forward (for example, the video sequence corresponding to a specific moment of the industrial site visit).

In conclusion, while numerous empirical studies should be made in order to support what is still only an hypothesis, we believe that it is through an adequate proportioning between the control offered to the learner and a flexible and individualized assistance proposed by the system as part of a relationship qualified as collaborative by CUMMING and SELF, that we must find the road capable to ensure the future of learning hyper-environments in a professional training context.

Chart 1: Functionalities available to the learner through an initiative cartridge

FUNCTION KEYS	ACCESSIBLE FUNCTIONALITIES	ICONS
F1	**Leave the present level and come back to the superior level.**	
F2	Recall a video sequence comment (unit III).	
F3	Look at or re-examine the video illustration of a piece to be processed (unit IV).	
F4	**Access program options.** These options let you modify the color of the screen, put yourself in learner mode (reserved for "formateurs" and users)	
F5	**Access theoretical and technical records.** Theoretical records offer explanations on course prerequisites. Technical records present a synthesis of the different anticorrosion processes.	
F6	**Move backward in the course.**	
F7	**Access the glossary.**	
F8	**Access help.** You can press at all times the F8 key in order to obtain explanations on: 1. The role of each function key (summary); 2. The way to answer the type of questions asked in the unit; 3. The general operation of the program; 4. Your present position in the program.	
F9	**Access the notebook.**	
F10	**Continue the course.**	

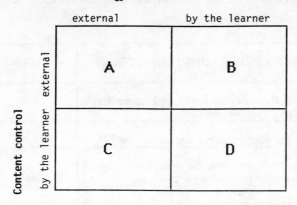

Strategy control

Figure 1. Origin of control in a teaching-learning situation

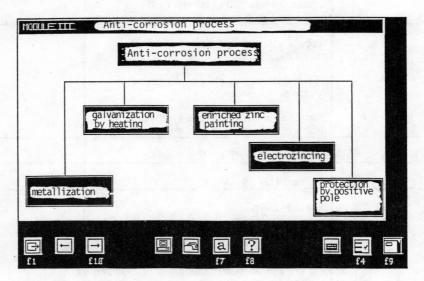

Figure 2. Presentation of the different industrial processes

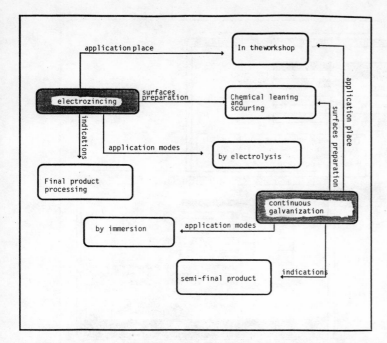

Figure 3. Conceptual network representation of electrozincing and continuous galvanization

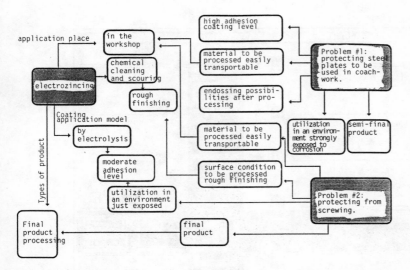

Figure 4. Representation of associations existing between electrozincing process and two corrosion problems

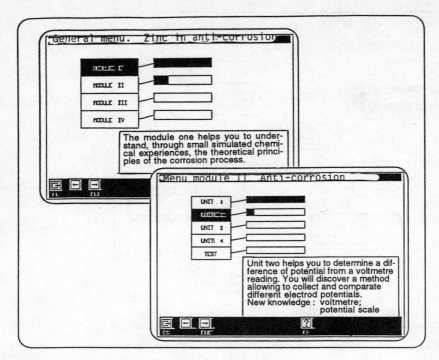

Figure 5. Board panel situating the learner in the lesson

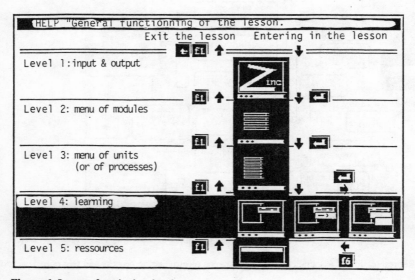

Figure 6. Lesson functioning levels

Module 3: Anti-corrosion process   Visiting a galvanization continuous line.

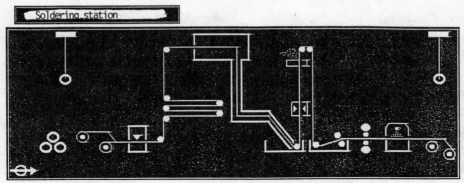

Soldering station

Move the cursor with the keys ← → and validate your choice with ENTER

Figure 7. Industrial process schematization (continuous galvanization) allowing direct access to every process step by the learner

Author Index

Subject Index

Printing: Druckhaus Beltz, Hemsbach
Binding: Buchbinderei Schäffer, Grünstadt

NATO ASI Series F

NATO ASI Series F

Including Special Programmes on Sensory Systems for Robotic Control (ROB) and on Advanced Educational Technology (AET)